A
Genealogical
Collection
of
Kentucky
Birth and Death
Records

Volume 1

Sherida K. Eddlemon

HERITAGE BOOKS
2007

HERITAGE BOOKS
AN IMPRINT OF HERITAGE BOOKS, INC.

Books, CDs, and more—Worldwide

For our listing of thousands of titles see our website
at
www.HeritageBooks.com

Published 2007 by
HERITAGE BOOKS, INC.
Publishing Division
65 East Main Street
Westminster, Maryland 21157-5026

International Standard Book Number: 978-0-7884-0677-9

DEDICATION

Leonard Eddleman (b. 1761ca. near Hagerstown, MD) enlisted in Capt. Gray's Co., March, 1781. He served as a private and was present at the siege at Yorktown and the surrender of Lord Cornwallis. After the surrender he remained about six weeks caring for the sick and wounded after which he marched as a guard for British prisoners to Fredericktown, MD. He went from there to Annapolis, MD where he was discharged.

Sometime after the close of the Revolutionary War, Leonard Eddleman settled in Greene Co., TN where he married Charity Bowman on Sep. 7, 1790. Not all their children are known at this time. Leonard and Charity did have three sons: Aaron, John, and Leonard, Jr.

By 1824, Leonard was living in Rush Co., IN with his family. After the death of his wife, Charity, on Apr. 3, 1839, Leonard moved to Harrison Co., KY and was living there with his son, Aaron Eddleman. Leonard and Charity's descendants settled in parts of Indiana, Tennessee, Kentucky and Missouri.

ACKNOWLEDGMENT

I want to thank my parents, P. Nelson and Amelia Eddlemon, for their continued support and encouragement.

CONTENTS

PREFACE

Birth and deaths were recorded in some counties as early as 1851.   It was not until January 1, 1911 that the state of Kentucky started officially requiring the registration of births and deaths. Copies of birth and death certificates after this date may be ordered from:

OFFICE OF VITAL STATISTCS
Department of Heath Services
275 East Main Street
Frankfort, KY 40621

Rates and other information requirements change over the years, so please contact the office before ordering to see what the current charges and procedures are for ordering

Birth and death records prior to 1911 for some counties are available from:

KENTUCKY HISTORICAL SOCIETY
P. O. Box H
Frankfort, KY 40621

The Society does not do personal research for individual.   If you contact the Society, please include an SASE and be as specific as possible.   Please remember that members are volunteers and replies to your inquiry could take awhile.
    Some of the death records indicated the possible maiden name of the woman. These maiden names appear in parentheses.   An index of these surnames is included at the end of this work for your convenience.   The entries are in alphabetical order.   The order is slightly affected because maiden names were included.   For example: Alice Carter and Alice Carter (Smith).   The sort option used by the program includes (Smith) as part of Alice Carter's name.
    An age at the time of death appears on some records.   This age was used to calculate the approximate birth date for the individual.   Ages do not appear on some records, or in some cases it was not legible.   These approximate birth dates were included for your convenience.   Please remember there could be some slight variation in the actual year simply because it was as accurate as the person supplying the information.   This approximate date when used with other sources will help to narrow down the birth year.   These records are indicated by using "ca."
    Many of these records were gathered over the last twenty years.   They were collected during vacation trips, cross country trips or sent by friends and family members who knew I was interested in this "old stuff" no matter where it came from. I am a genealogical pack rat. In several instances, it was the only "game" brought home during hunting season.   There will be several volumes in this series.   There are just a little over 6,600 individual records contained within this volume.
    Kentucky is a beautiful state with a rich heritage.   When you drive through Kentucky's mountains and valleys, you have to wonder about the strong pioneer spirit that our ancestors had.   They endured hardships that we can not even begin to imagine. Perhaps, your ancestor is within these pages. Good Luck.

COUNTY ABBREVIATIONS

COUNTY	CODE
Adair	Ada
Allen	All
Anderson	And
Ballard	Bal
Barren	Bar
Bath	Bat
Bell	Bel
Boone	Boo
Bourbon	Bur
Boyd	Boy
Boyle	Byl
Bracken	Bra
Breathitt	Bre
Breckinridge	Brk
Bullitt	Bul
Butler	But
Caldwell	Cal
Calloway	Cwy
Campbell	Cam
Carlisle	Crl
Carroll	Crll
Carter	Car
Daviess	Dav
Estill	Est
Fayette	Fay
Fulton	Ful
Grayson	Gra
Greenup	Grn
Hancock	Han
Hardin	Hdn
Harrison	Har
Henderson	Hen
Hopkins	Hop
Jefferson	Jef

COUNTY	CODE
Kenton	Ken
Kentucky	KY
Lewis	Lew
Lincoln	Lin
Logan	Log
Madison	Mad
McLean	McL
Menifee	Men
Muhlenberg	Muh
Nelson	Nel
Ohio	Oh
Rowan	Row
Simpson	Sim
Warren	War
Wayne	Way
Webster	Web
Woodford	Woo

SOURCE ABBREVIATIONS

SOURCE	CODE
A	Arkansas
Book	Bk
Cemetery	CEM
County Register	C
Korean War Military Record	KMIL
Marriage	Mar
Miscellaneous County Record	MCDR
Newspaper	NWS
NM	New Mexico
P	Page
Revolutionary Pension	RP
South Papers	SPF
T	Texas

Specific County Abbreviations

Newspapers	Addition	Code
Covington Licking Valley Register	Issue Date	NWS1
Maysville Bulletin	Issue Date	NWS2
Maysville Eagle	Issue Date	NWS3
Hopkinsville Gazette	Issue Date	NWS4
Kentucky Gazette	Issue Date	NWS5

Books
Encylcopedia of the New West	KY	BK1
Historic Families of Kentucky	KY	BK2

Miscelleanous
All Counties (Loose Records)		MCDR

Breckinridge County
County Death Register to 1903		C1

Breathitt County
County Death Register		C1

Butler County
Kentucky A History of the State	But	BK1
Pharris-Lindsey Cemetery		CEM1
Flint Springs Cemetery		CEM2

Caldwell County
Livingston Cemetery		CEM1

Carter
Birth Registers, 1904, 1906, 1907		C1
Kentucky A History of the State	Car	BK1
Death Registers, 1902, 1904, 1905		C2

Daviess County
Boulware Cemetery		CEM1
Salem Methodist Episcopal		CEM2
Travis Cemetery		CEM3
Death Register, 1852-1861		C1
Bethabara Baptist Church Cemetery		CEM4

Estill County
South Papers, Folder 1		SPF1

Fulton County
Alexander Cemetery CEM1
Asbell Cemetery CEM2
Bacon Cemetery CEM3
Beech Cemetery CEM4
Binford Cemetery CEM5
Bryan Cemetery CEM6
Harmony Cemetery CEM7

Grayson County
Marriage Records C1
Senior Citizen Reunion, Caneyville C2

Greenup County
Marriage Records Marr1
Death Register, 1853 .... C1
Death Register, 1877 .... C2

Hancock County
Kentucky A History of the State .... Han   Bk1

Hardin County
White Mills Baptist CEM1
Glendale Christian Church Cemetery CEM2
Old Union Cemetery CEM3

Harrison County
Oddville Methodist Episcopal CEM1
Raven Creek Burying Ground CEM2

Henderson County
Revolution War Soldiers, 1840 Census RC1840
McMullins Chapel Methodist Church Cemetery CEM1

Lewis County
Teager Cemetery CEM1

Logan County
Moore and Johnson Cemetery CEM1

McLean County
1900 School Census, Layton-Reeve School Sch1
New Salem Primitive Baptist Church CH1

Menifee County
Wills Cemetery CEM1

Last Name	First Name	I	Birth	Death	Co	Source
Aaron	Susan	T.	1867ca	Dec. 31, 1914	Ada	MCDR
Aaron (Slave)			1847ca	Aug. 28,1854	Brk	C1
Aaron (Slave)				Mar. 15, 1855	Brk	C1
Aaron (Slave)				Mar. 25, 1861	Brk	C1
Abate	Salvatore	A.	1914ca	Feb. 16, 1981	But	MCDR
Abbett	Chas.	A.	1886ca	Jan. 3, 1947	Jef	MCDR
Abbey	Harold	A.	1905ca	Sep. 28, 1981	Cam	MCDR
Abblett	Mary	A.	1856ca	Jan. 10, 1918	Bal	MCDR
Abbott	Avis	A.	1927ca	Nov. 19, 1985	But	MCDR
Abbott	Beatrice		1924ca	Dec. 18, 1986	Car	MCDR
Abbott	Beatrice		1924ca	Jul. 4, 1976	Byl	MCDR
Abbott	Ellen		May 5, 1907	May 18, 1989	Oh	MCDR
Abbott	John	T.	1881ca	Oct. 18, 1967	Cam	MCDR
Abbott	Leroy		1932	Aug. 17, 1950	KY	KMIL
Abbott	Tim		1888ca	Jan. 1, 1918	But	MCDR
Abbott	William	G.	1835		But	Bk1
Abel	Leah	T.	1889ca	Mar. 29, 1978	Fay	MCDR
Abel	Susan		1870ca	Feb. 8, 1935	Fay	MCDR
Abell	Bruce		1881ca	May 2, 1961	Byl	MCDR
Abell	Hugh		1915ca	Nov. 11, 1985	Ada	MCDR
Abell	Lawrence		1900ca	Jan. 9, 1981	Dav	MCDR
Abernathy	Lida		Jul. 20, 1907	Sep. 21, 1993	Ken	MCDR
Abernathy	Wendell		Sep. 28, 1904	Sep. ??. 1967	Ken	MCDR
Abert	Susan	B.	1852ca	Nov. 15, 1928	Cam	MCDR
Abney	Donald Lee		Mar. 4, 1953	Jul. 7, 1953	KY	KMIL
Abney	Susan	A.	1880ca	Mar. 7, 1915	Muh	MCDR
Aboumrad	William		Jun. 17, 1921	Dec. ??, 1982	Dav	MCDR
Abram	Bert		Jan. 6, 1922	Nov. ??, 1983	Fay	MCDR
Abram	Ella		Mar. 2, 1894	Jan. ??, 1978	Ken	MCDR
Abram	William		Apr. 17, 1890	Dec. ??, 1978	Ken	MCDR
Abrams	Ethel		1894ca		Grn	Marr1
Abrams	Isaac			Sep. 20, 1853	Grn	C1
Abrams	Louisa		1860ca		Grn	Marr1
Abrauer	Eddie		1876ca	Feb. 2, 1943	Dav	MCDR
Abrolat	Margaret		Jun. 29, 1904	Feb. ??, 1981	Fay	MCDR
Absher	Lester	D.	1889ca	Sep. 21, 1964	All	MCDR
Abston	Hugh		1919ca	May 4, 1970	Jef	MCDR
Ackerman	Abram		1843ca	Mar. 5, 1845	NWS1	4/12/1845
Ackerman	Theodore		Nov.13, 1882	Sep. ??, 1967	Cam	MCDR
Ackermann	Estella		1883ca	Oct. 22, 1948	Jef	MCDR
Ackridge	Susan	R.	1903ca	Nov. 18, 1974	Jef	MCDR
Acton	Hugh	C.	1871ca	May 22, 1948	Oh	MCDR
Adair	D.	L.	Nov. 26, 1824		Han	Bk1
Adair	Isaac	C.		1826	Han	Bk1
Adair	Mrs. Eddie		1864ca	Dec. 23, 1858	Jef	MCDR
Adams	Abbie		Feb. 3, 1881	Nov. ??, 1969	Ken	MCDR
Adams	Alfred	B.	1930	Nov. 27, 1950	KY	KMIL
Adams	Allie		1884ca		Grn	Marr1

Last Name	First Name	I	Birth	Death	Co	Source
Adams	Arthur	L.	1925	Aug. 13, 1950	KY	KMIL
Adams	Beatrice		1897ca	Jul. 2. 1925	Cam	MCDR
Adams	Beatrice		1903ca	May 17, 1952	Bell	MCDR
Adams	Bessie		1892ca		Grn	Marr1
Adams	Callie		Sep. 14, 1889	May ??, 1971	Dav	MCDR
Adams	Daniel		Feb. 8, 1907		Car	C1
Adams	Ed	W.	Nov. 9, 1844	Oct. 2, 1931	Ful	CEM7
Adams	Eddie	L.	1912ca	Oct. 7, 1968	Jef	MCDR
Adams	Eddie		1886ca	Jun. 25, 1946	Ken	MCDR
Adams	Edgar		Oct. 6, 1900	Apr. ??, 1967	Mad	MCDR
Adams	Helen		Apr. 24, 1919	Apr. ??, 1993	Fay	MCDR
Adams	Hugh		1896ca	Mar. 24, 1928	Jef	MCDR
Adams	J.	Q.	May 31, 1845		Han	Bk1
Adams	Jennie	M.	Apr. 1, 1881	Mar. 1, 1906	Ful	CEM7
Adams	Jerry	P.	1890ca	May 7, 1967	Jef	MCDR
Adams	John	S.	Jan. 4, 1870	Jul. 16, 1944	Ful	CEM7
Adams	Kathleen		Feb. 14, 1918	Jun. 23, 1992	Ken	MCDR
Adams	Lawrence	J.	1880ca	May 20, 1947	Fay	MCDR
Adams	Lawrence		1905ca	Jan. 16, 1974	Oh	MCDR
Adams	Leoto		Jun. 28, 1896	May ??, 1972	Ken	MCDR
Adams	Malinda	J.	Sep. 1, 1844	Aug. ??, 1911	Ful	CEM7
Adams	Maurice	C.	1896ca	Nov. 28, 1973	Fay	MCDR
Adams	Melvin	L.	1926ca	Mar. 19, 1983	Fay	MCDR
Adams	Melvin	R.	1903ca	Apr. 6, 1963	Fay	MCDR
Adams	Tamara		May 5, 1925	Jan. ??, 1980	Ken	MCDR
Adams	Troulius		1929	Nov. 28, 1950	KY	KMIL
Adams	Wallace		Jan. 27, 1920	Oct. ??, 1986	Fay	MCDR
Adams	William		Jul. 22, 1799		Han	Bk1
Adams (Crockett)	Margaret	J.	Jun. 15, 1850		Han	Bk1
Adams (Hawes)	Nancy	E.		1872	Han	Bk1
Adams (negro)	Unknown		Sep. 15, 1857		Sim	C1
Adams (Pitman)	Elizabeth		1832ca	Aug. 14, 1853	Dav	C1
Adamson	Hugh	P.	1913ca	Mar. 21, 1951	Jef	MCDR
Addison	Barbara		Jun. 27, 1942	May ??, 1985	Fay	MCDR
Addison	Claudie		Sep. 2, 1905	Aug. ??, 1980	Oh	MCDR
Aden	Aubrey	C.	Oct. 31, 1868	Aug. 12, 1948	Ful	CEM7
Aden	Louellen		Feb. 24, 1879	Oct. 11, 1946	Ful	CEM7
Adison (Robison)	Elizabeth		1825ca	Nov. 20, 1854	Brk	C1
Adiyan	Y.		May 13, 1923	Oct. ??, 1992	War	MCDR
Adkins	Beatrice		1905ca	Nov. 19, 1954	Dav	MCDR
Adkins	Beatrice			May 15, 1919	Car	MCDR
Adkins	Beecher	H.	1915ca	Jul. 28, 1983	Fay	MCDR
Adkins	Eddie	E.		Oct. 21, 1931	Jef	MCDR
Adkins	Eddie	L.	1960ca	May 10, 1983	Jef	MCDR
Adkins	Estill		Nov. 7, 1906	Jun. ??, 1972	Dav	MCDR
Adkins	Hugh	F.	1896ca	Aug. 24, 1966	Fay	MCDR
Adkins	Hugh	R.		Sep. 1, 1966	Jef	MCDR
Adkins	Lawrence	E.		Mar. 8, 1942	Car	MCDR

Last Name	First Name	I	Birth	Death	Co	Source
Adkins	Lenard		Aug. 7, 1918	Jun. 18, 1992	Ken	MCDR
Adkins	Melvin	L.		Jan. 28, 1936	Fay	MCDR
Adkins	Nellie		Jan. 28,1902	Feb. ??, 1984	Fay	MCDR
Adkins	Orvil		Dec. 27, 1924	Oct. ??, 1985	Hdn	MCDR
Adkins	Roy Wilbur		Aug. 15, 1906		Car	C1
Adkins	Susie		1884ca		Grn	Marr1
Adkinson	Hugh	B.	1922ca	Feb. 19, 1988	Fay	MCDR
Aebersold	Hugh	E.	1912ca	Jul. 3, 1973	Jef	MCDR
Agee	Melvin	T.	1911ca	Feb. 14, 1928	Dav	MCDR
Agner	Sadie		Dec. 12, 1900	Dec. 4, 1988	Dav	MCDR
Agnes (Slave)			1802ca	Mar. 15, 1857	Brk	C1
Ahart	Harold		May 30, 1916	May ??, 1984	Byl	MCDR
Ahl	Hyman	C.	1877ca	Dec. 18, 1878	Brk	C1
Ahl	Logan		1871ca	Jun. 29, 1878	Brk	C1
Ahnell	Karl		Sep. 19, 1892	Aug. ??, 1897	Dav	MCDR
Aiken	Henry		Aug. 21, 1903	Sep. ??, 1987	Dav	MCDR
Aikman	Alexander			Oct. 15, 1859	Bre	C1
Aikman	Armina			Aug. 5, 1852	Bre	C1
Ailsey (Slave)				Dec. 28, 1854	Brk	C1
Ainsworth	Bernadette		Jul. 23, 1894	Feb. ??, 1975	Fay	MCDR
Akeman	Margaret			Oct. 20, 1874	Bre	C1
Akeman	Peter		1826ca	Feb. 14, 1858	Bre	C1
Akers	Ambrose	G.	Apr. 15, 1855	Sep. 21, 1886	Hdn	CEM1
Akers	Dorothy		Dec. 19, 1923	May ??, 1989	Fay	MCDR
Akers	Hugh		1896ca	Mar. 1, 1941	Jef	MCDR
Akers	Hugh		1888ca	Mar. 19, 1940	Jef	MCDR
Akers, Jr.	Victor		1928	Aug. 18, 1950	KY	KMIL
Akin	Jerome	H.	1911ca	Oct. 14, 1981	Ada	MCDR
Alassey (Slave)			1831ca	Jul. 22, 1831	Brk	C1
Albani	Aniello		Jun. 5, 1928	May ??, 1982	Ken	MCDR
Albee	Zachariah		1849ca	May 9, 1933	Muh	MCDR
Albers	Bernard		Feb. 9, 1907	Kul. ??, 1981	Ken	MCDR
Albinson	Isaac		1845ca	Aug. 20, 1853	Grn	C1
Albrecht	Jay		Nov. 4, 1923	Nov. 13, 1988	Fay	MCDR
Albright	Eula		Jul. 6, 1911	Sep. ??, 1989	Dav	MCDR
Alcorn	Calvin	E.	1960ca	Apr. 15, 1978	Fay	MCDR
Alcorn	Estella	M.	1883ca	May 1, 1951	Byl	MCDR
Alcorn	William		Jun. 28, 1834		Est	SPF1
Aldemeyer	Albert		Mar. 10, 1884	Apr. ??, 1975	Ken	MCDR
Aldridge	Eddie	C.	1900ca	Nov. 27, 1946	Jef	MCDR
Aldridge	Henry	J.	1903ca	Jul. 30, 1904	Brk	C1
Aldridge	Lulu		1902ca	Feb. 10, 1904	Brk	C1
Aldridge	Miles	D.	1887ca	Oct. 30, 1918	Hdn	MCDR
Aldridge	William		Jan. 16, 1903	Oct. ??, 1979	Muh	MCDR
Aleshire	Ann		Jun. 12, 1906	Aug. ??, 1983	Ken	MCDR
Alexander	A.	E.	Nov. 23, 1844	Oct. 13, 1909	Ful	CEM7
Alexander	Betty		Nov. 29, 1903	Jan. ??, 1978	Ken	MCDR
Alexander	Betty		Nov. 29, 1903	Jan. ??, 1978	Ken	MCDR

Last Name	First Name	I	Birth	Death	Co	Source
Alexander	Brother		Jul. 17, 1891	Sep. 20, 1892	Sim	CEM1
Alexander	Calvin		1921ca	Apr. 30, 1975	Fay	MCDR
Alexander	Charles	G.	Aug. 26, 1868	Jan. 26, 1931	Ful	CEM1
Alexander	Charles		1873ca	Aug. 17, 1876	Brk	C1
Alexander	Charlotte		May 4, 1921	Sep. 20, 1988	Ken	MCDR
Alexander	Donald		Feb. 1, 1923	Jan. ??, 1966	Hdn	MCDR
Alexander	Dorothy		Aug. 17, 1897	Mar. ??, 1979	Hdn	MCDR
Alexander	Dr. J.	M.	Feb. 19, 1867	May 12, 1924	Ful	CEM1
Alexander	Dr. John	M.	May 28, 1818	Oct. 18, 1878	Ful	CEM1
Alexander	E.	E.	Feb. 4, 1892	Feb. 28, 1932	Ful	CEM7
Alexander	Elizabeth		Dec. 1, 1850	Feb. 20, 1899	Ful	CEM7
Alexander	Elizabeth	M.	Jul. 14, 1822	Sep. 26, 1887	Ful	CEM1
Alexander	Emma Bell		Nov. 4, 1859	Oct. 30, 1878	Ful	CEM1
Alexander	Enoch		1846ca	Feb. 15, 1852	Brk	C1
Alexander	James	R.	1757		All	RP1
Alexander	James	R.	Jul. 13, 1886	Apr. 6, 1926	Ful	CEM7
Alexander	John Loftus		Nov. 26, 1842	Apr. 24, 1848	Ful	CEM1
Alexander	John Thomas		1871	1949	Ful	CEM7
Alexander	Julia Samuel		Sep. 4, 1874	Mar. 28, 1951	Ful	CEM1
Alexander	Lizzie		Jan. 28, 1858	Mar. 26, 1862	Ful	CEM1
Alexander	M.	L.	Aug. 15, 1881	Aug. 31, 1881	Sim	CEM1
Alexander	Maj. Richard	B.	Dec. 20, 1801	Jun. 1, 1868	Ful	CEM1
Alexander	Male		Sep. 18, 1907	Sep. 18, 1907	Ful	CEM1
Alexander	Margaret Hall		Jun. 13, 1841	Dec. 23, 1939	Ful	CEM1
Alexander	Martha	L.	Aug. 11, 1852	Aug. 21, 1884	Ful	CEM1
Alexander	Mary	F.	Aug. 22, 1870	Dec. 6, 1876	Ful	CEM1
Alexander	Mary Marshall		Nov. 18, 1880	Mar. 8, 1885	Ful	CEM1
Alexander	Mary Mott		Oct. 8, 1824	Oct. 10, 1917	Ful	CEM1
Alexander	Maurice	F.	1911ca	Feb. 24, 1916	Byl	MCDR
Alexander	Maurice	M.	1890ca	Sep. 3, 1929	Fay	MCDR
Alexander	Myrtle		Nov. 22, 1896	Jan. 10, 1995	Sim	MCDR
Alexander	Nancy	H.	Jun. 11, 1879	Apr. 11, 1902	Ful	CEM7
Alexander	Nellie		May 4, 1886	Jun. 2, 1901	Dav	CEM3
Alexander	Nellie		Mar. 26, 1882	Apr. ??, 1971	Dav	MCDR
Alexander	Stella			Jul. 24, 1876	Brk	C1
Alexander	Susan	E.	Mar. 20, 1846	Aug. 14, 1863	Ful	CEM1
Alexander	Susan		1767ca	May 15, 1882	Grn	C1
Alexander	Susannah Allen		Jul. 18, 1784	Nov. 29, 1850	Ful	CEM1
Alexander	Thomas Lee		Aug. 18, 1943		Ful	CEM7
Alexander	Violet		May 23, 1904		Car	C1
Alexander	Wallace		1925	Mar. 12, 1951	KY	KMIL
Alexander	William Lock		Aug. 13, 1775	Dec. 31, 1851	Ful	CEM1
Alexander	William Lock		Apr. 22, 1808	Aug. 18, 1879	Ful	CEM1
Alexander (Rickman)	Mary Ann		Jan. 9, 1822	Dec. 2, 1901	Ful	CEM1
Alexander(Hoodenpyle)	Della		1888	19??	Ful	CEM7
Alf	Estella	H.	1889ca	Oct. 12, 1975	Cam	MCDR
Alford	Beatrice	H.	1941ca	Jun. 19, 1959	All	MCDR
Alford	Female		1862ca	Sep. 12, 1876	Dav	MCDR

Last Name	First Name	I	Birth	Death	Co	Source
Alford	Lottie		Mar. 2, 1910	Apr. 9, 1990	Ken	MCDR
Alford	Robert		Aug. 8, 1912	Oct. ??, 1985	Ken	MCDR
Alfred	Dan	O.	1929	Nov. 26, 1951	KY	KMIL
Algood	Addison			Jan. 3, 1854	Brk	C1
Allan	John		Feb. 8, 1921	Dec. 29, 1993	Dav	MCDR
Allan	W.	K.	1882ca	Jan. 12, 1946	Fay	MCDR
Allan	William		1783ca	Feb. 8, 1854	Bre	C1
Allard	Joseph		Apr. 5, 1933	Jan. ??, 1985	Hop	MCDR
Allario	Larry		Jan. 13, 1901	Jan. ??, 1977	Ken	MCDR
Allbaugh	Jerome		1845ca	Nov. 29, 1926	Ken	MCDR
Allen	Alice	B.	1889ca		Grn	Marr1
Allen	Ann	E.	1847ca	Oct. 2, 1852	Grn	C1
Allen	Anna Maria		1802		KY	BK2(P247)
Allen	Beatrice		1911ca	Feb. 4, 1985	Dav	MCDR
Allen	Billy		Feb. 1, 1927	Aug. 8, 1993	Ken	MCDR
Allen	Chas. Moorman		Aug. 7, 1877	Feb. 25, 1925	Ful	CEM7
Allen	Chris	H.	1876ca	Feb. 5, 1924	Dav	MCDR
Allen	Eddie		1901ca	Apr. 1, 1946	Fay	MCDR
Allen	Edmanda		1851ca	Jan. 7, 1852	Brk	C1
Allen	Eliza Sarah		Sep. ??, 1806		KY	BK2(P252)
Allen	Elizabeth		1859ca	Dec. 2, 1861	Brk	C1
Allen	Fannie Redman		Mar. 23, 1867	Jul. 9, 1953	Hdn	CEM2
Allen	Fielding	C.	1818ca	Apr. ??, 1852	Grn	C1
Allen	Garfield		Nov. 20, 1880	Jul. 17, 1955	Hdn	CEM3
Allen	Gorman		1912ca	Jan. 15, 1986	McL	MCDR
Allen	Henry		Nov. 8, 1909	Dec. ??, 1973	Fay	MCDR
Allen	Jane Logan		1808		KY	BK2(P271)
Allen	Jerome		1887ca	Mar. 17, 1972	Dav	MCDR
Allen	Jerome		1852ca	Oct. 1, 1912	Oh	MCDR
Allen	Jimmie		1929	Jul. 5, 1950	KY	KMIL
Allen	Jimmie		1929	Jul. 5, 1950	KY	KMIL
Allen	John	H.	1831ca	Oct. 23, 1853	Dav	C1
Allen	John		Dec. 30, 1771		KY	BK2(P233)
Allen	Katherine		1812ca	Sep. 25, 1852	Bre	C1
Allen	Lenore		Feb. 9, 1884	Aug. ??, 1970	Dav	MCDR
Allen	Livona			Nov. 15, 1878	Brk	C1
Allen	Lydia		1883ca		Grn	Marr1
Allen	M.			Feb. 19, 1888	Muh	Ch1
Allen	Peter		1872ca	Oct. 15, 1878	Brk	C1
Allen	Polka		1887ca		Grn	Marr1
Allen	Samuel		Aug. 5, 1899	Feb. ??, 1985	Ken	MCDR
Allen	Susan		1860ca	Oct. 14, 1878	Brk	C1
Allen	Tava		Aug. 13, 1877	Nov. 29, 1948	Hdn	CEM3
Allen	Tim		1900ca	Aug. 27, 1977	Web	MCDR
Allen	William		Jul. 29, 1901	Jul. ??, 1970	Fay	MCDR
Allen	William		Jun. 12, 1913	May ??, 1985	Jef	MCDR
Allen	William		Mar. 10, 1884	Apr. ??, 1975	Jef	MCDR
Allen	William Orson		Feb. 27, 1863	Mar. 28, 1960	Hdn	CEM2

Last Name	First Name	I	Birth	Death	Co	Source
Allen	William Thomas		Sep. 15, 1877	Jul. 8, 1955	Ful	CEM7
Allen (Daviess)	R.	C.	1829ca	Aug. 13, 1854	Dav	C1
Allen (Gray)	Mrs. Toni		1854ca	Jan. 23, 1904	Brk	C1
Allen, Jr.	Clyde			Nov. 25, 1952	KY	KMIL
Allen, Jr.	William	M.	1901	1937	Ful	CEM7
Allen, Jr.	Willie		1928	May 18, 1951	KY	KMIL
Allender	Robert Lee		Jun. 16, 1930	Jun. 10, 1951	KY	KMIL
Alley	James		Feb. 9, 1914	Nov. 17, 1988	Fay	MCDR
Alley	Martha	B.	1928ca	Jan. 11, 1983	Ada	MCDR
Alley	Miles	L.	1875ca	Mar. 14, 1920	Grn	Marr1
Alley	Ray	C.	1932	Jun. 16, 1953	KY	KMIL
Allgood	Aaron Shelby		Mar. 16, 1824	Nov. 17, 1889	Dav	CEM3
Allgood	Annie May		Dec. 6, 1894	Mar. 21, 1901	Dav	CEM3
Allgood	Elizabeth		1877ca	Aug. 23, 1878	Brk	C1
Allgood	Ella		Oct. 10, 1895	Aug. 11, 1902	Dav	CEM3
Allgood	Matilda		Nov. 3, 1832	Jan. 1, 1898	Dav	CEM3
Allgood	Robert Young		Mar. 16, 1869	Oct. 4, 1920	Dav	CEM3
Allgood	Unknown Male		1866ca	Aug. 13, 1875	Brk	C1
Allmond	Nettie		May 29,1908	Feb. ??, 1987	Hdn	MCDR
Almon	Eddie		1898ca	May 21, 1957	Fay	MCDR
Alrey	Jerome		1828ca	Mar. 15, 1920	Dav	MCDR
Alsip	Jake		1864	1954	Dav	CEM4
Alsip	Lizzie		1867	1934	Dav	CEM4
Alsip	Robert	L.	Nov. 14, 1866	Apr. 17, 1914	Dav	CEM4
Alsop	James		1829ca	Nov. 2, 1854	Dav	C1
Alsop (Terrill)	Duquincy	A.	1827ca	Jan. 28, 1854	Dav	C1
Alstork	Clarence		Feb. 13, 1911	Mar. ??, 1983	Dav	MCDR
Alter	Manny		Mar. 24, 1912	Jun. ??, 1981	Fay	MCDR
Alterr	William		Feb. 6, 1920	Mar. ??, 1986	Cam	MCDR
Alverson	Olive	J.	1858ca	Dec. 2, 1861	Brk	C1
Alves	James		Jul. 13, 1893	Sep. ??, 1968	Dav	MCDR
Alves	Walter		Jan. 22, 1911	Jan. 21, 1993	Dav	MCDR
Alvey	Bruce	T.	1955ca	Oct. 31, 1986	Fay	MCDR
Ambrose	Estella		1880ca	May 21, 1968	Dav	MCDR
Ament	Anthony			Sep. 8, 1844	Hdn	CEM3
Ament	Eliza Ann			Feb. 24, 1842	Hdn	CEM3
Ament	J.	C.	Sep. 14, 1839	Mar. 7, 1863	Hdn	CEM3
Ament	Jefferies		Sep. 15, 1861	Apr. 4, 1863	Hdn	CEM3
Ames	Katie		May 5, 1871	Apr. 27, 1877	Hdn	CEM1
Ames	Mary		1826ca	1861	Har	CEM2
Ames	Rev. Leonard		1843	1889	Hdn	CEM1
Amick	Elva		Sep. 4, 1896	Dec. ??, 1982	Fay	MCDR
Amilin	Grace		1883ca		Grn	Marr1
Amis	Bob	T.	1926	Aug. 12. 1950	KY	KMIL
Amis	Mae		Oct. 5, 1902	Jul. 23, 1989	Fay	MCDR
Amos	Audra		Aug. 6, 1896	Oct. ??, 1976	Fay	MCDR
Amruso	Louis		Sep. 6, 1911	Nov. ??, 1979	Fay	MCDR
Andersen	Minnie		Aug. 4, 1898	Sep. ??, 1979	Fay	MCDR

Last Name	First Name	I	Birth	Death	Co	Source
Anderson	A.	C.	1932	May 27, 1951	KY	KMIL
Anderson	A.	W.	Mar. 14, 1845	Mar. 31, 1910	Muh	CEM2
Anderson	Adjutant			1791ca	NWS5	11/12/1791
Anderson	Archibald		1776ca	Aug. 30, 1852	Brk	C1
Anderson	Eric	N.		Mar. 3, 1977	Fay	MCDR
Anderson	Estella	C.	1909ca	Aug. 10, 1984	Jef	MCDR
Anderson	Estella	D.	1910ca	Jan. 7, 1969	Jef	MCDR
Anderson	Esther		Jun. 18, 1897	Oct. ??, 1978	Fay	MCDR
Anderson	Garnett		1891ca		Grn	Marr1
Anderson	Geraldine		Feb. 14, 1928	May ??, 1980	Ken	MCDR
Anderson	Harold		Apr. 2, 1910	Jun. ??, 1976	Gra	MCDR
Anderson	James			1835	NWS4	8/14/1835
Anderson	James Edward		1872	1957	Muh	CEM2
Anderson	Jennie		Jun. 19, 1867	Mar. 16, 1946	Muh	CEM2
Anderson	Joe	H.	Nov. 1, 1869	Jan. 10, 1925	Muh	CEM2
Anderson	Lester	L.	1904ca	Mar. 15, 1978	Dav	MCDR
Anderson	Lusinda		1848ca	Aug. 14, 1852	Grn	C1
Anderson	Martha	B.	1879ca	Aug. 27, 1960	Bel	MCDR
Anderson	Martha	B.	1868ca	Jan. 5, 1939	All	MCDR
Anderson	Martha	F.	1831ca	Mar. 25, 1855	Dav	C1
Anderson	Martha		Oct. 15, 1893	Feb. ??, 1975	Ken	MCDR
Anderson	Mary	W.	Jan. 12, 1803	Feb. 13. 1863	Hdn	CEM1
Anderson	Mary		1797ca	Jul. ??, 1861	Dav	C1
Anderson	Miles	W.	1884ca	Oct. 16, 1932	Cam	MCDR
Anderson	Missouri	B.	1869ca	Feb. 2, 1947	Cam	MCDR
Anderson	Mollie	G.	1873	1925	Muh	CEM2
Anderson	Nelle		Jun. 15, 1902	May 12, 1992	Fay	MCDR
Anderson	Richard Clough		Jan. 12, 1750		KY	BK2(P171)
Anderson	Rose		Feb. 5, 1907	Apr. ??, 1987	War	MCDR
Anderson	Ruben		Feb. 7, 1904	Dec. ??, 1975	Fay	MCDR
Anderson	Rueben		1780ca	Oct. ??, 1853	Dav	C1
Anderson	Sadie		1885ca		Grn	Marr1
Anderson	Simeon		1843ca	Apr. 27, 1845	NWS1	5/10/1845
Anderson	W.	K.	1918ca	Apr. 10, 1970	Fay	MCDR
Anderson	Walter		Mar. 2, 1949	Jun. ??, 1979	Ken	MCDR
Anderson	Wm.		1823ca	Oct. 22, 1875	Brk	C1
Anderson (Elder)	Su.	J.	Nov. 24, 1833		Gray	C2
Anderson (McKenny)	Amanda		1822ca	Mar. 13, 1853	Dav	C1
Andress	Russel		Nov. 25, 1911	Jan. ??, 1983	Fay	MCDR
Andrews	Anna		May 20, 1907	Nov. ??, 1984	Dav	MCDR
Andrews	D.		Mar. 25, 1916	Aug. 7, 1995	Fay	MCDR
Andrews	Elisha		Mar. 1, 1844	Dec. 14, 1891	Sim	CEM1
Andrews	Eugene		Aug. 3, 1872	Aug. 13, 1873	Sim	CEM1
Andrews	M. Jane		Apr. 18, 1914	Sep. 5, 1993	Hdn	MCDR
Andrews	Male		Jul. 18, 1869	Jul. 16, 1880	Sim	CEM1
Andrews	Robert	E.	May 27, 1881	Jan. 22, 1872	Sim	CEM1
Andrews	Virginia		Nov. 19, 1846	Jun. 20, 1914	Sim	CEM1
Andriot	Maurice		1837ca	Apr. 19, 1916	Cam	MCDR

Last Name	First Name	I	Birth	Death	Co	Source
Angel	Archebala		1827ca	Apr. 14, 1857	Bre	C1
Angel	Franklin		1838ca	Jan. ??, 1854	Bre	C1
Angel	Haney		1821ca	Apr. 13, 1856	Bre	C1
Angel	Jane		1843ca	Mar. 1, 1854	Bre	C1
Angel	Ruby		Jan. 8, 1927	Mar. ??, 1987	Ken	MCDR
Angel	Unknown Female			Jan. 12, 1875	Bre	C1
Angle	Unknown			Apr. 27, 1853	Grn	C1
Ankrim	Hazel		1886ca		Grn	Marr1
Ann (Slave)			1828ca	Jul. 18, 1854	Brk	C1
Anterberg	Elizabeth		1821ca	Mar. ??, 1856	Dav	C1
Anthony	Mamie		Jan. 26, 1927	Apr. ??, 1990	Sim	MCDR
Antill	William		Apr. 3, 1916	Jan. ??, 1981	Muh	MCDR
Antis	Mary		1884ca		Grn	Marr1
Appel	Jule		Dec. 29, 1897	Aug. ??, 1972	Ken	MCDR
Apperson	M.	E.	Dec. 16, 1868	Nov. 25, 1895	Ful	CEM7
Apperson	W.	H.	May 3, 1862	Dec. 28, 1933	Ful	CEM7
Applegate	Ricie		Jul. 26, 1907		Car	C1
Appling	Hugh		Dec. 15, 1917	Apr. ??, 1976	Ken	MCDR
Apschnikat	Walter		May 19, 1918	Dec. ??, 1984	Sim	MCDR
Arble	Ruby		Mar. 9, 1888	Oct. ??, 1978	Dav	MCDR
Arcari	Frank		Oct. 28, 1914	Nov. 8, 1990	Har	MCDR
Archibald	Dr. Lorenzo	A.	Apr. 11, 1844		Web	Bk1
Archie, Sr.	Tuner		1887ca	Dec. 16, 1953	Fay	MCDR
Arcker	Jerome		1864ca	Nov. 12, 1924	Dav	MCDR
Arehart	Fred		Jul. 30, 1925	Dec. 14, 1994	Hdn	MCDR
Arehart	Theresa		Nov. 28, 1927	Jun. ??, 1977	Hdn	MCDR
Arendell	Reddick		1835		But	Bk1
Arkenau	Harry		Jan. 12, 1884	Oct. ??, 1978	Cam	MCDR
Arkle	Nancy		May 15 1897	May 22 1993	Fay	MCDR
Armell	William		Apr. 5, 1922	Feb. ??, 1988	Fay	MCDR
Armell	William		Apr. 5, 1922	Feb. ??, 1988	Fay	MCDR
Arms	Dr. William		Dec. 11, 1827		Gray	C2
Arms	William		1829ca		Gray	C1
Armstrong	David Newton			1835	NWS4	8/14/1835
Armstrong	James	L.		1835	NWS4	8/14/1835
Arnett	Alice		May 15, 1863	Aug. 29 1887	Hen	CEM1
Arnett	Dr. John	W.	Jul. 26, 1845	Jan. 12, 1882	Hen	CEM1
Arnett	Dr. Levin		May 11, 1852	Aug. 5, 1882	Hen	CEM1
Arnett	George	K.	Apr. 18, 1811	May 23, 1882	Hen	CEM1
Arnett	John	G.	1927	Sep. 22, 1950	KY	KMIL
Arnett	Nancy	C.	Mar. 18, 1820	Dec. 23, 1887	Hen	CEM1
Arnold	Ellery	S.	1903	1954	Har	CEM1
Arnold	George		Feb. 21, 1919	Jan. 4, 1995	Ken	MCDR
Arnold	J.	P.	1858	1911	Har	CEM1
Arnold	Lucy	S.	1877	1966	Har	CEM1
Arnold	Macel		Feb. 27, 1923	Apr. 19, 1994	Ken	MCDR
Arnold	Mae Haney		1904		Har	CEM1
Arnold	Rita		Jun. 28, 1912	Jan. ??, 1965	Ken	Misc11

Last Name	First Name	I	Birth	Death	Co	Source
Arnold	Alex.		Sep. 13, 1880	Oct. 15, 1936	Har	CEM1
Arnold, Jr.	Alex.		Nov. 16, 1922	Feb. 28, 1924	Har	CEM1
Arnott	Eric		1962ca	Jul. 28, 1966	Jef	MCDR
Arrick	Mary		Jul. 17, 1904	Feb. ??, 1985	Mad	MCDR
Arrington	Albert		Oct. 15, 1819	Apr. 18, 1899	Ful	CEM7
Arrington	Alice	E.	1860	1933	Ful	CEM7
Arrington	Ella		Mar. 25, 1873	Nov. 1, 1941	Ful	CEM7
Arrington	Ernest		Jun. 9, 1879	Jan. 27, 1905	Ful	CEM7
Arrington	Florella		Jul. 4, 1820	Feb. 6, 1821	Ful	CEM7
Arrington	Given		Oct. 12, 1828	Aug. 9, 1904	Ful	CEM7
Arrington	John		Oct. 7, 1875		Ful	CEM7
Arrington	Martha		Jan. 15, 1868		Ful	CEM7
Arrington	Nancy		Jan. 14, 1829	Jan. 9, 1877	Ful	CEM7
Arrington	R.	C.	Dec. 15, 1867	Dec. 22, 1918	Ful	CEM7
Arrington	Robert Mitchell		1940	1941	Ful	CEM7
Arrington	Sarah		Nov. 7, 1836	Mar. 10, 1911	Ful	CEM7
Arrington	William Sam		1854	1921	Ful	CEM7
Arrowood	Edward			Nov. 28, 1857	Bre	C1
Arrowood	Unknown Female			Jan. 6, 1856	Bre	C1
Arrowood	Unknown Male			Jan. ??, 1854	Bre	C1
Arthurs	Eulla		1893ca		Grn	Marr1
Artis	Ethel		1893ca		Grn	Marr1
Artis	Harry		Sep. 23, 1912	Mar. ??, 1971	Fay	MCDR
Artis	Stephen		1847ca	Jul. 25, 1853	Grn	C1
Artis	Vennie	D.	1892ca		Grn	Marr1
Asbell	Aaron	S.	Aug. 4, 1800	May 10, 1871	Ful	CEM2
Asbell	Elsie Viola		Feb. 11, 18?1	Jan. 26, 1894	Ful	CEM2
Asbell	Judge	B.	Oct. 28, 1880	Mar. 1, 1885	Ful	CEM2
Asbell	Katie	V.	Oct. 13, 1894	Feb. 20, 1861	Ful	CEM2
Asbell	Lydia Kay		Jun. 16, 1817	Nov. 22, 1892	Ful	CEM2
Asbell	Wm. Nelson		Jan. 11, 1834	Jul. 16, 1894	Ful	CEM2
Asbell (Bonner)	Elizabeth		Dec. 9, 1811	Feb. 3, 1843	Ful	CEM2
Asbell (Cloyce)	Sarah Elizabeth		Nov. 21, 1854	Nov. 30, 1893	Ful	CEM2
Ash	Garland	Y.	Dec. 21, 1888	Dec. 13, 1969	Hdn	CEM2
Ash	Joseph		Jan. 29, 1890	Aug. ??, 1971	War	MCDR
Ash	Mellie Katherine		May 25, 1897	Apr. 5, 1907	Hdn	CEM2
Ash	Myra	E.	Mar. 29, 1863	Dec. 13, 1947	Hdn	CEM2
Ash	Oliver		May 30, 1884	Nov. 15, 1961	Hdn	CEM2
Ash	Ree Thompson		Oct. 20, 1870	Nov. 1, 1958	Hdn	CEM2
Ash	Sarah Mildred		May 17, 1910	Dec. 18, 1913	Hdn	CEM2
Ash	Thomas		Apr. 7, 1844	May 16, 1904	Hdn	CEM2
Ash	W.	P.	Apr. 16, 1844	Apr. 20, 1965	Hdn	CEM2
Ashbrook	Frank		Oct. 17, 1876	Mar. 17, 1899	Har	CEM1
Ashby	Alfred	I.	Apr. 25, 1840		Oh	Cem3
Ashby	Billie Joe		Jun. 17, 1931	Nov. 29, 1950	KY	KMIL
Ashby	J.	W.	Feb. 6, 1825		Gray	C2
Ashby	James Monroe		Dec. 13, 1926	Dec. 15, 1926	Oh	CEM3
Ashby	Joseph		Dec. 14, 1911	Jun. ??, 1986	Fay	MCDR

Last Name	First Name	I	Birth	Death	Co	Source
Ashby	Susan	C.	May 17, 1833	Aug. 14, 1852	Web	CEM1
Ashcraft	Eric		1883ca	Jul. 9, 1955	Fay	MCDR
Ashcraft	Robert		Dec. 14, 1912	Feb. ??, 1981	Ken	MCDR
Ashcraft	Robert		Dec. 14, 1912	Feb. ??, 1981	Ken	MCDR
Ashcraft	Wade	W.	1878ca	Oct. 28, 1952	Cam	MCDR
Asher	Siegbert		Apr. 18, 1885	Mar. ??, 1975	Oh	MCDR
Ashkenaz	Estella		1909ca	Apr. 30, 1976	Jef	MCDR
Ashley	M.	J.	Apr. 22, 1836		Gray	C2
Ashley	Ruth		Jun. 11, 1908	Jun. ??, 1993	Mad	MCDR
Ashlock	Dr. J.	H.	1855	1933	Hdn	CEM2
Ashlock	Dr. Robert	L.	Aug. 1, 1824	Jun. 26, 1878	Hdn	CEM1
Ashlock	M.	G.	Nov. 1, 1832	May 1, 1891	Hdn	CEM1
Ashlock	Unadilla	E.	1854	1932	Hdn	CEM2
Ashlock	William	G.	Jan. 29, 1855	Sep. 30, 1874	Hdn	CEM1
Ashwel	A.		Apr. 1, 1928	May ??, 1992	Hdn	MCDR
Ashworth	Richard		Dec. 5, 1889	Sep. ??, 1971	Ken	MCDR
Ashworth	Richard		Dec. 5, 1889	Sep. ??, 1971	Ken	MCDR
Askins	James		May 17, 1913	Jul. 10, 1994	Dav	MCDR
Askins	John		1792ca	Apr. 21, 1876	Brk	C1
Askins	Treasy Jane		1860ca	Oct. 28, 1861	Brk	C1
Askins	Jackson			Jul. 3, 1852	Brk	C1
Aspden	John	J.	1929	Aug. 12, 1950	KY	KMIL
Astles	Agnes		Dec. 13, 1919	Mar. ??, 1986	Ken	MCDR
Atchison	Arthur		Mar. 12, 1901	Feb. ??, 1988	Fay	MCDR
Atherton	Dee		Aug. 22, 1896	Jul. ??, 1985	Dav	MCDR
Atkins	Benjamin		1769ca		NWS5	6/9/1792
Atkinson	Benny	C.	1922	Feb. 13, 1951	KY	KMIL
Atkinson	Elgie		Aug. 21, 1886	Nov. ??, 1976	Fay	MCDR
Atteberry	Dixie		1862	1932	Ful	CEM7
Atteberry	Edgar		1891	1953	Ful	CEM7
Atteberry	Ethel		1898		Ful	CEM7
Atteberry	Joseph		1863	1942	Ful	CEM7
Augustine	Daisy		1902ca	Aug. 7, 1976	Ken	MCDR
Augustine	Feda	A.	1902ca	Jul. 23, 1946	Cam	MCDR
Aulery	Weathly		1788ca	Sep. 28, 1858	Brk	C1
Aurelius	Mildred		Dec. 9, 1909	Dec. 12, 1992	Fay	MCDR
Aurs	Margarett		1860ca	Jul. 8, 1861	Brk	C1
Ausenbaugh	Mavorence		May 10, 1915	Oct. 25, 1900	Hop	MCDR
Aust	Unknown Male			Jan. 5, 1861	Brk	C1
Austin	Dorothy		Oct. 1, 1912	Oct. ??, 1985	Fay	MCDR
Austin	Estella		1895ca	Mar. 4, 1929	Jef	MCDR
Austin	Samuel	G.	1845		But	Bk1
Austin	Stella		Sep. 3, 1889	Mar. ??, 1972	Ken	MCDR
Austin	Thomas		May 19, 1919	Jul. ??, 1981	Fay	MCDR
Autry	French		Aug. 9, 1898	Apr. ??, 1971	McL	MCDR
Autry	Mary Jane		1869ca	Sep. 12, 1875	Dav	MCDR
Auxier	Carl	J.	1971ca	Apr. 6, 1981	Fay	MCDR
Auxier	Charles	G.	1911ca	Sep. 6, 1977	Fay	MCDR

Last Name	First Name	I	Birth	Death	Co	Source
Auxier	Darrell	D.	1928ca	Jun. 6, 1971	Fay	MCDR
Auxier	Fanny Martha		1889ca		Grn	Marr1
Averdick	Ruth		Jun. 28, 1912	Jan. ??, 1965	Ken	MCDR
Avery	Jay		Sep. 23, 1888	Jun. ??, 1970	Fay	MCDR
Avery	Orlena		Nov. 8, 1890	May ??, 1974	Fay	MCDR
Ayer	Adam		Oct. 28, 1894		McL	Sch1
Ayer	Alpha		Mar. 9, 1889		McL	Sch1
Ayers	Mattie		Apr. 11, 1894	Dec. ??, 1985	Fay	MCDR
Ayres	Capt. E.	K.	Mar. 13, 1839		Han	Bk1
Ayres	Thomas			1876	Han	Bk1
Ayres (Ebbert)	Sarah	E.		1844	Han	Bk1
B;and	Evaline English		Jan. 12, 1851	May 8, 1924	Hdn	CEM2
Babb	Augustine		1928ca	Sep. 26, 1979	Fay	MCDR
Babb	Lewis		Apr. 9, 1869	??? 2, 1893	Dav	CEM3
Back	Alfred		1845ca	Dec. 19, 1874	Bre	C1
Back	Catharine		1778ca	Sep. 1, 1858	Bre	C1
Back	Mary Ann		1843ca	Jan. 14, 1854	Bre	C1
Back	Mathew		1867ca	Nov. 1, 1877	Bre	C1
Back	Minerva	J.		Dec. 23, 1855	Bre	C1
Back	Rebecca		1848ca		Grn	Marr1
Back	Sanford		1850ca	Nov. 15, 1856	Bre	C1
Backus	Charles		Jan. 6, 1913	Feb. ??, 1985	Jef	MCDR
Bacon	Charles	P.	Jul. 27, 1877	Dec. 25, 1918	Ful	CEM3
Bacon	Elizabeth		Jun. 27, 1789	Jun. 27, 1870	NWS3	7/13/1870
Bacon	Margaret Eliz.		May 8, 1842	Dec. 5, 1911	Ful	CEM3
Bagwell	Bertha	L.	Jun. 21, 1894	Oct. 12, 1899	Muh	CEM3
Bagwell	Florence	E.	Apr. 12, 1896	Aug. 7, 1900	Muh	CEM3
Bahlmann	Jerome		1911ca	Aug. 16, 1979	Cam	MCDR
Bailey	Agnes		1889ca		Grn	Marr1
Bailey	Allen		Oct. 28, 1907		Car	C1
Bailey	Artelia Susan		Mar. 18, 1876	Sep. 22, 1877	Dav	CEM2
Bailey	Charles Wesley		May 10, 1862	Mar. 22, 1864	Dav	CEM2
Bailey	Donald		Nov. 24, 1925	Sep. 15, 1952	KY	KMIL
Bailey	Estella	L.	1908ca	Jul. 15, 1967	Jef	MCDR
Bailey	G.	W.	Apr. 4, 1848		Web	Bk1
Bailey	George	W.	Jul. 30, 1823	Dec. 11, 1908	Dav	CEM2
Bailey	Henry	C.	Jan. 3, 1841		Web	Bk1
Bailey	Ida	E.	1886ca		Grn	Marr1
Bailey	James	A.	1922	May 19, 1951	KY	KMIL
Bailey	James	W.		Oct. 23, 1853	Grn	C1
Bailey	John	G.	Jul. 28, 1833		Web	Bk1
Bailey	John	H.	1811		But	Bk1
Bailey	Wade	H.	1883ca	Mar. 9, 1949	Bell	MCDR
Bailey	Wilmer		1928	Oct. 4, 1951	KY	KMIL
Bailey	Winfield Scott		Oct. 21, 1870		Dav	CEM2
Bailey	Winfred	M.	Mar. 22, 1833	Aug. 7, 1902	Dav	CEM2
Bain	Alexander		1857ca	Jul. 10, 1932	Jef	MCDR
Bain	Allen	R.	1907ca	Jul. 22, 1913	Fay	MCDR

Last Name	First Name	I	Birth	Death	Co	Source
Bain	Andrew	D.	1895ca	Jun. 5, 1973	Ken	MCDR
Bain	Anna	N.	1842ca	Jan. 9, 1917	Fay	MCDR
Bain	Annie	E.	1892ca	Mar. 14. 1943	Jef	MCDR
Bain	Annie	L.	1860ca	Aug. 1, 1946	Fay	MCDR
Bain	Barbara		1858ca	Jul. 6, 1921	Jef	MCDR
Bain	Bessie		1884ca	Jun. 24, 1964	Ken	MCDR
Bain	Bettie	W.	1865ca	Jan. 13, 1915	Fay	MCDR
Bain	Birdie		1880ca	Nov. 29, 1956	Jef	MCDR
Baird (Rafferty)	M.	J.	1835ca	Oct. 12, 1853	Dav	C1
Baize	Wade	H.	1873ca	Nov. 12, 1928	Dav	MCDR
Baker	Eliza		1790ca	Jun. 3, 1853	Dav	C1
Baker	Ella		1871ca		Grn	Marr1
Baker	George	M.	Jan. 23, 1844		Web	Bk1
Baker	John	W.		Jan. 26, 1855	Bre	C1
Baker	John		1833		But	Bk1
Baker	Rebecca		1830ca	Nov. ??, 1857	Dav	C1
Baker	Robert	L.	1927	Oct. 18, 1951	KY	KMIL
Baker	Virgil	K.	1929	Jun. 11, 1953	KY	KMIL
Baker	W.	T.	Aug. 7, 1841		Web	Bk1
Baldwin	Edward		1762ca		Hen	RC1840
Baldwin	Louis	W.	Sep. 4, 1932	Jul. 26, 1953	KY	KMIL
Ball	Crystal	D.		Apr. 28, 1981	Nel	KMIL
Ball	Kenneth		1932	Sep. 3, 1950	KY	KMIL
Ballance	Jerome	L.	1874ca	May 30, 1958	Cam	MCDR
Ballance	Jerome	W.	1839ca	Sep. 2, 1923	Cam	MCDR
Ballard	James		1811ca	Sep. ??, 1876	Dav	MCDR
Ballard	John			Aug. ??, ????	Dav	MCDR
Ballard	Martha		1862ca	Jul. ??, 1876	Dav	MCDR
Ballew	Myrtle		1882ca		Grn	Marr1
Ballinger	Wm. Pitt		Sep. 25, 1825		KY	Bk1(P378)T
Balls	Wm. Tilden		Mar. 10, 1916	Oct. 24, 1918	Muh	CEM3
Balsh	Ensign			1791ca	NWS5	11/12/1791
Baltzell	Carinne	T.	1900ca	Oct. 15, 1935	Oh	MCDR
Baltzell	D.			Dec. 10, 1928	Oh	MCDR
Baltzell	Dearing	S.	1894ca	Sep. 23, 1961	Oh	MCDR
Baltzell	George		1857ca	Jan. 10, 1944	Oh	MCDR
Baltzell	Harriett	E.	1855ca	Feb. 25, 1921	Oh	MCDR
Baltzell	Stella	S.		Nov. 15, 1920	Oh	MCDR
Baltzell	Willie	L.	1888ca	Mar. 16, 1915	Oh	MCDR
Baltzwell	Stout		1857ca	Jun. 28, 1922	Oh	MCDR
Bandy	Ida			Sep. 15, 1888	Muh	Ch1
Bandy	Mary	A.	1862ca	Sep. 3, 1878	Brk	C1
Bandy	Nancy	J.	1851ca	Sep. 1, 1852	Brk	C1
Bandy	Unknown Female			Sep. 25, 1904	Brk	C1
Bandy (Claycomb)	Panthena		1833ca	Jul. 19, 1878	Brk	C1
Bandy (McKisson)	Eliz.		1797ca	Jul. 21, 1878	Brk	C1
Bank	Mahala			Aug. 12, 1852	Bre	C1
Banks	Eric		1935ca	Jul. 18, 1937	Fay	MCDR

Last Name	First Name	I	Birth	Death	Co	Source
Banks	Harrison			Apr. 1, 1874	Bre	C1
Banks	Mary Jane		1863ca	Mar. 15, 1875	Bre	C1
Banks	Ray	L.	1932	Sep. 10, 1950	KY	KMIL
Banks	Unknown Male			Nov. 10, 1855	Bre	C1
Banks	Unknown Male			Jul. 14, 1875	Bre	C1
Banks	Wm.			Oct. 15, 1854	Bre	C1
Banks	Unknown Male			Feb. 12, 1858	Bre	C1
Banks (Phelfry)	Rebecca		1852ca	Mar. 12, 1875	Bre	C1
Barbee	Jesse	T.		Mar. 30, 1855	Brk	C1
Barbee	John	F.		Jan. 14, 1861	Brk	C1
Barbee	Samuel		1788ca	Aug. 17, 1861	Brk	C1
Barbee	Thomas			Feb. 12, 1797	NWS5	2/22/1797
Barber	A.	B.	1874ca	Sep. 8, 1938	Fay	MCDR
Barber	Adam		Jun. 16, 1871	Jan. 5, 1926	Ful	CEM7
Barber	Charley		Feb. 20, 1903	Dec. 30, 1905	Ful	CEM7
Barber	Deward	B.	Jan. 17, 1888	May 25, 1946	Ful	CEM7
Barber	Edward		Jan. 25, 1818	Nov. 3, 1869	Dav	CEM1
Barber	Fred	R.	1892	1931	Ful	CEM7
Barber	G.	A.	Nov. 25, 1868	Dec. 2, 1927	Ful	CEM7
Barber	Harry		Feb. 20, 1890	Oct. 28, 1890	Ful	CEM7
Barber	Jacob			Dec. 4, 1853	Grn	C1
Barber	Lannom		Jan. 30, 1905	Oct. 13, 1905	Ful	CEM7
Barber	Mary Frances		Sep. 24, 1865	Apr. 16, 1941	Ful	CEM7
Barber	Nancy		Sep. 8, 1830	Jul. 22, 1897	Ful	CEM7
Barber	T.	E.	May 6, 1863	Mar. 15, 1929	Ful	CEM7
Barbey	John	C.	1924	Feb. 12, 1951	KY	KMIL
Barbour	Cora	M	1861	1950	Dav	CEM1
Barbour	Edwin		Feb. 23, 1898	Sep. 12, 1953	Dav	CEM1
Barbour	Juliet	C	Apr. 12, 1817	Mar. 30, 1878	Dav	CEM1
Barbour	Maurine		May 17, 1894	Sep. 20, 1961	Dav	CEM1
Barbour	Solon		1860	1942	Dav	CEM1
Bard	Warren	E.	1934ca	Mar. 21, 1976	Muh	MCDR
Bardin	Zachariah		1871ca	May 11, 1938	Ada	MCDR
Bare	Bessie		Jul. 31, 1907		Car	C1
Barger	Jerome	B.	1831ca	Sep. 26, 1852	Brk	C1
Barger	Sarah	E.	1834ca	Nov. 14, 1852	Brk	C1
Bargo, Jr.	Fred		1928	Sep. 9, 1951	KY	KMIL
Bargoss	Elizabeth		1784ca	Apr. 15, 1854	Brk	C1
Barker	Ettie		1891ca		Grn	Marr1
Barkley	A.	B.	1887ca	Oct. 20, 1967	Fay	MCDR
Barlow	Duncan		Oct. 2, 1907	Sep. ??, 1986	All	MCDR
Barlow	S.	W.	1853ca	Sep. 28, 1858	Brk	C1
Barlow (Brown)	Sarah		1837ca	Jul. 31, 1859	Brk	C1
Barnes	Augustine		1863ca	Oct. 12, 1932	Fay	MCDR
Barnes	Edwin	A.	Nov. 13, 1871	Apr. 19, 1954	Hdn	CEM2
Barnes	Miles		1878ca	May 8, 1958	Har	
Barnes	Persilla		Apr. 26, 1854		Sim	C1
Barnett	Cordelia		1890ca		Grn	Marr1

Last Name	First Name	I	Birth	Death	Co	Source
Barnett	Elizabeth			Nov. 1, 1877	Bre	C1
Barnett	Frankie	L.	1932	Sep. 7, 1950	KY	KMIL
Barnett	John	W.	1855ca	Nov. 23, 1878	Bre	C1
Barnett	John		1876ca	Nov. 15, 1877	Bre	C1
Barnett	S.	E.	Jan. 7, 1842	Jul. 31, 1878	Muh	CEM2
Barney	Elizabeth		1775ca	Aug. 18, 1852	Grn	C1
Barnhill	James	W.	Dec. 16, 1848		Web	Bk1
Barns	Elmina		1851ca	Sep. 3, 1857	Brk	C1
Baron	John Batiste		1769ca		NWS5	12/27/1794
Barr	Adaline Botts		Feb. 2, 1834	Apr. 24, 1855	Hdn	CEM2
Barr	Norman	F.	1926	Feb. 1, 1953	KY	KMIL
Barr	Sally		1859ca	Oct. 1, 1878	Brk	C1
Barr (Harden)	Martha		1810ca	Oct. 16, 1878	Brk	C1
Barret	James		1848ca	Feb. 24, 1853	Bre	C1
Barrett	Jesse		1933	Sep. 9, 1951	KY	KMIL
Barrett	John		1836ca	Apr. 11, 1874	Bre	C1
Barrett	John Pratt			Oct. 31, 1843	NWS1	11/11/1843
Barrett	Margaret		1831ca	Aug. 15, 1855	Dav	C1
Barrett	Mary	J.	1839ca	Jan. 29, 1855	Dav	C1
Barrett	Nancy	C.	1839ca	Jan. 31, 1855	Dav	C1
Barrette	Sally		1853ca	Nov. 10, 1856	Bre	C1
Barron	George	L.	1928	Jul. 16, 1950	KY	KMIL
Barrows	Miles	E.		Dec. 9, 1966	Hdn	MCDR
Barry	Jerome			Apr. 30, 1913	Fay	MCDR
Barry	William	T.		Aug. 30, 1835	NWS4	10/30/1835
Bartey	Lucy			Dec. 26, 1853	Grn	C1
Bartlett	Erma Clore		Nov. 26, 1878	Sep. 6, 1958	Dav	CEM1
Bartley	Elizabeth		1842ca	Mar. ??, 1852	Brk	C1
Barton	J.	H.	Dec. 4, 1818		Gray	C2
Barton	Miles		1879ca	Jul. 27, 1961	Jef	MCDR
Bascom	Mr. A.	W.		Apr. ??, 1845	NWS1	4/26/1845
Basham	D.	J.	Mar. 13, 1832		Gray	C2
Basham	Florence	E.	1856ca	Feb. 25, 1861	Brk	C1
Basham	James	T.		Sep. 6, 1852	Brk	C1
Basham	John	H.	1931	Apr. 25, 1951	KY	KMIL
Basham	John			Jan. 8, 1854	Brk	C1
Basham	Littleberry		1792ca	Oct. 27, 1855	Brk	C1
Basham	Madison	L.		Dec. 10, 1852	Brk	C1
Basham	Mary	A.	1860ca	Feb. 17, 1861	Brk	C1
Basham	Mary			Aug. 1, 1853	Brk	C1
Basham	Mary		1799ca	Nov. 6, 1878	Brk	C1
Basham	Nannie	B.		Jun. 16, 1878	Brk	C1
Basham	Sarah		1840ca	Sep. 24, 1855	Brk	C1
Basham	T.	D.	1846ca	Aug. 8, 1878	Brk	C1
Basham	Ann		1802ca	Oct. 5, 1852	Brk	C1
Basham (Fowler)	Mary	E.	1853ca.	Sep. 25, 1878	Brk	C1
Basham (Hall)	Fanny		1802ca	Oct. 6, 1852	Brk	C1
Basham (Hardin)	Theresa			Sep. 31, 1852	Brk	C1

Last Name	First Name	I	Birth	Death	Co	Source
Basham (Srueth)	Nancy		1845ca	Dec. 24, 1875	Brk	C1
Bassett	Dr. John	A.	Mar. 18, 1844		Web	Bk1
Bassham	Gideon			Jul. 15, 1861	Brk	C1
Bates	T.	E.	Apr. 6, 1827		Gray	C2
Bates	William			Aug. 15, 1853	Grn	C1
Batson	Annie Field			1949	Har	CEM1
Batson	Bettie		1860	1954	Har	CEM1
Batson	David	W.	1854	1916	Har	CEM1
Batson	Dr. J.	D.	1825	1901	Har	CEM1
Batson	Dr. J.	D.	1856	1925	Har	CEM1
Batson	Frank	R.	Nov. 1, 1901	Nov. 1, 1946	Har	CEM1
Batson	John	B.	1859	1909	Har	CEM1
Batson	Susannah Crow		1859	1909	Har	CEM1
Baughman	Jones	A.	1876ca	Dec. 28, 1966	Byl	MCDR
Baumgardner	Otis	B.	Aug. 12, 1899	Nov. 22, 1955	Hdn	CEM2
Bays	Izetta		1887ca		Grn	Marr1
Bays	Nyrtle	B.	1889ca		Grn	Marr1
Bays	Verna		1893ca		Grn	Marr1
Beachamp (Crockett)	Anna	M.	Dec. 22, 1836	May 11, 1878	Han	Bk1
Beale	Richard			Mar. 29, 1833	KY	P1812
Beale (Adams)	Mary		1796ca	Dec. 9, 1853	Dav	C1
Bealer (Dean)	Emaline		1833ca	Sep. 19, 1856	Brk	C1
Beall	Andrew			Feb. 24, 1856	KY	P1812
Beall	Margaret		1802ca	Dec. 18, 1852	Dav	MCDR
Beall (Forester)	Cynthia		1811ca	Dec. ??	Dav	C1
Beals	Margaret	L.	1890ca		Grn	Marr1
Beam	Donald		Aug. 20, 1933	Jul. 25, 1953	KY	KMIL
Bean	Jetson			Apr. 15, 1834	KY	P1812
Bear	Emma		1892ca		Grn	Marr1
Bear	Gladys		Nov. 4, 1902	Apr. ??, 1984	Byl	MCDR
Bear	Robert		Feb. 3, 1901	Jun. ??, 1982	Byl	MCDR
Beard	Johnson	H.	Jul. 15, 1834		Web	Bk1
Beark	Rassel		1809ca	May 18, 1854	Brk	C1
Beasley	Clifford	D.	1929	Dec. 1, 1950	KY	KMIL
Beasley	Kenneth Lee		Mar. 18, 1932	Apr. 6, 1953	KY	KMIL
Beasley	Silas	J.	Nov. 14, 1853		Sim	C1
Beathmott (Pumphrey)	Caroline		1797ca	Jul. 22, 1854	Brk	C1
Beatty	A.	J.	Sep. 12, 1834		Gray	C2
Beatty	Ensign			1791ca	NWS5	11/12/1791
Beatty	Frederick		1875ca	May 5, 1878	Brk	C1
Beatty	M.	M.	Oct. 6, 1832		Gray	C2
Beatty	Unknown Female			Aug. 30, 1878	Brk	C1
Beaty	Nancy	E.	1860ca	Mar. 4, 1861	Brk	C1
Beauchamp	David	T.	Jan. 26, 1835		Han	Bk1
Beauchamp	Robert	C.	1800	Sep. 9, 1884	Han	Bk1
Beauchamp (Stowers)	Ann		Sep. 9, 1811		Han	Bk1
Beaver	William	J.	1840ca	Jun. 16, 1857	Dav	C1
Beavin	Enfield	E.	1838ca	Apr. 1, 1852	Brk	C1

15

Last Name	First Name	I	Birth	Death	Co	Source
Beavin	Horace			Jul. 21, 1904	Brk	C1
Beavin	Nancy		1827ca	Feb. 4, 1861	Brk	C1
Beavin	W.	H.		Jul. 24, 1894	Brk	C1
Beck	Chris		1896ca	Feb. 22, 1977	Cam	MCDR
Beckelhymer	Ansel		1880ca	Jun. 16, 1972	Fay	MCDR
Becker	Missouri	C.	1886ca	Feb. 16, 1975	Cam	MCDR
Beckhan	Capt. R.	E.	Apr. 13, 1844		KY	Bk1(P207)T
Beckley	Willie		1929	May 24, 1951	KY	KMIL
Beckman	Frank Lloyd		May 18, 1924	Apr. 9, 1951	Cam	KMIL
Beecher	Marguerite	M.	1895ca	Mar. 1, 1971	Jef	MCDR
Beecher	Samuel		May 22, 1904	Jul. ??, 1986	Dav	MCDR
Beechman	Proctor		1892ca	Oct. 21, 1950	Gray	MCDR
Beeler	Charles		Oct. 9, 1836		Gray	C2
Beeler	Sue		Dec. 11, 1839		Web	C2
Beeson	Charles	F.	Mar. 20, 1841		But	Bk1
Belcher	Nellie		1888ca		NWS5	4/11/1799
Beler	Henry		1780ca		Grn	Marr1
Belford	Celia		1890ca		Grn	Marr1
Belford	Croa		1890ca		Grn	Marr1
Belford	Hattie	B.	1874ca		Grn	Marr1
Belford	Lomah		1895ca		Grn	Marr1
Belford	Tissie		1895ca		Bur	Marr1
Bell	Beecher		1854ca	May 29, 1936	Har	MCDR
Bell	Benson Brant		Sep. 8, 1872	Jan. 22, 1939	Har	CEM1
Bell	Bessie	B.	Nov. 2, 1898	Apr. 6, 1902	Hdn	CEM1
Bell	Bobbie		1868	1954	Grn	CEM2
Bell	Carrie		1890ca		Fay	Marr1
Bell	Chris		1884ca	Dec. 27, 1949	Hdn	MCDR
Bell	Denzel	L.	1897	1959	Dav	CEM2
Bell	Mary	E.	1834ca	Feb. 18, 1861	Hdn	C1
Bell	Samuel		1854	1931	Web	CEM2
Bell	Tim		1898ca	Mar. 1, 1915	Fay	MCDR
Bell	Whitney	C.	1917ca	Aug. 2, 1970	Grn	MCDR
Bellamy	James	W.		Oct. 10, 1853	KY	C1
Bellamy, Jr.	Roy	K.	1932	Feb. 12, 1951	KY	KMIL
Bellar	James	A.	1850		Ful	Bk1
Bellew	Mollie	E.	Aug. 26, 1857	Oct. 18, 1875	Ful	CEM7
Bellew	Uda May		Feb. 19, 1878	Sep. 19, 1892	Brk	C1
Bellow	Susan		1874ca	Nov. 12, 1878	Jef	MCDR
Belt	Ollie James		Jan. 24, 1931	Sep. 23, 1952	KY	KMIL
Belt	W.	R.		1835	NWS4	8/14/1835
Bendell	Stephen		1790ca	Sep. 28, 1852	Brk	C1
Bennett	Edna		1886ca		Grn	Marr1
Bennett	Grabella			May 4, 1904	Brk	C1
Bennett	Lucinda	G.	1854ca	Aug. 5, 1855	Brk	C1
Bennett	Mary	E.	1876ca	Sep. 29, 1878	Brk	C1
Bennett	Nat.		1771ca		NWS5	12/22/1792
Bennett	Rebecca		1811ca	Jul. 29, 1852	Brk	C1

16

Last Name	First Name	I	Birth	Death	Co	Source
Bennett	Sarah	J.		Apr. 6, 1852	Brk	C1
Bennett	William	M.	1930	Jun. 21, 1952	KY	KMIL
Bennett	Wm.			Jan. 8, 1878	Brk	C1
Bennett (Wilson)	Sarah	F.	1829ca	Apr. 3, 1856	Dav	C1
Bentley	James		Apr. 9, 1821		KY	Bk1(P209)T
Bentley	Laura		1896ca		Grn	Marr1
Benton	George	B.	1857ca	Aug. 15, 1861	Brk	C1
Benton	T.	A.	1856ca	Jun. 17, 1925	Dav	MCDR
Bergner	Robert		Mar. 14, 1919	Dec ??, 1984	Jef	MCDR
Berkley	Eddie	F.	Mar. 1, 1878	Jul. 5, 1878	Hdn	CEM1
Berkley	Farry	E.	Oct. 14, 1875	Apr. 7, 1890	Hdn	CEM1
Berkley	Ira	N.	Feb. 21, 1880	Mar. 31, 1885	Hdn	CEM1
Berkley	Rosa		Feb. 3, 1857	May 25, 1857	Hdn	CEM1
Bernhard	Eric	M.		Feb. 27, 1967	Cam	MCDR
Berry	Crystal	L.	1906ca	Jan. 23, 1981	Jef	KMIL
Berry	James	R.	1818		But	Bk1
Berry	Jasper	C.	1837		But	Bk1
Berry	Mrs. Rebecca		1822ca	Mar. 5, 1845	NWS1	4/12/1845
Berry	Turner		1901ca	Feb. 3, 1985	Dav	MCDR
Berry	William			Aug. 2, 1872	KY	P1812
Berry (Norris)	Mary	E.	1832ca	Jul. 20, 1854	Dav	C1
Bessette	Aldred		Nov. 30, 1924	Apr. 8, 1994	Dav	MCDR
Bessette	Fedora		Oct. 3, 1905	Sep. ??, 1992	Dav	MCDR
Best	Taca		Jan. 1, 1866	Sep. 1, 1946	Hdn	CEM3
Best	Theodore		Jan. 31, 1858	Feb. 28, 1921	Hdn	CEM3
Betley	Adina	M.	1936ca	Jun. 12, 1982	Fay	MCDR
Betley	Dr. A.	E.	Apr. 10, 1840		Web	Bk1
Beymer	Charles	A.	Jul. 6, 1855		Web	Bk1
Bickers	Missouri	A.	1858ca	Jul. 1, 1930	Ken	MCDR
Biddle	Moses		1844ca	Sep. 9, 1852	Brk	C1
Biggers	Ethel		Feb. 24, 1885		McL	Sch1
Biggers	Landie			Oct. 19, 1864	KY	P1812
Bigham	John	M.	1793	Apr. 6, 1872	KY	P1812
Bilbre	Female		May 29, 1903	May 29, 1903	Oh	CEM3
Bilbre	Male		Feb. 28, 1902	Feb. 28, 1902	Oh	CEM3
Billington	William			Feb. 14, 1868	KY	P1812
Billy (Slave)			1854ca	Sep. 30, 1857	Brk	C1
Binford	Anna Margaret		1920	1945	Ful	CEM7
Binford	Asa		Apr. 5, 1871	Aug. 11, 1902	Ful	CEM7
Binford	Atlanta		Jan. 28, 1867	Dec. 28, 1874	Ful	CEM5
Binford	Eddie	O.	Dec. 26, 1884	Sep. 22, 1886	Ful	CEM7
Binford	Ernest	E.	Jan. 6, 1888	Aug. 17, 1888	Ful	CEM7
Binford	Henderson		Mar. 30, 1901	Jun. 8, 1901	Ful	CEM7
Binford	Jessie	O.	Jul. 24, 1883	Feb. 13, 1884	Ful	CEM7
Binford	Lora	M.	Sep. 23, 1887	Jun. 14, 1889	Ful	CEM7
Binford	Nora	E.	Nov. 13, 1867		Ful	CEM7
Binford	P.	L.	Feb. 19, 1859		Ful	CEM5
Binford	R.	H.	Apr. 9, 1836	Feb. 23, 1906	Ful	CEM5

Last Name	First Name	I	Birth	Death	Co	Source
Binford	Robert	M.	Oct. 23, 1856	Feb. 20, 1930	Ful	CEM7
Binford	Robert Earl		1881	1962	Ful	CEM5
Binford	Sara	P.	Sep. 16, 1841	Nov. 9, 1911	Ful	CEM5
Binford	Unknown Male		Sep. 15, 1897	Oct. 31, 1897	Ful	CEM7
Binford	Virginia	B.	Aug. 27, 1869	Mar. 27, 1886	Ful	CEM5
Binford	W.	R.	Oct. 27, 1880	Mar. 10, 1901	Ful	CEM7
Binford	Walter		Aug. 27, 1869	Mar. 12, 1870	Ful	CEM5
Binford (Plumer)	Sarah Mae		1920	1945	Ful	CEM7
Binion	Ethel	J.	Apr. 18, 1912		Row	CEM1
Binion	Leroy		Apr. 17, 1909	May 30, 1996	Row	CEM1
Binion	Robert		Mar. 15, 1907		Car	C1
Binkley	James	F.	1930	Dec. 1, 1950	KY	KMIL
Birchfield	Unknown Male			Nov. 25, 1854	Bre	C1
Bird	Laura	B.	Jul. 7, 1867	Feb. 11, 1893	Hdn	CEM2
Bird	Mary	E.	Aug. 3, 1870	Jul. 17, 1895	Hdn	CEM2
Bird	V.	A.	1828	1905	Hdn	CEM2
Bird	Victor		Aug. 17, 1902	Oct. ??, 1972	Fay	MCDR
Bird	William			Feb. 14. 1869	KY	P1812
Birdsong	William			Sep. 13, 1863	KY	P1812
Birdsong (Allee)	Winaford			Jul. 25, 1886	KY	P1812
Birke	Helen		Dec. 16, 1901	Jan. ??, 1982	Jef	MCDR
Bishop	A.	T.	1866ca	May 29, 1941	Fay	MCDR
Bishop	Crystal	L.	1951ca	May 24, 1961	Jef	KMIL
Bishop	E.	G.	Sep. 28, 1857		Web	Bk1
Bishop	Laura		1887ca		Grn	Marr1
Bishop	Mary		1888ca		Grn	Marr1
Bishop	Samuel			Oct. 29, 1844	KY	P1812
Bishop	Thomas	C		Nov. 13, 1872	KY	P1812
Bissell	James	R.	1928	Dec. 6, 1950	KY	KMIL
Bissonnette	Ray		Jul. 12, 1953	Feb. ??, 1987	Ken	MCDR
Biven	Elizabeth	S.	1840ca	Mar. 3, 1861	Brk	C1
Bivin	John			Oct. 2, 1855	KY	P1812
Bivin (Dooley or Draley)	Margaret			Oct. ??, 1832	KY	P1812
Bivin (Griffith)	Hester Ann			1871	KY	P1812
Black	A.	T.	1890ca	May 20, 1941	Fay	MCDR
Black	Bessie Fay		Oct. 15, 1950	Mar. 5, 1931	Row	CEM1
Black	Charles	L.	Dec. 29, 1931	Sep. 24, 1990	Row	CEM1
Black	David		Mar. 11, 1861	Jul. 26, 1917	Row	CEM1
Black	Eliza Jane		Dec. 23, 1860		Row	CEM1
Black	Harlin	H.	Dec. 15, 1926	Feb. 11, 1929	Row	CEM1
Black	Jesse	L.	1809	1878	Row	CEM1
Black	Julia	V.	Aug. 27, 1933		Han	Bk1
Black	Louisa		1812	1857	Sim	C1
Black	Nettie Louisa		Oct. 30, 1882		Row	CEM1
Black	Robert			1850	Han	Bk1
Black	Vada	M.	Jun. 30, 1906	Jul. 17, 1925	Han	Bk1
Black	William			May 30, 1851	Row	CEM1
Black	Rebecca Epperhart		Nov. 19, 1834	Nov. 25, 1922	Row	CEM1

Last Name	First Name	I	Birth	Death	Co	Source
Blair	Mary	A.	1846ca	Mar. 9, 1852	Fay	MCDR
Blair	Thos.		1819ca	Sep. 25, 1854	Grn	C1
Blan	William		1846ca	Sep. 13, 1852	Brk	C1
Bland	Douglas	K.	1922	Jun. 9, 1952	KY	KMIL
Bland	Fannie Wilson	A.	Feb. 1, 1850	Dec. 27, 1934	Hdn	CEM2
Bland	Gilbert	O.	1888	1966	Hdn	CEM2
Bland	H.	W.	Feb. 23, 1844	Apr. 21, 1933	Hdn	CEM2
Bland	Harve	O.	Dec. 10, 1868	May 10, 1956	Hdn	CEM2
Bland	Hattie		1882	1946	Hdn	CEM2
Bland	Hugh	E.	Apr. 21, 1882	Aug. 24, 1946	Hdn	CEM2
Bland	John	W.	Sep. 3, 1885	Apr. 30, 1956	Hdn	CEM2
Bland	Julia Ann			Sep. 8, 1854	Hdn	CEM2
Bland	W. Churchill		1879	1934	Brk	C1
Bland (Ash)	Mayme		Apr. 21, 1886	May 15, 1953	Hdn	CEM2
Bland (Buckles)	Sallie Belle		1862	1934	Hdn	CEM2
Bland (Cleaver)	Mary E.		Oct. 12, 1882	Apr. 29, 1942	Hdn	CEM2
Bland (Nall)	Nell		1878	1962	Hdn	CEM2
Bland (Van Metre)	Lena		May 14, 1871	Feb. 22, 1953	Hdn	CEM2
Blankenship	Charlie		1928	Sep. 2, 1951	KY	MIL
Blankenship	Essie	V.	1905	1906	Hdn	CEM3
Blankenship	James		1851ca	Sep. 4, 1852	Hdn	CEM3
Blankenship	Jno.		1869ca	Aug. 26, 1876	Hdn	CEM3
Blanton	Stella		1889ca		Grn	Marr1
Blazer	Stuart		1927	Oct. 14, 1952	KY	KMIL
Bledsoe	Effie Susan		Feb. 1, 1907		Car	C1
Blentlinger	Rachel		1892ca		Grn	Marr1
Blentlinger	Ruby		1887ca		Grn	Marr1
Blevens	Samantha		1892ca		Grn	Marr1
Blevins	Ada Lee		Jan. 1, 1907		Car	C1
Blevins	Mary Dicey		1895ca		Grn	Marr1
Blevins	Ray		Aug. 12, 1904		Car	C1
Blevins	Unknown Male		Jun. 1, 1907		Car	C1
Blevins	William	H.	1930	Jul. 28, 1950	KY	KMIL
Blowing	Licia		Feb. 7, 1907		Car	C1
Blue	Bartlett	W.	1872ca	Dec. 8, 1930	Fay	MCDR
Blume	Carrie	A.	1872ca		Grn	Marr1
Blunk	Joseph		1833		But	Bk1
Blye	Eric		1940ca	Sep. 9, 1982	Fay	MCDR
Blythe	Juda		1836ca	Jul. 14, 1911	Sim	MCDR
Board	Brigley			Jul. 24, 1904	Brk	C1
Board	Edgar		1859ca	Aug. 20, 1861	Brk	C1
Board	Eugene			Aug. 1, 1894	Brk	C1
Board	Fletcher		1839ca	Jun. 23, 1856	Brk	C1
Board	James		1800ca	Jul. 29, 1875	Dav	MCDR
Board	Jefferson		1831ca	Sep. 15, 1852	Brk	C1
Board	John	T.		Aug. 1, 1852	Brk	C1
Board	Unknown Female			Oct. 10, 1859	Brk	C1
Board (Arington)	Judith		1785ca	Sep. 9, 1854	Brk	C1

Last Name	First Name	I	Birth	Death	Co	Source
Board (Compton)	Martha		1825ca	Jan. 2, 1856	Brk	C1
Board (Compton)	Mary	E.	1825ca	Oct. 27, 1859	Brk	C1
Boaz	Wm. Jesse		1840		KY	Bk1(P97)T
Bodine	George	A.	Jun. 8, 1860	Dec. 4, 1882	Muh	CEM3
Boeker	Wayne		Jan. 11, 1903	22-Mar-95	Fay	MCDR
Boggs	Bish		1922	Jul. 29, 1950	KY	KMIL
Boggs	Hannah		1879ca		Grn	Marr1
Boggs	James	V.	1931	Sep. 6, 1952	KY	KMIL
Boggs	Sarah		1889ca		Grn	Marr1
Boggs	Virgil		1927	Oct. 29, 1950	KY	KMIL
Bohannon	Unknown Female			Jan. 20, 2855	Bre	C1
Bolduc	Delisca		May 9, 1917	May ??, 1986	Jef	MCDR
Bolen	Turner		1922ca	Feb. 27, 1979	Fay	MCDR
Boley	Crystal	D.		May 27, 1976	Jef	KMIL
Bolin	Fannie		1891ca		Grn	Marr1
Boling	Huda		1839ca	Sep. 15, 1875	Bre	C1
Boling	Sarah Elizabeth			Dec. 3, 1859	Brk	C1
Boling	Mary Ann	P.	1818ca	Auf. 5, 1858	Bre	C1
Boling (Riley)	Nancy		1834ca	Jan. 12, 1856	Bre	C1
Boling (Rily)	Nancy		1836ca	Jan. 12, 1857	Bre	C1
Bolling	Thomas	E.	1927	Feb. 16, 1951	KY	KMIL
Bolton	James	J.	1837		But	Bk1
Boon	Isiah	H.		Aug. 22, 1835	NWS4	8/28/1835
Boone	Alice		1871ca	Oct. 4, 1875	Dav	MCDR
Boone	W.	K.	1873ca	Jul. 17, 1911	Fay	MCDR
Boothe	Kenneth Jordan		Apr. 14, 1930	Sep. 28, 1951	KY	KMIL
Booton	Denman	G.	1926	Sep. 26, 1951	KY	KMIL
Borders	Peter		1759		All	RP1
Borders, Jr.	Roscoe		1928	Oct. 5, 1951	KY	KMIL
Borkland	Alfred	G.	1924	Aug. 19, 1951	KY	KMIL
Bosley	Jack Winstead		Oct. 29, 1918	Oct. 31, 1918	Dav	CEM1
Bostick	Maggie		1888ca		Grn	Marr1
Boston	Charles		Jul. 3, 1920	Mar. 9, 1988	Jef	MCDR
Boswell(Cromwell)	Elizabeth	M.	1818ca	Aug. ??, 1856	Dav	C1
Botanica	Margaret		Aug. 21, 1905	Aug. ??, 1986	Jef	MCDR
Bottom	Ansel			Aug. 13, 1917	Byl	MCDR
Bottoms	Ansel		1895ca	Nov. 15, 1954	Byl	MCDR
Botts	Bessie Marie		Jun. 9, 1895	Sep. 28, 1896	Hdn	CEM2
Botts	Clinton	C.	1870	1961	Hdn	CEM2
Botts	Lou Thompson		1867	1941	Hdn	CEM2
Botts	Louise		Nov. 27, 1901	Oct. 15, 1902	Hdn	CEM2
Botts	Seth		Dec. 17, 1794	Sep. 20, 1873	Hdn	CEM2
Botts	Seth		May 21, 1894	Jul. 29, 1894	Hdn	CEM2
Boucher	Roland		Aug. 24, 1932	Jun. ??, 1977	Muh	MCDR
Boudreau	Normand		Apr. 22, 1928	Jun. 28, 1994	Hdn	MCDR
Boulds	Thomas		1820ca	Aug. ??, 1853	Dav	C1
Boultinghons	William		1807ca	Nov. 20, 1878	Brk	C1
Boulware	Clarence		Aug. 27, 1849	Oct. 11, 1889	Dav	CEM1

Last Name	First Name	I	Birth	Death	Co	Source
Boulware	Jessie Barbour		Dec. 18, 1851	Apr. 24, 1920	Dav	CEM1
Boulware	Milron Fountain		Jul. 10, 1881	Sep. 23, 1970	Dav	CEM1
Bourner	Robert	H.	1840ca	Aug. 16, 1876	Brk	C1
Bowe	Juda		1878ca	Jul. 10, 1930	Muh	MCDR
Bowen	John			Aug. 20, 1835	NWS4	8/21/1835
Bowers	Raymond Trammell		Aug. 1, 1925	Nov. 29, 1950	KY	KMIL
Bowlds	James	J.	1816ca	May 2, 1852	Dav	MCDR
Bowles	David		1873ca	Aug. 12, 1878	Brk	C1
Bowley	Milton		1875ca	May ??, 1878	Brk	C1
Bowling	Mittie		1875ca	Jul. ??, 1878	Brk	C1
Bowling	Mrs. H.	C.	1840ca	Jun. 1, 1875	Brk	C1
Bowling	Warren		Mar. 29, 1929	Nov. 30, 1950	KY	KMIL
Bowman	Crystal	G.		Aug. 14, 1957	Jef	KMIL
Bowman	John			Jun. 20, 1780	KY	BK2(P19)
Bowman	Martha		1836ca	May 17, 1853	Bre	C1
Bowman	Rachel			Nov. 16, 1857	Bre	C1
Bowman	Unknown Female			Dec. 10, 1856	Bre	C1
Bowman (Rice)	Mary		1817ca	Mar. 16, 1857	Brk	C1
Bowmer	Catherine		1782ca	Feb. 13, 1861	Brk	C1
Bowmer (Westerfield)	Ellen		1861ca	Feb. 14, 1894	Brk	C1
Boyd	Beatrice		Mar. 27, 1903	Oct. ??, 1976	Jef	MCDR
Boyd	Howard	R.	1931	Feb. 12, 1951	KY	KMIL
Boyd	Howard	R.	1931	Feb. 12, 1951	KY	KMIL
Boyd	Isabella		Feb. 28, 1847	Oct. 21, 1904	Hdn	CEM2
Boyd	John	A.	Nov. 14, 1846	Jul. 5, 1925	Hdn	CEM2
Boyd	Lieut.			1791ca	NWS5	11/12/1791
Boyd	William	T.	1929	May 19, 1950	KY	KMIL
Boydson	Rosie Lee		May 19, 1896	Sep. 12, 1876	Ful	CEM7
Boyer	Lewis		1756ca	Mar. 23, 1843	NWS1	9/30/1843
Boyle	John	W.	1815ca	Nov. 25, 1845	NWS1	12/13/1845
Brack	Polly		1806ca	Oct. 15, 1854	Brk	C1
Braden	Perry	O.	Jun. 27, 1933	May 10, 1953	KY	KMIL
Braden	Widow Elizabeth		1871ca		Grn	Marr1
Bradford	Maj.			1791ca	NWS5	11/12/1791
Bradley	Agnes		1893ca		Grn	Marr1
Bradley	Juda		1834ca	Aug. 25, 1918	But	MCDR
Bradley	Robert		Feb. 24, 1902	Dec. ??, 1983	Bal	MCDR
Bradly	William		1846ca	Aug. 12, 1876	Bre	C1
Bradshaw	David	F.	1932	Nov. 26, 1950	KY	KMIL
Bradshaw	Female			Feb. 22, 1852	Grn	C1
Bradshaw	James			Sep. 7, 1842	KY	P1812
Bradshaw	James		1852	Jul. 3, 1852	Grn	C1
Bragg	Charles	W.	1932	Sep. 4, 1950	KY	KMIL
Bramble	Eric			Oct. 27, 1937	Jef	MCDR
Brame	Andrew	J.	Jun. 18, 1830		Web	Bk1
Bramlett	Martha			Sep. 27, 1852	Brk	C1
Brandenburg	Clifton		Jan. 8, 1930	Sep. 16, 1952	KY	KMIL
Brandon	John			May 19, 1861	KY	P1812

Last Name	First Name	I	Birth	Death	Co	Source
Brandon	N.	Y.	Jan. 1, 1919	Oct. 10, 1950	KY	KMIL
Brandon (Gray)	Anna			Jan. 17, 1885	KY	P1812
Branham	Clyde		1931	Mar. 28, 1953	KY	KMIL
Branham	George			Sep. 5, 1873	KY	P1812
Branham	Leota		Sep. 25, 1888	Aug. 12, 1972	Row	CEM1
Branley	Lillie		1874ca		Grn	Marr1
Brann	Joseph			Mar. 20?, 1837	KY	P1812
Brann	Thomas	M		Jul. 16, 1850	KY	P1812
Brannock	Mary	M.	Mar. 18, 1815	Nov. 26, 1861	Har	CEM1
Brasfield	James			Sep. 22, 1839	KY	P1812
Brashear	Edwin		Dec. 29, 1842		Han	Bk1
Brashear	R.	A.	1812	1859	Han	Bk1
Brashear	William	E.	1926	Nov. 2, 1950	KY	KMIL
Brashear (Cox)	Margaret		1814	1874	Han	Bk1
Brashear (Younger)	Jennie		1844		Han	Bk1
Brashears	Otho			Dec. 23, 1875	KY	P1812
Brashears (Jackson)	Julia Ann			Jan. 29, 1900	KY	P1812
Brasher	James		1850ca	Jul. 17, 1852	Brk	C1
Brashere	Louie	D.	1928	Mar. 6, 1951	KY	KMIL
Brashers	William			Feb. 23, 1868	KY	P1812
Bratcher	E.	C.	1925ca	Nov. 19, 1926	But	MCDR
Bratcher	Elzor		1822ca		Gray	C1
Bratcher	John	W.	1830ca		Gray	C1
Bratcher	Juda	D.	1887ca	Mar. 26, 1932	Oh	MCDR
Bratcher	Margaret		Mar. ??, 1822		Gray	C2
Bratcher	William		1831ca		Gray	C1
Bratcher (Wale)	Ann		1794ca	Sep. 12, 1858	Brk	C1
Brawner	Laetitia Cofer		Oct. 18, 1910		Hdn	CEM2
Brawner	William	R.	Aug. 5, 1911	Feb. 6, 1974	Hdn	CEM2
Brawner	William			Mar. 30, 1820	KY	P1812
Brayfield	Burt	S.	1879ca	Nov. 18, 1953	Fay	MCDR
Brayfield	Cammie	B.	1888ca	Apr. 27, 1960	Fay	MCDR
Brayfield	Harvey	R.	1872ca	Jan. 28, 1945	Fay	MCDR
Brayfield	Marjorie	W.	1914ca	Jan. 2, 1984	Fay	MCDR
Brayfield	Mary	P.	1885ca	Jun. 8, 1978	Fay	MCDR
Breckenridge	Eddlyn			Jul. 14, 1875	KY	P1812
Breeden	William		Feb. 18, 1841		KY	Bk1(P17)NM
Breeding	Eric	E.	1980ca	Jan. 8, 1981	Jef	MCDR
Brevard	Alfred	A.	Jan. 10, 1790	Oct. 17, 1865	Ful	CEM1
Brevard	Archibald	D.	Feb. 14, 1850	Sep. 21, 1851	Ful	CEM1
Brevard	Cythnia	A.	Apr. 29, 1838	Aug. 11, 1887	Ful	CEM1
Brevard	John	M.	1884	1891	Ful	CEM1
Brevard	John M.	T.	Dec. 3, 1843	Apr. 12, 1862	Ful	CEM1
Brevard	Mary	B.	Mar. 14, 1805	Aug. 3, 1887	Ful	CEM1
Brevard	Sallie Malone		1852	1935	Ful	CEM1
Brevard	Susan	A.	Oct. 12, 1856	Aug. 12, 1858	Ful	CEM1
Brevard	Susan Ann		Oct. 24, 1823	Sep. 1, 1851	Ful	CEM1
Brevard	T. M.	L.	Mar. 21, 1885	Sep. 7, 1859	Ful	CEM1

Last Name	First Name	I	Birth	Death	Co	Source
Brewer	Meridette	W.	1873ca	Mar. 5, 1875	Bre	C1
Brewer	Unknown Female			Mar. 27, 1875	Bre	C1
Brewer	Unknown Male			Mar. 15, 1877	Bre	C1
Breye	Viola		Jul. 18, 1875	May 10, 1915	But	CEM2
Brickey	Harriet			Jun. 10, 1878	Brk	C1
Brickey	Robt.		1846ca	Sep. 17, 1894	Brk	C1
Bridges	Eric	D.	1893ca	Jun. 17, 1967	Jef	MCDR
Bridges	John	R.	1927	Jun. 13, 1953	KY	KMIL
Bridges	Joseph			Mar. 29, 1836	KY	P1812
Bridges	Thomas			Apr. 15, 1874	KY	P1812
Bridwell	Amanda	F.	1833ca	May 20, 1855	Brk	C1
Bright	Tim		1921ca	May 3, 1937	Fay	MCDR
Brill	Gregory		Nov. 25, 1835		Web	Bk1
Brilly	Katherine		1836ca	Apr. 20, 1861	Brk	C1
Brinley	Thomas	F.	1874ca	Aug. 13, 1875	Dav	MCDR
Brite	Pauline			Oct. 26, 1904	Brk	C1
Brock	Louisa	J.	1843ca	Aug. 25, 1878	Brk	C1
Brodie	Female		1843ca	Sep. 18,1844	NWS1	9/29/1844
Brokaw	Guy	H.	Oct. 5, 1890	Jan. 7, 1933	Hdn	CEM2
Brokaw	John	H.	Jan. 10, 1849	Dec. 2, 1940	Hdn	CEM2
Brokaw	Margaret Bell	D.	Jul. 27, 1862	Feb. 15, 1933	Hdn	CEM2
Bromley	Floyd		Aug. 12, 1900	Dec. ??, 1967	Grn	MCDR
Brook	John		1754		All	RP1
Brooks	Ann		Jun. 17, 1816	Oct. 9, 1895	Har	CEM2
Brooks	Church		1830ca	Jun. 30, 1914	Fay	MCDR
Brooks	Colby		Aug. 27, 1806	Feb. 27, 1895	Har	CEM2
Brooks	Courtland		Nov. 29, 1904	Sep. 25, 1906	Dav	CEM3
Brooks	Ensign			1791ca	NWS5	11/12/1791
Brooks	Rebecca		1890ca		Grn	Marr1
Brooks	Robert Franklin		Nov. 20, 1930	Jun. 9, 1951	KY	KMIL
Brooks	T.	A.	1876ca	Jun. 26, 1931	Fay	MCDR
Brooks	Willis Cornelius		Jan. 8, 1859		Web	Bk1
Broolks	Jewell		1919	Dec. 25, 1950	KY	KMIL
Brown	A.	M.	1829ca	Sep. 16, 1857	Dav	C1
Brown	Alma		Feb. 10, 1902	Jan. 1, 1903	Dav	CEM3
Brown	Beulah May Hite		Nov. 11, 1925	May 13, 1996	Row	CEM1
Brown	Charles	W.	1928	Sep. 19, 1951	KY	KMIL
Brown	Clayton		Oct. 13, 1928	Oct. ??, 1984	Har	MCDR
Brown	Clora	L.	1885ca		Grn	Marr1
Brown	Cora		1883ca		Grn	Marr1
Brown	David	J.	1863	1945	Ful	CEM7
Brown	Dorcas	C.	Jul. 24, 1829	??? 21, 1901	Ful	CEM7
Brown	Dotson		Nov. 24, 1886	Oct. 16, 1946	Ful	CEM7
Brown	Edmona	S.	1867	1947	Ful	CEM7
Brown	Ellie Louise		Dec. 22, 1862	Jul. ??, 1948	Ful	CEM7
Brown	Emma		1861ca	Jul. ??, 1878	Brk	C1
Brown	Eric	P.		May 6, 1978	Jef	MCDR
Brown	Florence Pearl		Sep. 25, 1881	Oct. 29, 1902	Dav	CEM3

Last Name	First Name	I	Birth	Death	Co	Source
Brown	Frances Ethel		Mar. 19, 1886	Jun. 29, 1912	Ful	CEM2
Brown	G. Washington		1840		But	Bk1
Brown	Grace	A.	1887ca		Grn	Marr1
Brown	James	N.	Mar. 29, 1826	Mar. 14, 1901	Ful	CEM7
Brown	James Eugene		Sep. 20, 1943	Oct. 27, 1943	Row	CEM1
Brown	John Henry		Oct. 29, 1820		KY	Bk1(P131)T
Brown	Juda		1891ca	Apr. 6, 1974	Grn	MCDR
Brown	Katie		1874ca		Grn	Marr1
Brown	Lela Mae		May 31, 1891	Jan. 1, 1957	Ful	CEM7
Brown	Lena May		Sep. 16, 1894	Oct. 23, 1894	Ful	CEM7
Brown	Lon Nathaniel		Sep. 26, 1887		Ful	CEM7
Brown	Lucy		1902	1972	Row	CEM1
Brown	Maggie		Oct. 2, 1861	Jan. 2, 1905	Dav	CEM3
Brown	Maj.			1791ca	NWS5	11/12/1791
Brown	Mary	A.	1891ca		Grn	Marr1
Brown	Mary		1783ca	Dec. 16, 1853	Grn	C1
Brown	Meade	M.	Jun. 26, 1916	Aug. 25, 1951	KY	KMIL
Brown	Mr.			1800	NWS5	5/29/1800
Brown	Oliver	L	1842ca	Feb. 9, 1844	NWS1	2/10/1844
Brown	Oswald John		Jan. 13, 1850	Apr. 11, 1903	Ful	CEM2
Brown	Roy	A.	Aug. 16, 1920	Aug. 16, 1921	Hdn	CEM2
Brown	Roy		Apr. 28, 1918	Jun. 7, 1983	Row	CEM1
Brown	Sarah Milner		Oct. 9, 1896		Ful	CEM7
Brown	W.	M.	1875ca	Aug. 3, 1878	Brk	C1
Brown	Wade	H.	Jun. 8, 1860	Feb. 28, 1923	Ful	CEM7
Brown	Wheeler		1890	1959	Row	CEM1
Brown	William	A.	Sep. 10, 1942	Oct. 26, 1964	Row	CEM1
Brown(McKay)	Mary	H.	1810ca	Jul. 15, 1844	Dav	C1
Brown(Trimble)	Clarrissa		1824ca	Mar. 24, 1856	Dav	C1
Bruce	Charlotte		1828ca	Aug. 25, 1858	Brk	C1
Bruce	James		1855ca	Aug. 20, 1876	Brk	C1
Bruce	Lisa		1898ca	Oct. 10, 1903	Brk	C1
Bruce	Mary	E.	1873ca	Dec. 1, 1878	Brk	C1
Bruington	Geo.		1837ca	Feb. ??, 1878	Brk	C1
Bruington	Jos.		1808ca	Feb. 28, 1894	Brk	C1
Brumagen	Daniel	T.	1931	Sep. 1, 1950	KY	KMIL
Brumfield	Newton	C.	1811ca	Nov. 4, 1878	Brk	C1
Bruner	J.	C.	1853ca	Seo. 7, 1861	Brk	C1
Bruner	John	B.	1825ca	May 29, 1876	Brk	C1
Bruner	Umphrey		1874ca	Mar. 1, 1878	Brk	C1
Brunson	Stout		1756		All	RP1
Bryan	Barton		1790ca	Apr. ??, 1853	Dav	C1
Bryan	Mary Jane			Sep. 10, 1852	Grn	C1
Bryan	William	A.	Mar. 30, 1823	Sep. 23, 1876	Ful	CEM6
Bryan (Blair)	Rebecca		Feb. 19, 1827	Mar. 3, 1874	Ful	CEM6
Bryant	Agnes		1777ca	Oct. 3, 1852	Brk	C1
Bryant	Paul	C.	1929	Apr. 24, 1951	KY	KMIL
Bryant	Thomas	J.	1850ca	Aug. 27, 1852	Brk	C1

Last Name	First Name	I	Birth	Death	Co	Source
Bryant (Kult)	Nancy	A.	1826ca	Feb. 21, 1852	Brk	C1
Bryson	Andrew	J.	1852ca	Feb. 17, 1877	Grn	C2
Bryson	Ronald		12-May-37	Mar. 28, 1995	Hdn	MCDR
Bryson	Tally		1863ca	Feb. ??, 1877	Grn	C2
Buchanan	Charles	N.	Jan. 20, 1831	1824	Han	Bk1
Buchanan	Georginia		Mar. 26, 1891	Aug. ??, 1979	Jef	MCDR
Buchanan	Mary	C.	1844ca	Sep. 19, 1856	Brk	C1
Buchanan (Brent)	Florinda			1848	Han	Bk1
Buckles	Albert	L.	1897	1946	Hdn	CEM2
Buckles	Annie	B.	1873	1962	Hdn	CEM2
Buckles	Evaline English		1899		Hdn	CEM2
Buckles	Female		Aug. 12, 1900	Aug. 12, 1900	Hdn	CEM2
Buckles	James	H.	Jul. 16, 1877	Sep. 21, 1910	Hdn	CEM2
Buckles	John	R.	1864	1950	Hdn	CEM2
Buckles	Lamana		1849	1935	Hdn	CEM1
Buckles	Lucy		Feb. 17, 1908	Feb. 5, 1909	Hdn	CEM2
Buckles	Male		Dec. 26, 1886	Dec. 26, 1886	Hdn	CEM2
Buckles	Mary	A.	May 5, 1805	Jun. 19, 1892	Hdn	CEM2
Buckles	Mary Catherine		Aug. 11, 1958	Aug. 11, 1958	Hdn	CEM2
Buckles	Maud May		Oct. 6, 1891	Apr. 25, 1894	Hdn	CEM2
Buckles	Robert	H.	Sep. 21, 1921	Dec. 1, 1959	Hdn	CEM2
Buckles	Ruth		Jan. 2, 1926	Jan. 22, 1926	Hdn	CEM1
Buckles	Viola		1864	1922	Hdn	CEM2
Buckles	William	E.	1860	1923	Hdn	CEM2
Buckles	William Robert		1893	1918	Hdn	CEM2
Buckner	Thomas		1795ca	Jun. ??, 1844	NWS1	6/22/1844
Bugg	L.	E.	Oct. 23, 1856	Aug. 3, 1876	Ful	CEM7
Bugg (Davis)	Alice		Feb. 21, 1872	Oct. 10, 1930	Ful	CEM7
Bullin	Alse		1805ca	May 20, 1855	Brk	C1
Bunch	Alvin	G.	1923	Jul. 31, 1950	KY	KMIL
Bundy	Annie		1893ca		Grn	Marr1
Bunger	Mary Jane		1831	1914	Hdn	CEM2
Bunger	P.	G.	1827	1903	Hdn	CEM2
Burchett	Bobby	G.	1930	Oct. 11, 1950	KY	KMIL
Burchfield	Eliza		1842ca	Aug. 28, 1859	Bre	C1
Burchfield	Polly		1820ca	Jan. 4, 1859	Bre	C1
Burchfield (Taulbee)	Nancy		1794ca	Mar. 23, 1852	Bre	C1
Burdell	Unknown Male			Mar. 12, 1859	Brk	C1
Burdet	John	R.		Aug. 15, 1854	Brk	C1
Burdett	Stpehen		1822ca	Dec. 16, 1861	Brk	C1
Burdett (Walls)	Eliza	J.	1830ca	Aug. 16, 1861	Brk	C1
Burdette	Donald		1927	Apr. 8, 1952	KY	KMIL
Burditt (Arglebright)	Malinda Jane		1835ca	Apr. 1, 1855	Brk	C1
Burdon	De. John LeMaster		Nov. 2, 1843		Web	Bk1
Buren	Cynthia		1847ca	Jul. 15, 1852	Brk	C1
Burgess	Adjutant			1791ca	NWS5	11/12/1791
Burgess	Columbia			1835	NWS4	8/14/1835
Burgess	Oma	A.	1892ca		Grn	Marr1

Last Name	First Name	I	Birth	Death	Co	Source
Burk	Michael		1761ca		NWS5	12/27/1788
Burk	Unknown		1816ca	Apr. 10, 1853	Dav	C1
Burke	Fred		Jun. 4, 1884	Apr. ??, 1975	Sim	MCDR
Burke	J.	H.		Aug. 16, 1864	KY	CMIL2
Burke	Thomas		Sep. 14, 1917	Mar. ??, 1987	Jef	MCDR
Burker	W.	N.		Jan. 12, 1866	KY	CMIL2
Burkhardt	Bertha		1887ca		Grn	Marr1
Burks	Avilla		1856ca	Sep. 27, 1878	Brk	C1
Burnett	John		1828ca		Gray	C1
Burnett	Willis		1874ca	Jul. 15, 1875	Dav	MCDR
Burns	Chadwick Otis		Nov. 30, 1929	Aug. 8, 1950	KY	KMIL
Burns	Lizzie		1872ca		Grn	Marr1
Burns	Martha		Dec. 6, 1842	Nov. 10, 1895	Ful	CEM7
Burns	W.	M.	Jun. 18, 1835	Jun. 16, 1897	Ful	CEM7
Burris	Columbus	W.	Sep. 8, 1846		KY	Bk1(P31)C
Burriss	John	H.	1822		But	Bk1
Burton	A.	C.	1838ca	Oct. 30, 1855	Dav	C1
Burton	Almeda		1858ca	Aug. 8, 1861	Brk	C1
Burton	Amanda		1859ca	Aug. 2, 1861	Brk	C1
Burton	Ida		1892ca		Grn	Marr1
Burton	Rachel	M.	1885ca		Grn	Marr1
Bush	Armina			Feb. 20, 1856	Bre	C1
Bush	C;arence	M.	1921	Jul. 16, 1952	KY	KMIL
Bush	Catherine		1849ca	Nov. 2, 1853	Grn	C1
Bush	John		Mar. 21, 1767	Aug. 5, 1845	NWS1	8/9/1845
Bush	Mary		1852ca	Sep. 1, 1858	Bre	C1
Bush	Mrs. Mary Jane		Nov. 28, 1826	Sep. 27, 1844	NWS1	10/5/1844
Bush	Mrs. Mattie		1835ca	Nov. ??, 1875	Dav	MCDR
Bush	William		1851ca	May 15, 1853	Grn	C1
Bussiere	Henry		Jul. 7, `907	Dec. 18, 1993	Har	MCDR
Bustestter	Sophia		1887ca		Grn	Marr1
But;er	Glassell		Jan. 22, 1898	Apr. ??, 1971	Har	MCDR
Butcher	Hazel		1888ca		Grn	Marr1
Butler	Edward		Mar. 20, 1762		KY	BK2(P252)
Butler	Eleanor		Dec. 31, 1763		KY	BK2(P252)
Butler	Gen.			1791ca	NWS5	11/12/1791
Butler	Jabeze		1850ca	Dec. 29, 1855	Brk	C1
Butler	Julia		1897	1978	Row	CEM1
Butler	Lizzy	S.	1852ca	Oct. 15, 1858	Bre	C1
Butler	Mary		Nov. 3, 1749		KY	BK2(P252)
Butler	Mrs.			Jul. 28, 1867	KY	BK2(P268)
Butler	Nannie		Jul. 21, 1840		KY	BK2(P270)
Butler	Pierce		Apr. 4, 1760		KY	BK2(P252)
Butler	Pierce		Oct. 4, 1794		KY	BK2(P267)
Butler	Pierce			1851	KY	BK2(P268)
Butler	Rebecca		Sep. 19, 1751		KY	BK2(P252)
Butler	Richard		Apr. 1, 1743		KY	BK2(P252)
Butler	Stephen		1828ca	Oct. 15, 1855	Brk	C1

Last Name	First Name	I	Birth	Death	Co	Source
Butler	Susan		1856ca	Nov. 17, 1858	Brk	C1
Butler	Thomas		Apr. 6, 1720		KY	BK2(P252)
Butler	Thomas		May 28, 1748		KY	BK2(P252)
Butler	Thos.	V.	1872ca	Oct. 15, 1878	Brk	C1
Buttram	James			Jul. 25, 1853	Brk	C1
Buxton	Ilse		Apr. 21, 1920	Jun. ??, 1989	Grn	MCDR
Byers	Amanda		Aug. 8, 1826		Fay	C2
Byers	E.		1834ca	May 7, 1894	Gray	C1
Byers	Iredell		1829		Brk	Bk1
Byers	W.	B.	Jun. 26, 1837		But	C2
Bynum	Adam		1869	1940	Gray	CEM7
Bynum	Blanche		Jun. 12, 1889	Aug. 27, 1890	Ful	CEM7
Bynum	Jackson		May 17, 1819	May 14, 1894	Ful	CEM7
Bynum	James Harwell		Feb. 27, 19-3	Apr. 2, 1905	Ful	CEM7
Bynum	James Lowry		May 16, 1919	Sep. 11, 1919	Ful	CEM7
Bynum	Mark		1863	1946	Ful	CEM7
Bynum	Mary Ann		Apr. 24, 1823	Sep. 8, 1898	Ful	CEM7
Bynum (Lannan)	Patsy		1852	1896	Ful	CEM7
Bynum (Tap)	A.	T.	1850	1927	Ful	CEM7
Byrant	Rollins Mason			May 28, 1952	Ful	KMIL
Cain	Mary			Dec. 17, 1878	KY	C1
Cain (Calhoun)	Emily		1833ca	Dec. 28, 1855	Brk	C1
Caldwell	Georgiana			1835	Dav	8/14/1835
Caldwell	Infant (2X)			1835	NWS4	8/14/1835
Caldwell	Samuel	J.	1840		NWS4	Bk1
Calhoon	Derutha			Nov. 10, 1855	But	C1
Calhoon	Malvina		1851ca	May 12, 1855	Bre	C1
Calhoun	Barthena		1852ca	May 11, 1854	Bre	C1
Calhoun	Lillian		1885ca		Bre	Marr1
Calhoun	Unknown Female			Jan. 15, 1874	Grn	C1
Callihan	Elizabeth		1890ca		Bre	Marr1
Callihan	Ethel	H.	1886ca		Grn	Marr1
Callihan	John	H.		Jul. 17, 1853	Grn	C1
Callihan	Sarah			Sep. 25, 1853	Grn	C1
Calloway	M.		1842ca	Mar. 2, 1861	KY	BK2(P194)
Calrton	John Thomas			Feb. 16, 1860	Dav	C1
Calvert	Forest	C.	Dec. 28m 1903		Hdn	CEM3
Calvert	Richard		1832ca	Apr. ??, 1857	Hdn	CEM2
Calvert	Ruth Chitwood		Nov. 12, 1912		Dav	C1
Camp	Ruth	P.	Feb. 26, 1878	Feb. 25, 1899	Hdn	CEM2
Camp	William	H.	1850ca	Feb. 19, 1904	Muh	CEM2
Campbell	Caleb		1831ca	Apr. 21, 1859	Brk	C1
Campbell	Carrlene		Dec. 17, 1842	Jun. 1, 1860	Bre	C1
Campbell	Charles		1780ca		Ful	CEM7
Campbell	Col. William			Nov. 20, 1800	NWS5	6/13/1798
Campbell	David	L.	1930	Jul. 25, 1950	NWS5	11/24/1800
Campbell	Dr. George	W.	Dec. 28, 1822		KY	KMIL
Campbell	Dr. John	C.	1812		Web	Bk1

Last Name	First Name	I	Birth	Death	Co	Source
Campbell	Eva			Oct. 25, 1877	KY	BK2(P60)
Campbell	Jackie	A.	1933	Feb. 13, 1951	Bre	C1
Campbell	John	B.	1928	Jul. 20, 1950	KY	KMIL
Campbell	John			Sep. 15, 1874	KY	KMIL
Campbell	Lewis		1840ca	Feb. 16, 1859	Bre	C1
Campbell	Lucinda		1849ca	May 1, 1854	Bre	C1
Campbell	Lucy	E.	1863	1949	Bre	C1
Campbell	Lucy		1879ca		Ful	CEM7
Campbell	Mary	L.	1885ca		Grn	Marr1
Campbell	Pearl		Sep. 11, 1884	May 4, 1904	Grn	Marr1
Campbell	Robert	M.	1856	19125	Ful	CEM7
Campbell	Robert		Apr. 22, 1822	Oct. 21, 1904	Ful	CEM7
Campbell	William			Apr. ??, 1845	Ful	CEM7
Campbell (Coals)	Delila		1829ca	Jul. 28, 1859	NWS1	4/26/1845
Canary	W.	A.		Oct. 10, 1894	Bre	C1
Candel	John		1840ca	Feb. 19, 1858	Brk	C1
Candill (Burns)	Elizabeth		1835ca	Sep. 19, 1874	Bre	C1
Candle	John		1797ca	Jul. 15, 1859	Bre	C1
Candler	Zachariah		1773ca		Bre	C1
Cannon	Crystal	J.		Jun. 26, 1980	NWS5	1/12/1793
Cantrell	Odes	I.	1929	Sep. 1, 1950	KY	KMIL
Cardwell	William	B.	1841		Muh	CEM2
Carico(Harrison)	Elizabeth		1833ca	Feb. 22, 1854	But	Bk1
Carline (Colored)			1835ca	Jan. 5, 1855	Dav	C1
Carlyle	Iva	H.	1876	1954	Bre	C1
Carlyle	Martin	S.	1866	1948	Hdn	CEM2
Carlyle	Martin		Feb. 17, 1916	Feb. 7, 1923	Hdn	CEM2
Carman	Edward	N.	1852ca	Apr. 16, 1878	Hdn	CEM2
Carman	Hardin	A.	1847ca	Jul. 20, 1874	Brk	C1
Carman	Jas.		1870ca	Aug. 23, 1878	Brk	C1
Carman	Margaret		1826ca	Jan. 21, 1894	Brk	C1
Carman	William			Aug. 20, 1878	Brk	C1
Carman (Horsley)	Elizabeth		1808ca	Apr. 20, 1855	Brk	C1
Carman (Sosh)	Emeline		1832ca	Jun. 10, 1952	Brk	C1
Carman (Thornhill)	Mary		1846ca	Aug. 1, 1878	Brk	C1
Carman (Whitworth)	Sarah		1827ca	Apr. 14, 1857	Brk	C1
Carnett	Unknown Female			Jan. 16, 1875	Brk	C1
Carney	James Charles		Jul. 12, 1930	Mar. 23, 1952	KY	KMIL
Carpenter	Fielding		1767ca	Jun. 25, 1853	Bre	C1
Carpenter	Irene		1889ca		Grn	Marr1
Carpenter	Martha		Feb. 14, 1832	May 15, 1873	Dav	CEM2
Carpenter	Mary		1879ca		Grn	Marr1
Carpenter	Richard Joel			Jul. 5, 1845	NWS1	7/19/1845
Carpenter	Unknown Female			May 15, 1875	Bre	C1
Carr	Clifford	L.	1927	May 27, 1951	KY	KMIL
Carr	Cora		1894ca		Grn	Marr1
Carr	Lottie		1886ca		Grn	Marr1
Carrico	Joseph	A.	1817ca	Apr. 30. 1854	Dav	C1

Last Name	First Name	I	Birth	Death	Co	Source
Carroll	Day	S.	1814ca		Gray	C1
Carroll	Dr. Clyde	C.	Dec. 7, 1878	Dec. 4, 1945	Hdn	CEM2
Carroll	Geo.	W.	Jan. 7, 1907		Car	C1
Carroll	James	A.	1926	Dec. 30, 1952	KY	KMIL
Carroll	Leonard		Jan. 1, 1907		Car	C1
Carroll	Robert	L.	Mar. 12, 1894	Oct. 22, 1975	Hdn	CEM2
Carroll	S.	S.	Nov. 12, 1835		Gray	C2
Carroll	Winnie		1887ca		Grn	Marr1
Carroll (Boyd)	Elizabeth		Jun. 19, 1880	Jun. 30, 1968	Hdn	CEM2
Carroll (Bunger)	Elizabeth	A.	May 17, 1855	Dec. 30, 1935	Hdn	CEM2
Carroll, Jr.	Charles Paten		Apr. 14, 1929	Sep. 19, 1950	KY	KMIL
Carson	Thomas	C.	1823		But	Bk1
Carter	C.		Oct. 22, 1838		Gray	C2
Carter	Cammie	A.	1897ca	Sep. 27, 1915	All	MCDR
Carter	Cammie	L.	1906ca	Oct. 4, 1933	All	MCDR
Carter	Clyde	M.	1931	Nov. 29, 1950	KY	KMIL
Carter	Dicy		1811	1926	Row	CEM1
Carter	Douglas	E.	1930	Aug. 2, 1950	KY	KMIL
Carter	Francis	A.		Jun. 21, 1853	Brk	C1
Carter	J.		Aug. 30, 1831	Jul. 7, 1873	Dav	CEM3
Carter	Joe	D.	1924	Sep. 4, 1950	KY	KMIL
Carter	Joe	D.	1924	Sep. 4, 1950	KY	KMIL
Carter	Joel		1779ca	Dec. 23, 1861	Brk	C1
Carter	Maggie		1885ca		Grn	Marr1
Carter	Richd.	F.	1790ca	Mar. 20, 1853	Brk	C1
Carter	Von			Sep. 12, 1957	Fay	MCDR
Carter	Widow Mary		1851ca		Grn	Marr1
Carwile	Cammie	J.		Mar. 12, 1959	Jef	MCDR
Carwile	Chas.			Jan. 6, 1878	Brk	C1
Carwile	E.	L.		Mar. 16, 1894	Brk	C1
Cary	Joseph		1844ca	May 4, 1845	NWS1	5/10/1845
Casebier	Martha	A.	Sep. 11, 1837	Apr. 17, 1899	Muh	CEM3
Casebier	Melissa		Feb. 16, 1871	Mar. 30, 1880	Muh	CEM3
Casebier	Ollie		Sep. 28, 1906	Oct. 29, 1934	Muh	CEM3
Casebier	R.	G.	Apr. 18, 1878	Sep. 16, 1896	Muh	CEM3
Casey	John	E.	1835ca	Mar. 18, 1875	Dav	MCDR
Casey	John		1824ca		Gray	C1
Casey	Martha			Oct. 25, 1878	Brk	C1
Cash	Elvree		Aug. 11, 1835	Dec. 1, 1899	Hdn	CEM2
Cash	Male		Dec. 19, 1883	Dec. 19, 1883	Hdn	CEM2
Cash	R.	T.	Jan. 3, 1830	May 12, 1912	Hdn	CEM2
Cash	Thomas	T.	May 14, 1866	Feb. 26, 1944	Hdn	CEM2
Cashman	Charles			Jun. 22, 1861	Brk	C1
Cashman	Grace	A.	1892ca	Aug. 20, 1894	Brk	C1
Cashman	Thomas	J.	1828ca	May 5, 1852	Brk	C1
Castle	Robert	E.	1930	Jul. 31, 1950	KY	KMIL
Castleman	William		1930	May 17, 1951	KY	KMIL
Caudill	Benton		Mar. 29, 1903	Nov. 12, 1965	Row	CEM1

Last Name	First Name	I	Birth	Death	Co	Source
Carter	J.		Aug. 30, 1831	Jul. 7, 1873	Dav	CEM3
Carter	Joe	D.	1924	Sep. 4, 1950	KY	KMIL
Carter	Joe	D.	1924	Sep. 4, 1950	KY	KMIL
Carter	Joel		1779ca	Dec. 23, 1861	Brk	C1
Carter	Maggie		1885ca		Grn	Marr1
Carter	Richd.	F.	1790ca	Mar. 20, 1853	Brk	C1
Carter	Von			Sep. 12, 1957	Fay	MCDR
Carter	Widow Mary		1851ca		Grn	Marr1
Carwile	Cammie	J.		Mar. 12, 1959	Jef	MCDR
Carwile	Chas.			Jan. 6, 1878	Brk	C1
Carwile	E.	L.		Mar. 16, 1894	Brk	C1
Cary	Joseph		1844ca	May 4, 1845	NWS1	5/10/1845
Casebier	Martha	A.	Sep. 11, 1837	Apr. 17, 1899	Muh	CEM3
Casebier	Melissa		Feb. 16, 1871	Mar. 30, 1880	Muh	CEM3
Casebier	Ollie		Sep. 28, 1906	Oct. 29, 1934	Muh	CEM3
Casebier	R.	G.	Apr. 18, 1878	Sep. 16, 1896	Muh	CEM3
Casey	John	E.	1835ca	Mar. 18, 1875	Dav	MCDR
Casey	John		1824ca		Gray	C1
Casey	Martha			Oct. 25, 1878	Brk	C1
Cash	Elvree		Aug. 11, 1835	Dec. 1, 1899	Hdn	CEM2
Cash	Male		Dec. 19, 1883	Dec. 19, 1883	Hdn	CEM2
Cash	R.	T.	Jan. 3, 1830	May 12, 1912	Hdn	CEM2
Cash	Thomas	T.	May 14, 1866	Feb. 26, 1944	Hdn	CEM2
Cashman	Charles			Jun. 22, 1861	Brk	C1
Cashman	Grace	A.	1892ca	Aug. 20, 1894	Brk	C1
Cashman	Thomas	J.	1828ca	May 5, 1852	Brk	C1
Castle	Robert	E.	1930	Jul. 31, 1950	KY	KMIL
Castleman	William		1930	May 17, 1951	KY	KMIL
Caudill	Benton		Mar. 29, 1903	Nov. 12, 1965	Row	CEM1
Caudill	Donna Maxine		1927	1928	Row	CEM1
Caudill	Estil		1923	1928	Row	CEM1
Caudill	Eulas		Oct. 27, 1992		Row	CEM1
Caudill	Flora	M.	1903	1951	Row	CEM1
Caudill	Henry	C.	Aug. 24, 1874	Jul. 16, 1941	Row	CEM1
Caudill	Henry	C.	Oct. 14, 1891	May 5, 1935	Row	CEM1
Caudill	James	C.	1933	Jun. 7, 1951	KY	KMIL
Caudill	John	D.	Jan. 29, 1901	Jul. 26, 1973	Row	CEM1
Caudill	John	T.	1870	1957	Row	CEM1
Caudill	John Monroe		Nov. 29, 1910	Dec. 14, 1930	Row	CEM1
Caudill	Joseph		1886	1957	Row	CEM1
Caudill	Mabel				Row	CEM1
Caudill	Martha	E.	1874	1958	Row	CEM1
Caudill	Martha Alice		Mar. 26, 1933		Row	CEM1
Caudill	Martha Ann		1874	1947	Row	CEM1
Caudill	Nancy	J.	Feb. 6, 1905	Sep. 28, 1984	Row	CEM1
Caudill	Ottis		Mar. 24, 1911	Mar. 25, 1911	Row	CEM1
Caudill	Rachel		Jan. 31, 1872	Mar. 26, 1954	Row	CEM1

Last Name	First Name	I	Birth	Death	Co	Source
Caudill	Ralph	K.	1931	Nov. 27, 1950	KY	KMIL
Caudill	Sally		Aug. 9, 1900	Mar. 30, 1993	Row	CEM1
Caudill	Teddy	R.	1938	1967	Row	CEM1
Caudill	William	M.	1870	1933	Row	CEM1
Caudill	Willis	C.	Oct. 25, 1899	Oct. 20, 1992	Row	CEM1
Caudill	Wilson		May 3, 1899	Jan. 22, 1975	Row	CEM1
Caudle	Halcie		1890ca		Grn	Marr1
Cavelle	Preston		1835ca	May 15, 1859	Bre	C1
Cavender	George		1778ca		NWS5	3/12/1796
Cawthorn	Norman	G.	1927	Jul. 5, 1950	KY	KMIL
Cecil	Bessie		Aug. 15, 1897	Sep. 2, 1966	Hdn	CEM2
Cecil	Charlie		Aug. 15, 1893	Sep. 15, 1967	Hdn	CEM2
Cecil	William	A.	1929	Sep. 24, 1951	KY	KMIL
Cecil	William	U.	1859ca	Mar. 7, 1914	Hdn	MCDR
Chadwell	Bertha	K.	1892ca	Aug. 7, 1950	Dav	MCDR
Chaffin	Clifford		1931	Dec. 2, 1950	KY	KMIL
Chaffins	Leo		1930	Sep. 12, 1951	KY	KMIL
Chafins	Mahala		1889ca		Grn	Marr1
Chambers	Elisha		1778ca	Aug. 11, 1859	Bre	C1
Chambers	Mrs. Elizabeth		1825ca	1845	NWS1	6/7/1845
Chambers	N.	B.	Jun. 19, 1852		Han	Bk1
Chambers (Williams)	Letticia		1821	1882	Han	Bk1
Chambers, Jr.	G.	W.	1814	1860	Han	Bk1
Chandler	James	M.	Aug. 13, 1827		Web	Bk1
Chandler	Prentice		1928	Apr. 27, 1953	KY	KMIL
Chandler	William	M.	Jan. 16, 1829		Web	Bk1
Chaney	Maggie		1880ca		Grn	Marr1
Chapen	James		1779ca	Dec. 15, 1874	Brk	C1
Chapin	George	H	1822ca	Mar. 30, 1844	NWS1	4/13/1844
Chapman	Anthony			Aug. 9, 1835	NWS4	8/14/1835
Chapman	Aristexes			Oct. 25, 1853	Grn	C1
Chapman	Bertha	L.	1887ca		Grn	Marr1
Chapman	Edmond		1796ca	Mar. 11, 1859	Bre	C1
Chapman	Elide		1883ca		Grn	Marr1
Chapman	Fayatte		1839ca	Nov. 23, 1852	Bre	C1
Chapman	John			Mar. 20, 1859	Bre	C1
Chapman	Whitney	C.		Mar. 10, 1974	Dav	MCDR
Chapman	William	R.	1841		But	Bk1
Chappell	Ellis	T.	1885	1938	Muh	CEM3
Chappell	Gennevie		1887		Muh	CEM3
Charles	James	O.	1931	Mar. 23, 1953	KY	KMIL
Charles (Slave)				Nov. 15, 1861	Brk	C1
Chase	Ensign			1791ca	NWS5	11/12/1791
Chatfield	Fred	T.	1930	Dec. 1, 1950	KY	KMIL
Cheanult	Ellen Carroll		Feb. 21, 1889	Sep. 13, 1970	Hdn	CEM2
Cheanult	George	M.	Aug. 9, 1871	Jul. 4, 1938	Hdn	CEM2
Chenault	Hugh	F.	Dec. 13, 1891	Dec. 30, 1947	Hdn	CEM2

Last Name	First Name	I	Birth	Death	Co	Source
Chenault	Mabel		1894	1970	Hdn	CEM2
Chenault	Clyde Coleman		Apr. 1, 1886	Jan. 4, 1966	Hdn	CEM2
Chenault (Van Meter)	Alice		Apr. 8, 1872	Mar. 20, 1949	Hdn	CEM2
Childers	W.	P.	May 7, 1851	Oct. 20, 1870	Ful	CEM7
Childress	Margarett			Jul. 27, 1835	NWS4	8/7/1835
Chilton	Owen	D.	1927	Nov. 4, 1951	KY	KMIL
Chinn	Louis	O.	1930	Jun. 23, 1951	KY	KMIL
Chinn	Mary		1886ca		Grn	Marr1
Chinn	Melissa			Oct. 22, 1845	NWS1	11/15/1845
Chitwood	Charlie Thomas		1880	1960	Hdn	CEM2
Chitwood	Edward	F.	Oct. 3, 1882	Aug. 1, 1964	Hdn	CEM2
Chitwood	Lee	E.	1884	1911	Hdn	CEM2
Chitwood	Roger Larue		1910	1937	Hdn	CEM2
Chitwood	Rose	P.	Jul. 9, 1888	Mar. 30, 1974	Hdn	CEM2
Chitwood	Virgie Lee		1889	1917	Hdn	CEM2
Christian	Andrew	J.	1930	May 31, 1951	KY	KMIL
Christian	Unknown Male			Jun. 20, 1861	Brk	C1
Church	Alfred	L.	1930ca	Sep. 19, 1986	Fay	MCDR
Church, Jr.	Ray		1929	Oct. 14, 1952	KY	KMIL
Cinthia (Slave)			1847ca	Jun. 10, 1855	Brk	C1
Cirnett	Richard		1831ca	Oct. 22, 1852	Brk	C1
Clack	Mary Elizabeth		Aug. 18, 1857		Sim	C1
Clark	Bertha		1892ca		Grn	Marr1
Clark	Fannie Duncan		Jul. 27, 1856	Dec. 11, 1882	Ful	CEM1
Clark	Fleming	J.	1836		But	Bk1
Clark	James		Apr. ??, 1786	Jan. 26, 1844	NWS1	2/3/1844
Clark	John		1820ca	Dec. 2, 1875	Dav	MCDR
Clark	Jonathan		1771ca		NWS5	1/12/1793
Clark	Joseph	E.	1929	Oct. 6, 1952	KY	KMIL
Clark	Kisah		1801ca	Apr. 10, 1857	Dav	C1
Clark	Maj.			1791ca	NWS5	11/12/1791
Clark	Presely	M.	1829		But	Bk1
Clark	Sylvania		1891ca		Grn	Marr1
Clark	Thomas	J.		Aug. 20, 1855	Brk	C1
Clark	W.	T.		Feb. 8, 1868	Ful	CEM7
Clark	William	B.	Mar. 9, 1835		Web	Bk1
Clark	Wm.	B.	1809ca	Mar. 17, 1856	Brk	C1
Clark	James	M.	Mar. 25, 1828		Web	Bk1
Clark (Bowman)	Catherine		1871ca	Mar. ??, 1894	Brk	C1
Clark, Jr.	Herbert	F.	1926	Oct. 12, 1951	KY	KMIL
Clarke	Loueller		Nov. 19, 1859		Sim	C1
Clarkson	Thomas	S.	1927	Sep. 1, 1950	KY	KMIL
Clater	L.		1888ca	Feb. ??, 1894	Brk	C1
Claudio	Ramon	N.	1925ca	Sep. 28, 1953	Jef	MCDR
Clawferd	Unknown Male			Dec. 16, 1854	Bre	C1
Claycomb	Adam		1810ca	Apr. 29, 1855	Brk	C1
Claycomb (Wales)	Unknown Female		1850ca	Aug. 18, 1894	Brk	C1

Last Name	First Name	I	Birth	Death	Co	Source
Clayton	Elizabeth		1825ca	Apr. 4, 1853	Grn	C1
Clayton	Geprge		1821ca	Jul. 24, 1861	Dav	C1
Clayton	Judge P.	D.	Dec. 25, 1811		Web	Bk1
Clemens	John	J.	1932	Sep. 19, 1951	KY	KMIL
Clements	J.	H.	1831ca	Jul. 22, 1861	Dav	C1
Clements (Nelson)	Ann	M.	1827ca	Apr. 22, 1861	Dav	C1
Clemmans	Leander			Aug. 23, 1877	Bre	C1
Clemmons	Polly		1836ca	Feb. 29, 1859	Bre	C1
Clemmons	Samuel		1850ca	Jan. 5, 1856	Bre	C1
Clemmons	Unknown Male			Apr. 15, 1876	Bre	C1
Clemmons (Jones)	Rebecca		1841ca	Apr. 15, 1876	Bre	C1
Clemons	Ansel	S.	1891ca	Sep. 29, 1953	Jef	
Clemons	Carey		1789ca	Jul. 8, 1844	NWS1	8/3/1844
Clemons	Clifford		1930	Jul. 03, 1953	KY	KMIL
Clemons	William	A.	1852ca	May 20, 1853	Bre	C1
Clemons (Miller)	Fanny		1819ca	Jul. 15, 1854	Bre	C1
Cleveland	Charles	L.	Aug. 25, 1844		KY	Bk1(P53)T
Clevenger	James	M.	1928	Nov. 4, 1950	KY	KMIL
Click	Leslie	D.	1932	Dec. 6, 1950	KY	KMIL
Cline	George Hay		Mar. 15, 1930	Jun. 11, 1951	KY	KMIL
Cline	John	S.	Jan. 25, 1838		Gray	C2
Clough	Abram		1855ca	Oct. 9, 1932	Bur	MCDR
Clough	Abram		1855	1932	Har	CEM1
Clough	Agnes			Mar. 11, 1919	Bur	MCDR
Clough	Alex.	Z.	1857	1936	Har	CEM1
Clough	Alexander		1858ca	Feb. 7, 1936	Har	MCDR
Clough	Alice	L.	Jul. 6, 1877	Nov. 23, 1899	Har	CEM1
Clough	Anna	L.	1882ca	Apr. 7, 1932	Har	MCDR
Clough	Anna L. Wheeler		Apr. 30, 1882	Jan. 7, 1932	Har	CEM1
Clough	Arena	B.	1851	1928	Har	CEM1
Clough	Beadie		1883	1919	Har	CEM1
Clough	Beadie		1886ca	Feb. 18, 1919	Har	MCDR
Clough	Bessie Lee		Feb. 25, 1877	Jan. 10, 1878	Har	CEM1
Clough	Bula	M.	1906ca	Dec. 16, 1958	Lin	MCDR
Clough	C.	C.	1914ca	Feb. 27, 1915	Bur	MCDR
Clough	Carlos	B.	1878ca	Mar. 24, 1964	Byl	MCDR
Clough	Carlos	C.	1932ca	Oct. 23, 1965	Lew	MCDR
Clough	Carlos			Feb. 27, 1919	Har	MCDR
Clough	Carma		1896ca	Mar. 14, 1927	Car	MCDR
Clough	Carolos		1917		Har	CEM1
Clough	Claudy		Mar. 22, 1887	Apr. 28, 1890	Har	CEM1
Clough	Doc		1924ca	Oct. 7, 1986	Har	MCDR
Clough	Drusa	L.	1892ca	Mar. 21, 1972	Fay	MCDR
Clough	Earl	T.	1898ca	Nov. 3, 1976	Woo	MCDR
Clough	Earl			Apr. 16, 1937	Woo	MCDR
Clough	Elbert		Jul. 20, 1875	Jul. 22, 1936	Har	CEM1
Clough	Ethel		1894ca	Jun. 7, 1912	Bur	MCDR

Last Name	First Name	I	Birth	Death	Co	Source
Clough	Fannie Duncan		1870ca	Mar. 28, 1931	Oh	MCDR
Clough	Franklin			Dec. 6, 1920	Har	MCDR
Clough	Garlan	C.	1924ca	Oct. 7, 1986	Har	MCDR
Clough	George	W.	May 23, 1912	Jun. 18, 1933	Har	CEM1
Clough	George		1912ca	Jun. 18, 1933	Har	MCDR
Clough	Gerald	C.	1959ca	Mar. 12, 1986	Mad	MCDR
Clough	Guss	T.	1883ca	Jul. 12, 1964	Bur	MCDR
Clough	Helen Whalen		Aug. 31, 1912	Oct. 20, 1942	Har	CEM1
Clough	Inez		Jun. 11, 1887	Jun. 11, 1887	Har	CEM1
Clough	Infant		Jun. 31, 1890	Jun. 31, 1890	Har	CEM1
Clough	James	T.	1845	1902	Har	CEM1
Clough	John	W.	1861	1946	Har	CEM1
Clough	Maggie J. McF.		1859	1936	Har	CEM1
Clough	Mart		Oct. 19, 1883	Jan. 26, 1951	Har	CEM1
Clough	Mary T. Arnold		Jun. 12, 1862	Aug. 7, 1932	Har	CEM1
Clough	Ransom		Aug. 3, 1820	Feb. 18, 1861	Har	CEM1
Clough	Ruth	A.	1860	1948	Har	CEM1
Clough	Samuel		Dec. 11, 1881	Aug. 29, 1890	Har	CEM1
Clough	Susan		1827ca	Mar. 7, 1876	Har	CEM1
Clough	Veach		1890	1929	Har	CEM1
Clough	W.	L.	Jun. 13, 1860	Mar. 24, 1933	Har	CEM1
Clouse	George Wash.		May ??, 1844	Apr. ??, 1892	Dav	CEM3
Cloyce	Elizabeth Boyd	K.	1823	Sep. 20, 1861	Ful	CEM2
Cloyce	Elvira		Oct. 31, 1856	Feb. 20, 1861	Ful	CEM2
Cloyce	Lydia Frances		Feb. 21, 1850	Oct. 23, 1850	Ful	CEM2
Clutter	William		1831ca	Jun. 17, 1852	Brk	C1
Clutts	Mary	A.	1815ca	May 6, 1853	Grn	C1
Coakley	Ernest	L.	1928	Oct. 13, 1951	KY	KMIL
Cobbs	Ensign			1791ca	NWS5	11/12/1791
Cochran	Lucy		1881ca		Grn	Marr1
Cockeral	William		1830ca		Gray	C1
Cockrill	Henry		1860ca	Nov. 31, 1875	Bre	C1
Cockwell	Simon		1771ca	Sep. 13, 1856	Bre	C1
Cockwell	Susan Elizabeth		1852ca	Sep. ??, 1854	Bre	C1
Cockwill (Smith)	Polly		1795ca	May 7, 1855	Bre	C1
Cody	Whitney			Nov. 18, 1986	Ken	MCDR
Cody	William	F.	1925	Jul. 12, 1950	KY	KMIL
Coelman	Charles		1927	Mar. 22, 1953	KY	KMIL
Coffee	Ambrose		1789ca	May 13, 1852	Grn	C1
Coffee	William	W.	1932	Feb. 13, 1951	KY	KMIL
Coffey	Clifford	V.	1931	Jan. 12, 1951	KY	KMIL
Coffey	Gordon	R.	1929	Mar. 26, 1953	KY	KMIL
Coffman	Charles	G.	1927	Oct. 26, 1952	KY	KMIL
Coffman	John Perry		Jan. 8, 1840		Web	Bk1
Coffman	Richard Franklin		Mar. 6, 1834		Web	Bk1
Cohron	Henry		1833		But	Bk1
Cole	Fannie		Feb. 25. 1858	Jan. 7, 1900	Ful	CEM4

Last Name	First Name	I	Birth	Death	Co	Source
Cole	Jefferson	T.	1904ca	May 14, 1972	Fay	MCDR
Cole	R.	S.	May 17, 1827	Dec. 3, 1898	Ful	CEM4
Colegrove	Ethel		1892ca		Grn	Marr1
Colegrove	Oliver		1930	Aug. 16, 1950	KY	KMIL
Colemaan	James	L.	1851ca	Mar. 12, 1852	Brk	C1
Coleman	Charles		1927	Mar. 22, 1953	KY	KMIL
Coleman	Gilbert	T.	1927	Aug. 27, 1951	KY	KMIL
Coleman	Grover	W.	1918	Nov. 20, 1951	KY	KMIL
Coleman	John Francis		Jun. 23, 1869	Aug. 25, 1871	Web	CEM1
Coleman	Malissa		Nov. 7, 1874	Feb. 19, 1890	Dav	CEM2
Coleman	Prof. William	S.	Dec. 25, 1844		Web	Bk1
Coleman	W.	S.	Dec. 8, 1833	May 13, 1887	Ful	CEM7
Coles	Jack		1845ca	Nov. ??, 1854	Bre	C1
Collier	Crystal	J.	1978ca	Sep. 6, 1981	Jef	MCDR
Collins	David		Nov. 20, 1931	Dec. 7, 1951	KY	KMIL
Collins	James	E.	1925	Nov. 29, 1950	KY	KMIL
Collins	John	P.	1811ca	Jan. 20, 1877	Grn	C2
Collins	John Soulard		Mar. 30, 1919	Jan. 31, 1954	KY	KMIL
Collins	Orman	E.	1910ca	Dec. 5, 1961	Grn	MCDR
Collins	Rev. John			Aug. 22, 1845	NWS1	9/6/1845
Collins	S.	H.		Oct. 19, 1875	Bre	C1
Collins	Terrie		1842ca	Nov. 14, 1852	Grn	C1
Collins	Widow Naomi		1881ca		Grn	Marr1
Collins	William	U.	1893ca	Dec. 26, 1956	Jef	MCDR
Colston	Gorman			Jan. 1, 1925	Ken	MCDR
Colvin	Charles	W.	1874	1912	Har	CEM1
Colvin	Ruth	N.	1876		Har	CEM1
Coman	Stephen		1806ca	Feb. 15, 1853	Grn	C1
Combs	Alexander		1851	Mar. 23, 1852	Bre	C1
Combs	Andrew		1836ca	Oct. ??, 1852	Bre	C1
Combs	Anthony		1931	Oct. 14, 1951	KY	KMIL
Combs	Benjamin		1788ca	Nov. 6, 1858	Bre	C1
Combs	Bobby	V.	1930	Oct. 2, 1952	KY	KMIL
Combs	Calvin		1847ca	Oct. 15, 1877	Bre	C1
Combs	Emilia		1837ca	Sep. ??, 1852	Bre	C1
Combs	Granvill		1841ca	Sep. ??, 1852	Bre	C1
Combs	Malony		1856ca	Jun. 20, 1859	Bre	C1
Combs	Nancy			Sep. 10, 1875	Bre	C1
Combs	Preston		1802ca	Oct. 4, 1877	Bre	C1
Combs	Susan			Nov. 23, 1877	Bre	C1
Combs	Unknown Female			Dec. 14, 1857	Bre	C1
Combs	Unknown Male			Nov. 13, 1876	Bre	C1
Combs (Davis)	Eliza Jane		1851	Mar. 15, 1854	Bre	C1
Combs (Davis)	Tempy		1815ca	Dec. 5, 1854	Bre	C1
Combs (Strong)	Sarah		1850ca	Nov. 5, 1876	Bre	C1
Comer	Emma		Jan. 1, 1871	Mar. 19, 1904	Dav	CEM3
Comer	Henry	A.	Aug. 12, 1864		Dav	CEM3

Last Name	First Name	I	Birth	Death	Co	Source
Compton	Caleb		1821ca	Jun. ??, 1861	Brk	C1
Compton	Jerry	D.	1803ca	Oct. 4, 1859	Brk	C1
Compton	Mary		1801ca	Nov. 8, 1861	Brk	C1
Compton	Nataline		1849	1852	Grn	C1
Compton (Parsons)	Sarah	F.	1860ca	Jul. 17, 1904	Brk	C1
Comstock	Sarah	E.	1853ca	Mar. 6, 1861	Brk	C1
Conaghan	William	U.	1913ca	Aug. 25, 1984	Gm	MCDR
Conger	Osia	L.	1883ca		Grn	Marr1
Conklin	David		1830ca		Gray	C1
Conklin	David		1797ca	Dec. 11, 1858	Brk	C1
Conklin	Sindarells		1829ca		Gray	C1
Conley	Myrtle		1884ca		Grn	Marr1
Conly	Elizabeth		1821ca	Aug. 14, 1853	Grn	C1
Conly	James			May 21, 1857	Bre	C1
Connaway	Lucinda Francis			Jul. 31, 1858	Brk	C1
Connely	Alexander			Sep. 30, 1845	NWS1	9/6/1845
Conner	Davis	M.	1829		Han	Bk1
Conner	George	W.	1927	Dec. 12, 1950	KY	KMIL
Conner	M.	H.	Feb. 11, 1851		Han	Bk1
Conner	Raymond	E.	1927	Nov. 1, 1951	KY	KMIL
Conner (Prentiss)	Maria	L.	1828		Han	Bk1
Conway	J.	N.	Jan. 6, 1841		Gray	C2
Conway	John	N.	1841		But	Bk1
Cook	Douglas		1917	1921	Hdn	CEM2
Cook	Edward		1881	1957	Hdn	CEM2
Cook	George	E.	Jul. 17, 1913	Oct. 4, 1969	Hdn	CEM2
Cook	George	H.	Apr. 26, 1799	Mar. 27, 1876	Hdn	CEM1
Cook	George		1874	1876	Hdn	CEM1
Cook	Ible			1887ca	Grn	Marr1
Cook	James	L.	Feb. 19, 1931	Jul. 25, 1953	KY	KMIL
Cook	James	M.	1832		But	Bk1
Cook	Mary	S.	1885	1924	Hdn	CEM2
Cook	Mary Eloise		1923	1944	Hdn	CEM2
Cook	Mattie		Jun. 3, 1874	Jul. 29, 1874	Muh	CEM3
Cooke	A.	V.	Dec. 10, 1868	Jan. 31, 1941	Hdn	CEM2
Cooke (Hatfield)	Beatrice		Jun. 10, 1870	Sep. 3, 1961	Hdn	CEM2
Coomes	Lucy	J.	Jan. 17, 1873	Dec. 7, 1898	Dav	CEM3
Coomes	Marie		Jun. 23, 1894	Jun. 23, 1894	Dav	CEM3
Coon	Lucy		Feb. 30, 1833	Feb. 15, 1895	Dav	CEM3
Coons	Malnor	G.		Nov. 10, 1845	NWS1	11/15/1845
Cooper	Harold	R.	1912	Dec. 2, 1950	KY	KMIL
Cooper	James		1764ca		NWS5	12/27/1788
Cooper	Lillie		1891ca		Grn	Marr1
Cooper	W.	K.	1893ca	Jul. 28, 1940	All	MCDR
Cooper	W.	M.	Sep. 29, 1836		Gray	C2
Cooper	William	E.	1920	Apr. 4, 1951	KY	KMIL
Cooper (Hoover)	Miley		1821ca	Sep. 2, 1854	Dav	C1

Last Name	First Name	I	Birth	Death	Co	Source
Cope	Deal		1833ca	Sep. 11, 1857	Bre	C1
Cope	Eliza Jane		1829ca	Jul. 26, 1856	Bre	C1
Cope	Greenville		1842ca	Aug. 23, 1853	Bre	C1
Cope	Jas.	P.	1785ca	Feb. 27, 1857	Bre	C1
Cope	Leander			Dec. 19, 1854	Bre	C1
Cope	Ree Allice			Jul. 20, 1874	Bre	C1
Cope	William	D.	1825ca	Mar. 28, 1854	Bre	C1
Cope (Hargis)	Sabina		1831ca	May 24, 1858	Bre	C1
Copeland	Ellis	H.	1931	Nov. 27, 1950	KY	KMIL
Copher	Adina		1906ca	Sep. 26, 1981	Bat	MCDR
Copher	Andrew	F.	1889ca	Oct. 10, 1966	Bat	MCDR
Copher	Andy		1871ca	Feb. 16, 1940	Bat	MCDR
Copher	Anzy	N.	1912ca	Mar. 16, 1973	Bat	MCDR
Copher	Carolyn		1942ca	Apr. 18, 1959	Fay	MCDR
Copher	Chris		1913ca	Jun. 21, 1964	Fay	MCDR
Copher	Clark	V.	1896ca	Jan. 26, 1965	Bat	MCDR
Copher	Corbett	J.	1909ca	Jan. 22, 1972	Bat	MCDR
Copher	David		1842ca	Oct. 10, 1922	Bat	MCDR
Copher	Elzie			Apr. 18, 1928	Bat	MCDR
Copher	Emmie	C.	1893ca	Nov. 25, 1980	Bat	MCDR
Copher	Ethel	R.	1931ca	Feb. 14, 1956	Bat	MCDR
Copher	Flossie	P.	1929ca	Nov. 10, 1985	Bat	MCDR
Copher	Francis	L.	1902ca	Oct. 5, 1912	Bat	MCDR
Corbett	Joseph		Sep. 22, 1829		Web	Bk1
Cord	Lillian		1876ca		Grn	Marr1
Corder	John	W.	1834		But	Bk1
Cormett	Crystal	L.		Dec. 4, 1985	Jef	KMIL
Cornett	Unknown Female			Jan. 15, 1875	Bre	C1
Corns	Etta		1891ca		Grn	Marr1
Corriell	Emma	F.	1886ca		Grn	Marr1
Corrington	Joseph		1851	Sep. ??, 1852	Grn	C1
Corum	A.	W.	Oct. 18, 1852	Nov. 20, 1919	Ful	CEM7
Corum	Lizzie		Nov. 28, 1863	Jul. 15, 1923	Ful	CEM7
Corum	Mattie		Nov. 14, 1893	Dec. 17, 1936	Ful	CEM7
Corum	W.	N.	Mar. 9, 1848	Jul. 4, 1886	Ful	CEM7
Corum	Zachary	T.	1849		But	Bk1
Corwile	Jas.		1849ca	May 5, 1904	Brk	C1
Cottell	Ansel	C.	1914ca	Mar. 23, 1966	Fay	
Couch	Andrew		1806ca	May 15, 1856	Bre	C1
Couch	Cintha		1843ca	Sep. 15, 1856	Bre	C1
Couch	Dr. L.	J.	1847		Web	Bk1
Couch	Powhatan	J.	Oct. 24, 1839		Web	Bk1
Countzler	Peter		Sep. 1, 1838		Web	Bk1
Courm	Rosie Nina		Aug. 18, 1897	May 25, 1962	Ful	CEM7
Cox	Boyd	E.	1928	Jul. 5, 1950	KY	KMIL
Cox	Lorenzo	D.		Jun. 28, 1855	Brk	C1
Cox	Nancy			Mar. 18, 1843	NWS1	4/1/1843

Last Name	First Name	I	Birth	Death	Co	Source
Cox	Vina		1873ca		Grn	Marr1
Coyle	Martha		1838ca	Feb. 29, 1852	Brk	C1
Crabtree	A.			May 7, 1912	Dav	MCDR
Crabtree	Agnes	F.	1901ca	Jan. 24, 1963	Dav	MCDR
Crabtree	Albert	T.	1892ca	Feb. 23, 1951	Byl	MCDR
Crabtree	Albert		1900ca	Oct. 26, 1962	Dav	MCDR
Crabtree	Albert			Apr. 4, 1935	Dav	MCDR
Crabtree	Alex		1847ca	Nov. 29, 1919	Dav	MCDR
Crabtree	Alexander		1884ca	Apr. 20, 1941	Dav	MCDR
Crabtree	Alexander		1836ca	Oct. 23, 1916	Dav	MCDR
Crabtree	Alfred	J.	1925ca	May 24, 1945	Dav	MCDR
Crabtree	C.	A.	1831ca	Nov. 17, 1855	Dav	C1
Crabtree	David	E.	1934	May 3, 1952	KY	KMIL
Crabtree	Effie		Feb. 12, 1902	Feb. 9, 1941	Dav	CEM2
Crabtree	Jacob		1805ca	Jan. 25, 1855	Dav	C1
Crabtree	Myra		1817ca	Feb. 20, 1854	Dav	C1
Crady	Eugene		Oct.16, 1887	Jan. 15, 1954	Hdn	CEM2
Craft	Angeline			Nov. 5, 1859	Bre	C1
Craft	Effie		1895ca		Grn	Marr1
Craft	Essie		1895ca		Grn	Marr1
Craft	Esther	B.	1893ca		Grn	Marr1
Craft	Winnie		1890ca		Grn	Marr1
Crafton	Margaret			Apr. 12, 1854	Brk	C1
Craig	C.	G.	1946	1926	Hdn	CEM2
Craig	Charles	H.	Dec. 8, 1851	Nov. 11, 1930	Hdn	CEM2
Craig	Chester	A.	Oct. 17, 1881	Feb. 7, 1949	Hdn	CEM2
Craig	Eliza	S.	Jul. 4, 1854	Nov. 18, 1934	Hdn	CEM2
Craig	Ella		Nov. 22, 1882	Nov. 22, 1923	Hdn	CEM2
Craig	James		Mar. 25, 1840		Gray	C2
Craig	James	E.	Nov. 14, 1857	Nov. 19, 1935	Hdn	CEM2
Craig	James			1874	Han	Bk1
Craig	Jessye		Mar. 21, 1892	Jan. 15, 1976	Hdn	CEM2
Craig	Male		1912	1912	Hdn	CEM2
Craig	Mary	E.	Feb. 26, 1861	May 25, 1950	Hdn	CEM2
Craig	Will	H.	Jul. 5, 1874	Mar. 2, 1928	Hdn	CEM2
Craig (Egemann)	Gussie		Jul. 8, 1883	May 15, 1947	Hdn	CEM2
Crain	Annah Melloan		Jul. 15, 1880	Jun. 24, 1944	Hdn	CEM2
Crain	Fred Lee		Aug. 14, 1871	Dec. 27, 1962	Hdn	CEM2
Crain	Henry Lee			Oct. 28, 1935	Hdn	CEM2
Crain	John Houghton		Oct. 15, 1900	Oct. 27, 1972	Hdn	CEM2
Crain (Richardson)	Margaret		Dec. 31, 1901		Hdn	CEM2
Crawford	Clell		Jul. 11, 1864	Jan. 2, 1906	Hdn	CEM2
Crawford	Edward			Jul. 19, 1875	Bre	C1
Crawford	George		1871ca	May 20, 1874	Bre	C1
Crawford	Kenneth	E.	1931	Jun. 14, 1953	KY	KMIL
Crawford	Mary	F.		Jul. 15, 1875	Bre	C1
Crawford	Nancy		1789ca	Feb. 28, 1854	Bre	C1

Last Name	First Name	I	Birth	Death	Co	Source
Crawford	Nettie	C.	1887ca		Grn	Marr1
Crawford	Tarlton		1857ca	Mar. 20, 1876	Bre	C1
Crawford (Malony)	Nancy		1795ca	Feb. 29, 1855	Bre	C1
Crawford (Slave)			1857ca		Brk	C1
Craycraft	Thadeous		Apr. ??, 1852	Sep. ??. 1852	Grn	C1
Creamer	Elizabeth		1866ca		Grn	Marr1
Creech	Elizabeth			Jun. 9, 1857	Bre	C1
Creek	Bobbie	R.		Jan. 6, 1939	All	MCDR
Creek	Dosia	A.	1868ca	Apr. 3, 1928	Muh	MCDR
Creek	Elizabeth		1928ca	Jun. 27, 1930	All	MCDR
Creek	Ethel	M.	1910ca	Apr. 1, 1969	All	MCDR
Creighton	Mrs. Ann		1798ca	May 10, 1845	NWS1	5/17/1845
Cremeans	Dellie		1889ca		Grn	Marr1
Cremeans	Myrtle		1881ca		Grn	Marr1
Cremeans	Ollie		1888ca		Grn	Marr1
Crenshaw	Ansel	G.	1927ca	Aug. 19, 1986	Jef	
Crenshaw	R.	B.	Jun. 11, 1850	Aug. 27, 1858	Ful	CEM1
Crenshaw	William Fletcher		Nov. 3, 1821	Aug. 9, 1896	Ful	CEM1
Crews	D.	H.	Jan. 17, 1840		Web	Bk1
Crews, Jr.	Elwood Stone		Mar. 3, 1930	Dec. 7, 1950	KY	KMIL
Cribbs	Capt.			1791ca	NWS5	11/12/1791
Crihfield	Arthur	Q	1826ca	Sep. 3, 1844	NWS1	9/7/1844
Crisp	Minnie		1889ca		Grn	Marr1
Criston	Charity		1852ca	Jun. 15, 1878	Bre	C1
Critchloe	Tilden		1877ca	Mar. 5, 1878	Brk	C1
Crookshanks	Mr. B.	B.		Aug. 23, 1845	NWS1	9/6/1845
Cross	Von	O.	1935ca	Aug. 25, 1984	Fay	MCDR
Crossman	Charles	V		Dec. ??, 1843	NWS1	12/9/1843
Crostic	J.	G.	Oct. 15, 1827	Sep. 12, 1879	Ful	CEM7
Crostic	LaMay		Jun. 6, 1893	Oct. 11, 1894	Ful	CEM7
Crostic	Mary		1852	1918	Ful	CEM7
Crostic	W.	S.	1851	1943	Ful	CEM7
Crow	Jane		1846ca	Oct. 18, 1854	Har	CEM1
Crow	Josiah		1836ca	Aug. 5, 1855	Har	CEM1
Crow	Mary		1840ca	Dec. 5, 1861	Dav	C1
Crow	Mrs. Jemina		1819ca	Feb. 1, 1875	Dav	MCDR
Crow	Nancy	P.	1843ca	Mar. 10, 1853	Har	CEM1
Crow	Nancy		Feb. 18, 1809	Mar. 5, 1887	Har	CEM1
Crow	Nancy H. T.		No Date	No Date	Har	CEM1
Crow	Rev. J.	C.	Mar. 1, 1802	Apr. 25, 1885	Har	CEM1
Crowder	Elizabeth			Jul. 31, 1876	Brk	C1
Crowley	Edmund	G.	Aug. 31, 1838		Web	Bk1
Crowley	W.	D.	Oct. 16, 1832		Web	Bk1
Cruce	Martha		Apr. 17, 1819	May 19, 1854	Ful	CEM2
Cruce	William Marshall		Jan. 12, 1851	May 11, 1914	Ful	CEM2
Cruce (Asbell)	Martha Alice		Sep. 24, 1832	Jan. 15, 1903	Ful	CEM2
Cruce (Farris)	Rachel Virginia		1857	1880	Ful	CEM2

Last Name	First Name	I	Birth	Death	Co	Source
Cruce (Workman)	Theococia Anne		May 18, 1859	Jan. 29, 1922	Ful	CEM2
Crume	Ansel	P.	1904ca	Mar. 30, 1959	Jef	
Crume	James	T.	1846ca	Apr. 5, 1852	Brk	C1
Crume (Nottingham)	Jane		1828ca	Apr. 7, 1857	Brk	C1
Cummins	Ada		1902ca	Jun. 14, 1923	Fay	MCDR
Cummins	Alfred	P.	1898ca	Dec. 26, 1962	Fay	MCDR
Cummins	Elza	M.	1927	Sep. 2, 1950	KY	KMIL
Cummins	Lue	D.	1904		Har	CEM1
Cummins	William			Aug. 6, 1865	KY	CMIL2
Cundiff	Bertha Lee		1875	1944	Muh	CEM3
Cundiff	Eunice		1904	1940	Muh	CEM3
Cundiff	Isaac		1777ca	Sep. 30, 1855	Dav	C1
Cundiff	J. Milton		Dec. 17, 1898	Jan. 24, 1927	Hdn	CEM3
Cundiff	Mary Ann		Nov. 14, 1867	Sep. 6, 1950	Hdn	CEM3
Cundiff	Nancy		1840ca	Nov. ??, 1857	Dav	C1
Cundiff	Nancy		1865ca	Jul. 24, 1877	Bre	C1
Cundiff	Sammie	A.	1895	1941	Muh	CEM3
Cundiff	Wm. Jasper		Feb. 8, 1865	Jan. 27, 1943	Hdn	CEM3
Cunning	America		Jan. 14, 1872	Aug. 14, 1900	Men	CEM1
Curl	Carl	S.	1932	Nov. 1, 1950	KY	KMIL
Currens	Calvin Kenneth		1920	Jul. 3, 1951	KY	KMIL
Currey	Catherine		Oct. 29, 1834	Feb. 13, 1908	Hen	CEM1
Currey	John		Apr. 15, 1803	Apr. 3, 1877	Hen	CEM1
Curry	Henry	L.	1933	Mar. 12, 1953	KY	KMIL
Curry	Henry	L.	1933	Mar. 13, 1953	KY	KMIL
Curry	Mary	J.	1890ca		Grn	Marr1
Curtis	Bertha	M.	Dec. 10, 1897	Apr. 20, 1926	Row	CEM1
Curtis	Bessie	E.	1926	1928	Row	CEM1
Curtis	Lloyd	N.	1928	Sep. 20, 1951	KY	KMIL
Curtiss	William	S.	Apr. 11, 1904		Car	C1
Cyrus	Hallie May		1892ca		Grn	Marr1
Dale	Emily	M.	1892ca		Grn	Marr1
Dalton	Lloyd		1930	Sep. 20, 1950	KY	KMIL
Dancy	Richard		1892ca	May 26. 1895	Ful	CEM7
Dancy	W.	H.	1863ca	Nov. 1, 1902	Ful	CEM7
Daniel	????		1825ca	Aug. 29, 1853	Dav	C1
Daniel	Asher		1932	Nov. 29, 1950	KY	KMIL
Daniel	Asher		1932	Nov. 29, 1950	KY	KMIL
Daniel (Slave)			1834ca	Nov. 24, 1854	Brk	C1
Daniels	Nellie		1893ca		Grn	Marr1
Daniels	Paul	L.	1931	Jan. 7, 1951	KY	KMIL
Daniels	Susie		1894ca		Grn	Marr1
Dannels	Mary	E.	1889ca		Grn	Marr1
Darby	Addie	A.	1889ca		Grn	Marr1
Darby	James			Oct. 24, 1853	Grn	C1
Darby	Martha		1850ca	Jul. 1, 1853	Grn	C1
Daugherty	Mary Jane		Nov. 22, 1838	Feb. 13, 1890	Hdn	CEM1

Last Name	First Name	I	Birth	Death	Co	Source
Daugherty	Moses	J.	Apr. 27, 1906		Hdn	CEM2
Daughtery	Frances	M.	1850		But	Bk1
Daughtery	Thomas		Jul. 11, 1836	Apr. 30, 1908	Hdn	CEM1
Daughtery	W.	R.	Nov. ??, 1838		Gray	C2
Dauphin	Louise		1889ca		Grn	Marr1
Davenport	Antha	A.	Jun. 20, 1854	Aug. 4, 1932	Muh	CEM3
Davenport	Mrs. Elizabeth		1780ca	Aug. 5, 1845	NWS1	8/16/1845
David (Slave)			1823ca	Jul. 1, 1857	Brk	C1
Davidson	Auce		1840ca	May 18, 1904	Brk	C1
Davidson	Louisa		1875ca	Jul. 20, 1878	Bre	C1
Davidson	Polly		1872ca	Sep. 12, 1875	Bre	C1
Davidson	Thomas		1776ca	Mar. 27, 1852	Brk	C1
Davidson	Unknown Female			Oct. 28, 1855	Bre	C1
Daviess (Neill)	Ann		1791ca	Sep. 9, 1861	Dav	C1
Davis	Barbara	E.	Nov. 4, 1853	Mar. 16, 1922	Dav	CEM3
Davis	Bernard	N.	1930	Jul. 10, 1950	KY	KMIL
Davis	Bobby		1932	Dec. 19, 1950	KY	KMIL
Davis	Elizabeth		Aug. 23, 1851		Dav	CEM2
Davis	Elizabeth		1807ca	Mar. 12, 1853	Grn	C1
Davis	Jessee		1850ca	Apr. 21, 1853	Brk	C1
Davis	John	H.	Sep. 8, 1850	Nov. 1, 1933	Dav	CEM3
Davis	Joseph		May 5, 1816	Aug. 27, 1865	Muh	CEM3
Davis	Lillian	B.	1888ca		Grn	Marr1
Davis	Lora Belle		1883ca		Grn	Marr1
Davis	Martha		Jun. 5, 1809	Aug. 3, 1883	Ful	CEM7
Davis	Matilda		1840ca	Jul. 2, 1853	Grn	C1
Davis	Morgan		1850ca	Dec. 23, 1855	Bre	C1
Davis	Rachael		1808ca	Apr. 11, 1852	Grn	C1
Davis	Robert	A.	1923	Mar. 25, 1951	KY	KMIL
Davis	Roy Anderson		Sep. 15, 1923	Oct. 2, 1951	KY	KMIL
Davis	Russell		1930	Aug. 8, 1950	KY	KMIL
Davis	Unknown Male			Aug. 15, 1852	Brk	C1
Davis	W.	N.	Apr. 6, 1856	Jan. 28, 1916	Dav	CEM2
Davis	William	E.	1927	Feb. 4, 1953	KY	KMIL
Davis (Guill)	Laura		1878ca	Jun. 18, 1904	Brk	C1
Davison (Robinson)	Wesly		1791ca	Mar. 19, 1878	Brk	C1
Davisson	George		1853ca	Jan. 14, 1877	Grn	C2
Dawson	Harrison		1807ca	Mar. 16, 1855	Dav	C1
Dawson	Mary	M.	1836ca	Oct. 1, 1855	Dav	C1
Day	Billie	W.	1930	Oct. 16, 1951	KY	KMIL
Day	Edward	E.		Nov. 28, 1876	Bre	C1
Day	Eva Maude		1885ca		Grn	Marr1
Day	Glen	W.	Jun. 30, 1918		Hdn	CEM2
Day	Huldah		1837ca	Mar. 23, 1853	Bre	C1
Day	Lucinda	C.	1852ca	Oct. 30, 1855	Bre	C1
Day	Nancy Jane		1851ca	Mar. 16, 1854	Bre	C1
Day	Patricia	S.	Dec. 27, 1938		Hdn	CEM2

Last Name	First Name	I	Birth	Death	Co	Source
Day	Sarah		Oct. 20, 1833		Gray	C2
Day	Whitten		1840ca	Apr. 1, 1853	Bre	C1
Dean	Cordelia		1885ca	Apr. 11, 1904	Brk	C1
Dean	Ellen		1856ca	Apr. ??, 1878	Brk	C1
Dean	H.	R.	1828ca	1894	Brk	C1
Dean	Thos.	R.	1829ca	Sep. 13, 1894	Brk	C1
Dean	William	H.	Apr. 22, 1922	Dec. 1, 1950	KY	KMIL
Dean, Jr.	Ben	J.	1878ca	Feb. ??, 1904	Brk	C1
Deaton	Jane		1872ca	Apr. 1, 1875	Bre	C1
Deaton	John		1807ca	Dec. 15, 1877	Bre	C1
Deaton	Lewis		1848ca	Jul. 25, 1855	Bre	C1
Deaton	Malinda		1802ca	Nov. 23, 1875	Bre	C1
Deaton	Rachel			May 14, 1874	Bre	C1
Deaton	Reece			Jan. 16, 1854	Bre	C1
DeBoard	Della	M.	1894ca		Grn	Marr1
Deboard	Wid. Mary Eliza.		1870ca		Grn	Marr1
Deckard	John	W.	1831ca		Gray	C1
Dedman	Eugene		1930	Jul. 31, 1950	KY	KMIL
DeHaven	Ira		1868ca	Jul. 20, 1904	Brk	C1
DeHaven (Landrum)	Elizabeth		1870ca	Jul. 28, 1894	Brk	C1
Dejarnett	George	T.	1840ca	Mar. 26, 1861	Brk	C1
DeJernette	George		1875ca	Sep. 3, 1876	Brk	C1
	John Glendale		Jul. 27, 1931	Jul. 7, 1953	KY	KMIL
Delany	Col. W. S.		Sep. 18, 1825		KY	Bk1(P399)T
Delany	Xavier		1894ca	May 5, 1916	Cam	MCDR
Denney	Warren	E.	1915ca	Aug. 13, 1976	Fay	MCDR
Dennis	Henry Rufus		May 8, 1906	Jul. 30, 1913	Muh	CEM3
Dennis	Josiah		1834ca		Gray	C1
Dennis	Lena		1884	1922	Muh	CEM3
Dennis	W.	M.	1873	1933	Muh	CEM3
Dent	Ulliss	G.	1826ca	Nov. 22, 1852	Brk	C1
Dent (Phillips)	Mattie	A.	1820ca	Apr. 25, 1855	Brk	C1
Denton	S. Thomas		1867	1949	Hen	CEM1
Denton	Susan	R.	1872	1939	Hen	CEM1
Depeyster	Cordelia		Dec. 18, 1856	Aug. 30, 1877	Muh	CEM3
Depeyster	Porst	H.	1800		Muh	CEM3
Depeyster	Sallie Ann		Aug. 31, 1831	Feb. 8, 1882	Muh	CEM3
DeRossette	Blanche	W.	1881	1912	Hdn	CEM2
Deweese	Thomas		May 14, 1831		Gray	C2
DeWeese	Virgil	M.	1840		But	Bk1
DeWitt	Hattie	B.	1886ca		Grn	Marr1
Dewitt	Shelton		1848ca	Dec. 18, 1878	Brk	C1
Dexter	Isaac	B.	1843		But	Bk1
Dial	John	B.	1850		But	Bk1
Dials	Granville		1850ca	May ??, 1852	Grn	C1
Dickison	Charles	R.	1929	Aug. 11, 1950	KY	KMIL
Dickman	B.	C.		Sep. 2, 1904	Brk	C1

Last Name	First Name	I	Birth	Death	Co	Source
Diecks	Mary Margaret	M.	Feb. 27, 1909	Nov. 3, 1957	Hdn	CEM2
Diederich	Minnie		1860ca		Grn	Marr1
Dillingham	Mart.		1833	1917	Hdn	CEM2
Dillingham	Menerda Jane		Apr. 9, 1843	Jan. ??, 1922	Hdn	CEM2
Dillingham	Pheobe		1844		Hdn	CEM2
Dillingham	R.	L.	Apr. 20, 1842	Aug. 31, 1895	Hdn	CEM2
Dillingham	Thomas		Jul. 14, 1879	Dec. 30, 1884	Hdn	CEM1
Dillingham	Von		1916ca	Aug. 21, 1917	Fay	MCDR
Dillow	Mary	M.	1890ca		Grn	Marr1
Dillow	Phoeba		1883ca		Grn	Marr1
Dillow	Widow Anna		1844ca		Grn	Marr1
Dingus	Louellen		1889ca		Grn	Marr1
Dingus	Maude		1890ca		Grn	Marr1
Dinsmore	Nobile Wm.	F	Feb. 9, 1829		KY	RP1
Dismukes	Charles	E.	1928	Dec. 1, 1950	KY	KMIL
Dixon	Mary Jane		1867ca	Jan. 20, 1875	Bre	C1
Docie (Slave)			1814ca	Aug. 15, 1861	Brk	C1
Dockery	J.	A.	Jun. 27, 1837		Gray	C2
Dockery	John	A.	1837		But	Bk1
Dodge	Eugene	E.	Dec. 10, 1930	Jul. 25, 1953	KY	KMIL
Dohoney	Ebenezer	L.	Oct. 13, 1832		KY	Bk1(P394)T
Dohoney	Peyton		1807		KY	Bk1(P394)T
Donelion	James		1762ca		NWS5	3/22/1788
Donovan	Mrs. Mildred			May 18, 1845	NWS1	5/24/1845
Dooley	Henry		1802ca	Nov. 15, 1852	Brk	C1
Doolin	Frances	A.	1840		But	Bk1
Doran	Dr. Thomas	M.	1849		But	Bk1
Doris	C.	A.	Dec. 16, 1860		Cam	MCDR
Doron	Agnes	M.	1887ca		Grn	Marr1
Doss	Cammie	S.	1881ca	May 16, 1952	All	MCDR
Douglas	Carrie		1858ca	May 14, 1874	Brk	C1
Douglas	Emma	A.	1853	1857	Har	CEM1
Douglas	John	W.	1861	1946	Har	CEM1
Douglas	Richard Leland		Dec. 15, 1898	Sep. 27, 1959	Har	CEM1
Douglas	Sue	C.	1863	1929	Har	CEM1
Douglass	John	R.	1814	1893	Har	CEM1
Douglass	Sarah	A.	1819	1894	Har	CEM1
Douglass	Shirley		Sep. 9, 1956		Har	CEM1
Douglass	William	R.	May 21, 1818	Jan. 21, 1873	Har	CEM1
Dougthett	James		1808ca	May 21, 1853	Dav	C1
Dowel	Mattie		1859ca	Aug. 1, 1861	Brk	C1
Dowell	M.		1873ca	Oct. 8, 1878	Brk	C1
Dowell	Nancy		1839ca	Jan. 26, 1852	Brk	C1
Dowell	Thom.		1846ca	Oct. 19, 1876	Brk	C1
Downey	Ben	T.	May 28, 1879	Nov. 9, 1969	Hdn	CEM2
Downey	Emma Akers		May 1, 1879	Feb. 27, 1968	Hdn	CEM2
Downey	Mary	E.	Jan. 6, 1887	Nov. 14, 1972	Hdn	CEM2

Last Name	First Name	I	Birth	Death	Co	Source
Downey	William	W.	Dec. 30, 1870	Feb. 1, 1950	Hdn	CEM2
Downing (Churchill)	Elizabeth		1762ca	Aug. 9, 1787	NWS5	9/29/1787
Downs	Rosa		1887ca		Grn	Marr1
Downs	William			Jul. 30, 1886	McL	CH1
Doyle	A.	H.	1872ca	Apr. 9, 1894	Brk	C1
Drain	Joseph		Dec. 12, 1859	Jan. 7, 1860	Hdn	CEM1
Drake	William			Jan. 4, 1845	NWS1	1/11/1845
Drew	Percy	M.	Mar. 11, 1871	Feb. 22, 1919	Ful	CEM7
Drew (Oates)	Mary	G.	1842		Ful	CEM7
Drewry	Eva		Mar. 2, 1877		Dav	CEM3
Drewry	William		Mar. 4, 1872	Nov. 6, 1902	Dav	CEM3
Driskell	Nannie	E.	1858ca	Oct. 30, 1874	Brk	C1
Druen	Mary	F.	Jan. 20, 1900	Dec. 15, 1970	Hdn	CEM2
Druen	Rufus	L.	Mar. 25, 1897	Oct. 8, 1978	Hdn	CEM2
Drune	Elizabeth		1805ca	Nov. 22, 1854	Brk	C1
Duff	Elizabeth	B.	Mar. 26, 1900	Jul. 2, 1977	Hdn	CEM2
Duff	George	A.	1931	Jul. 18, 1953	KY	KMIL
Duff	Gorman	M.	1897ca	Nov. 18, 1973	Grn	MCDR
Duff	John	S.		Dec. 1, 1876	Bre	C1
Duff	Rachel			Mar. 12, 1853	Bre	C1
Duff	Robert	W.	Nov. 27, 1894	Jul. 7, 1961	Hdn	CEM2
Duggins	H.		Jan. 2, 1840		Gray	C2
Duggins	William		1821ca		Gray	C1
Duko	D.	B.	May 26, 1835		Gray	C2
Duncan	Archie		Mar. 18, 1826	Jan. 17, 1908	Har	CEM1
Duncan	Benjamin		1801ca	Feb. 10, 1875	Dav	MCDR
Duncan	Bessie		1897ca		Grn	Marr1
Duncan	Cora	J.	Jan. 2, 1855	Dec. 17, 1925	Hdn	CEM1
Duncan	Dr. R.	W.	Jan. 28, 1850	Mar. 1, 1906	Hdn	CEM1
Duncan	Elizabeth	M.	Apr. 11, 1852	Feb. 28, 1875	Hdn	CEM1
Duncan	Gretta		1895ca		Grn	Marr1
Duncan	Hattie	E.	1885ca		Grn	Marr1
Duncan	Houson		Feb. 27, 1815	Jan. 27, 1890	Hdn	CEM1
Duncan	James	T.	1831ca	Nov. 20, 1855	Brk	C1
Duncan	John	G.	1802		Han	Bk1
Duncan	John	W.	Nov. 27, 1831		KY	Bk1(P25)A
Duncan	Judge Robert	E.	Jan. 22, 1846		Han	Bk1
Duncan	Lem.			Sep. 24, 1878	Brk	C1
Duncan	Lizzie Claggert		Jul. 19, 1855	Jan. 23, 1885	Hdn	CEM1
Duncan	Lucretia	F.	Nov. 9, 1818	Mar. 20, 1899	Hdn	CEM1
Duncan	Margaret		Aug. 18, 1898	Oct. 19, 1920	Har	Cem1
Duncan	Nancy	S.	1887ca		Grn	Marr1
Duncan	Robert			1830	Han	Bk1
Duncan	Susan	E.	1853ca	Feb. 4, 1854	Brk	C1
Duncan	Thos.		1810ca	Oct. 2, 1878	Brk	C1
Duncan	Virgie	M.	1889ca		Grn	Marr1
Duncan	William	G.	Feb. 11, 1847		Cam	MCDR

44

Last Name	First Name	I	Birth	Death	Co	Source
Duncan (Beauchamp)	Eliza Bell		1808ca	Oct. 4, 1854	Dav	C1
Dunlap	Mrs. Rose			May 10, 1845	NWS1	5/24/1845
Dunn	Charles		1873ca	Oct. ??, 1878	Brk	C1
Dunn	Maj. Isaac	B.		Jun. 28, 1789	NWS5	7/4/1789
Dunn	Marce	P.	Jul. 27, 1928	Jun. 16, 1954	KY	KMIL
Dunnaway	Elizabeth		Dec. ??, 1833		KY	RP1
Dunnaway	Levi Harrison		Feb. 23, 1844		KY	RP1
Dunnaway	Mary Ann		Nov. 7, 1836		KY	RP1
Dunnaway	Sinthe Ann		Feb. 26, 1837		KY	RP1
Dunnaway	William	F	Mar. 30, 1835		KY	RP1
Dunning	John	A.	1932	Jul. 27, 1950	KY	KMIL
Dura	John		1816ca	Feb. 10, 1875	Bre	C1
Durham	John		1761		All	RP1
Durham	Mrs. Lunetty			Oct. 17, 1884	Muh	Ch1
Durham	Simon	B.	1852ca	Oct. 24, 1874	Brk	C1
Durkee	William	L.	1832		But	Bk1
Dykes	Ramon		1901ca	Nov. 7, 1975	Fay	MCDR
Dynmitt	John		1772ca	Sep. 10, 1854	Brk	C1
Dysard	Simpson		1831ca	Jun. 22, 1852	Grn	C1
Eades	Catherine		Jan. 3, 1856	Mar. 31, 1939	Hdn	CEM2
Eades	Female		1821ca		Way	C1
Eads	James	R.	Jan. 25, 1856	Jan. 16, 1899	Muh	CEM2
Eads	Lucy	E.	1885	1924	Hdn	CEM2
Eads	Sarah	A.	Feb. 29, 1836	Dec. 27, 1892	Muh	CEM2
Eads	Thomas	C.	1879	1943	Hdn	CEM2
Eakins	Isiah		Dec. 12, 1819		Cam	MCDR
Easley	Steph. Davenport		1811		But	Bk1
Easley	Wiley	R.	1807		But	Bk1
Eastwood	Ramon	D.	1894ca	Sep. 19, 1946	Jef	MCDR
Eaton	Robert		1931	Nov. 29, 1950	KY	KMIL
Ebirt	Infant			1835	NWS4	8/14/1835
Eblen	Ida Alice		1861	1939	Hen	CEM1
Eblen	Thomas	J.	1853	1936	Hen	CEM1
Edds	Cammie	V.	1901ca	Mar. 7, 1973	Dav	MCDR
Edminston	Robert	L.	Jun. 26, 1866	Jan. 12, 1903	Ful	CEM6
Edwards	John		1882	1904	Ful	CEM4
Edwards	Nannie		1882	1926	Ful	CEM4
Edwards	Rev. Algernon		May 5, 1826		Cam	MCDR
Edwards	V.	L.	Jul. 5, 1859		Sim	C1
Edwards	William	H.	Jan. 19, 1852		Sim	C1
Edwards (Decker)	Elizabeth		1815ca	Sep. 15, 1859	Brk	C1
Egeen	Virginia	E.	1908	1943	Hdn	CEM2
Eggen	C.	S.	Jul. 10, 1862	Jan. 11, 1914	Hdn	CEM2
Eggen	Nora Gray		Feb. 10, 1873		Hdn	CEM2
Eggen	Robert Gray		Nov. 5, 1909	Jun. 19, 1910	Hdn	CEM2
Eggers	Julia		1885ca		Grn	Marr1
Eidson	Henry		1797	Apr. 14, 1883	Dav	CEM3

45

Last Name	First Name	I	Birth	Death	Co	Source
Eidson	Rebecca		Jan. 24, 1801	Sep. 21, 1880	Dav	CEM3
Elder	Hannah			Jan. 3, 1819	Cal	CEM1
Elder	Henry		1845		But	Bk1
Elder	Mary			Mar. 15, 1878	Brk	C1
Elder	Pius	L.	1810ca	May 9, 1878	Brk	C1
Elder	Robert	J.		Sep. 16, 1915	Cal	CEM1
Elder	Robert			J?n. 14, 1821	Cal	CEM1
Elder	E.	C.	1822ca	Dec. 16, 1904	Brk	C1
Elder	John			Oct. 21, 1799	Cal	CEM1
Elder (McGill)	Sutan		1809ca	Nov. 20, 1852	Brk	C1
Elder (Walker)	Martha		1831ca	Feb. 3, 1894	Brk	C1
Eldridge	John	C.	1897	Aug. 13, 1965	Row	CEM1
Eldridge	Lena Fay		Aug. 2, 1923	Jun. 10, 1988	Row	CEM1
Eldridge	Levi		1867	1939	Row	CEM1
Eldridge	Lyda		Nov. 4, 1906	Oct. 17, 1908	Row	CEM1
Eldridge	Martha	J.	1866	1957	Row	CEM1
Eldridge	Maud	D.	1892	May 23, 1961	Row	CEM1
Eldridge	Mollie	O.	Jan. 19, 1892	Nov. 25, 1980	Row	CEM1
Eldridge	Nancy	M.	1895ca		Grn	Marr1
Eldridge	Nellie		1918		Row	CEM1
Eldridge	Preston		1904	1948	Row	CEM1
Eldridge	Russell		1917	1951	Row	CEM1
Eldridge	Sarah	J.	Dec. 19, 1912	Feb. 1, 1913	Row	CEM1
Eldridge	Vernon		Jun. 27, 1924	Jul. 13, 1927	Row	CEM1
Eldridge	Virgil		Aug. 4, 1919		Row	CEM1
Eldridge	William	E.	1961	1968	Row	CEM1
Elgin	Thomas	P.		Mar. 17, 1836	NWS4	3/19/1836
Elisha (Slave)			1840ca	Mar. 31, 1857	Brk	C1
Elizabeth (Slave)			1852ca	Mar. 27, 1855	Brk	C1
Ellen (Slave)			1835ca	Dec. 2, 1861	Brk	C1
Elliott	Allen			Jul. 15, 1857	Brk	C1
Elliott	Elizabeth		1825ca	Jun. 1, 1843	NWS1	6/3/1843
Elliott	Elizabeth		1831ca	Jan. 20, 1852	Brk	C1
Elliott	Huston		1822ca	Feb. 29, 1852	Brk	C1
Elliott	Jacob		1831ca	Apr. 14, 1854	Brk	C1
Elliott	James		1829ca	Mar. 30, 1852	Brk	C1
Elliott	Jemina		1800ca	Aug. 11, 1852	Brk	C1
Ellis	Sarah		1833ca	Apr. 14, 1856	Dav	C1
Ellis	Sarah Douty		1844ca	Jul. 14, 1845	KY	7/19/1845
Embry	B.	T.	Apr. 19, 1820		KY	Bk1(P117)A
Embry	Forest		1929	Jun. 24, 1953	KY	KMIL
Embry	I.	J.	Aug. 4, 1834		Gray	C2
Embry	Malachi		1838		But	Bk1
Embry	Mason		1826		But	Bk1
Embry	Tine		Feb. 24, 1839		Gray	C2
Embry	Viola		1872ca	Feb. 28, 1959	But	CEM2
Embry	Wes		Sep. 26, 1835		Gray	C2

Last Name	First Name	I	Birth	Death	Co	Source
Embry	William	U.	1922ca	Sep. 23, 1939	But	MCDR
Emery	Jesse	H.	1845		But	Bk1
Emery	Rosa		1888ca		Grn	Marr1
Emitt	R.	S.		1835	NWS4	8/14/1835
England	John		Aug. 2, 1832		Gray	C2
England	Louisa		1850ca	Dec. 8, 1853	Grn	C1
England	Mary Belle		Mar. 3, 1866	Apr. 1, 1901	Dav	CEM3
England	Maude		Mar. 12, 1898	Mar. 15, 1898	Dav	CEM3
England	Sarah		1823ca	Jan. 28, 1877	Grn	C2
England	William	H.	1849ca	Dec. 6, 1853	Grn	C1
England	William	W.	Feb. 26, 1897	Feb. 27, 1897	Dav	CEM3
English	A.	S.		Feb. 4, 1904	Brk	C1
English	Earl	L.	1898	1951	Hdn	CEM2
English	Fannie	W.	1871	1939	Hdn	CEM2
English	Fannie		Jan. 10, 1818	Feb. 7, 1908	Hdn	CEM2
English	Hortense	P.	1863	1910	Hdn	CEM2
English	J.	M.	1862	1945	Hdn	CEM2
English	Nancy		Jan. 26, 1840	Nov. 30, 1928	Hdn	CEM2
English	Noah		Dec. 6, 1909	Jun. 21, 1884	Hdn	CEM2
English	Ted		1929	Jul. 31, 1952	KY	KMIL
Epperhart	Chester		Dec. 17, 1916	May 25, 1985	Row	CEM1
Epperhart	David		1893	1941	Row	CEM1
Epperhart	Lacy		1902	1985	Row	CEM1
Epperhart	Norma	J.	Feb. 24, 1933	Nov. 22, 1938	Row	CEM1
Epperhart	Roger	G.	Jun. 14, 1940	Feb. 22, 1941	Row	CEM1
Epperhart	William	D.	May 27, 1925	Sep. 9, 1927	Row	CEM1
Estep	Eugene		1931	Mar. 25, 1951	KY	KMIL
Estes	Sally Ann		1819ca	Feb. 12, 1855	Dav	C1
Eubank	Gipson Taylor		Jun. 9, 1839	Jul. 13, 1916	Dav	CEM3
Eubank	Henry		1818ca	Mar. 29, 1861	Dav	C1
Eubank	Infant		Jul. 31, 1904	Jul. 31, 1904	Dav	CEM3
Eubank	Jesse		Jul. 24, 1870	Aug. 1, 1819	Dav	CEM3
Eubank	Martha	E.	Feb. 2, 1844	Dec. 3, 1885	Dav	CEM3
Eubank	Mrs. Martha		1811ca	Dec. 23, 1843	Dav	MCDR
Evans	Earl		1925	Jan. 2, 1951	KY	KMIL
Evans	Edward		1853ca	Dec. 12, 1876	Bre	C1
Evans	Mary Allice			Nov. 20, 1876	Bre	C1
Evans	Nancy	J.	1894ca		Grn	Marr1
Evans	S.	W.	1840ca	Dec. 28, 1861	Dav	C1
Evans	Thomas	F.	1806ca	Jul. 20, 1854	Brk	C1
Evans	Ulysses		1865ca	Apr. ??, 1877	Grn	C2
Evans (Tery)	Edward		1852ca	Oct. 26, 1876	Bre	C1
Evely	William		1865ca	Jul. 20, 1876	Brk	C1
Evins	Morris	M.	1832CA	Apr. 2, 1855	Dav	C1
Ewell	Whitney	M.		Sep. 30, 1986	Fay	MCDR
Ewing	Elizabeth	A.	1853	1939	Har	CEM1
Ewing	Harriett		1844ca	Aug. 25, 1853	Grn	C1

Last Name	First Name	I	Birth	Death	Co	Source
Ewing	Josie		1886	1969	Har	CEM1
Fain	James	E.	1932	Oct. 14, 1952	KY	KMIL
Fairchild	Ray Palmer		Jan. 1, 1929	Nov. 27, 1950	KY	KMIL
Fairmein	Martha		1837ca	Sep. 21, 1844	NWS1	9/29/1844
Faith	Jakie		Apr. 23, 1890	Dec. 4, 1893	Dav	CEM3
Faith	Joseph	T.	Dec. 6, 1877	Dec. 25, 1908	Dav	CEM3
Faith	Laura		Oct. 7, 1852	Sep. 1, 1895	Dav	CEM3
Faith	Martha		May 11, 1846	Aug. 10, 1918	Dav	CEM3
Faith	William Cook		Nov. 3, 1868	Jan. 31, 1905	Dav	CEM3
Faith	Wm. Mortimer		No Date	No Date	Dav	CEM3
Falls (Rice)	Emala		1831ca	Sep. 27, 1854	Brk	C1
Fannin	Becca		1893ca		Grn	Marr1
Fannin	Bessie		1895ca		Grn	Marr1
Fannin	Clara		1887ca		Grn	Marr1
Fannin	Emma		1888ca		Grn	Marr1
Fannin	Glenn	W.	1933	Sep. 22, 1951	KY	KMIL
Fanny (Slave)			1786ca	Mar. 10, 1861	Brk	C1
Farmer	Archie		Jan. 4, 1889	Jan. 8, 1889	Dav	CEM3
Farmer	Fannie		Nov. 24, 1854	Apr. 14, 1891	Dav	CEM3
Farmer	John		1829ca	Jan. 25, 1853	Grn	C1
Farmer	Kenneth	W.	1921	Dec. 2, 1950	KY	KMIL
Farmer	Levinia	M.	1829ca	May 25, 1853	Grn	C1
Farmer	Paul	C.	1930	Nov. 8, 1950	KY	KMIL
Farmer	Robert	P.	1843ca	Sep. 1, 1853	Grn	C1
Farris	Clofus	O.	1931	Jul. 17, 1953	KY	KMIL
Farrow	Elizabeth		1821ca	May 30, 1854	Brk	C1
Feaman (Beard)	Sarah		1844ca	Nov. 9, 1876	Brk	C1
Fellowes	Benjamin	C.	1843ca	Aug. ??, 1844	NWS1	8/10/1844
Feltner	Harlon	C.	1931	Aug. 17, 1950	KY	KMIL
Feltner	Harlon	C.	1931	Aug. 17, 1950	KY	KMIL
Felts	Bennie		Dec. 27, 1889	Oct. 17, 1931	Ful	CEM7
Felty	Belle		1887ca		Grn	Marr1
Felty	Sena		1886ca		NWS4	Marr1
Ferguson	Maj.			1791ca	NWS5	11/12/1791
Ferguson	Russell		May 22, 1904		Car	C1
Ferguson	William	J.	1844		But	Bk1
Ferman	William		1832ca		Gray	C1
Fetters	Timmie		1888ca		Grn	Marr1
Field	Benjamin		Feb. 19, 1829	Mar. 8, 1873	Oh	CEM4
Field	Betsy	P.	Jul. 8, 1805	Apr. 1, 1845	Oh	CEM4
Field	Capt. Benj.		1755	1842	Oh	CEM4
Field	Curtis		Aug. 27, 1842	Sep. 2, 1853	Oh	CEM4
Field	Edward		Apr. 3, 1839	Aug. 8, 1863	Oh	CEM4
Field	Elizabeth		Sep. 7, 1821	May 24, 1847	Oh	CEM4
Field	Emma		Jul. 13, 1834	Aug. 24, 1864	Oh	CEM4
Field	Henrietta		Oct. 22, 1858	Nov. 4, 1860	Oh	CEM4
Field	John		1757		Oh	CEM4

Last Name	First Name	I	Birth	Death	Co	Source
Field	Joshua		Nov. 16, 1830	Feb. 6, 1859	Oh	CEM4
Field	Lucy	G.	Oct. 10, 1860	Dec. 6, 1861	Oh	CEM4
Field	Lucy	G.	Sep. 4, 1797	Aug. 29, 1880	Oh	CEM4
Field	Merit		Aug. 29, 1842	Sep. 2, 1853	Oh	CEM4
Field	Merit		Dec. 10, 1836	Aug. 9., 1840	Oh	CEM4
Field	Mildred		1768	1853	Oh	CEM4
Field	Nancy		1798	Sep. 7, 1824	Oh	CEM4
Field	Reubin		Sep. 19, 1930	Dec. 1, 1950	KY	KMIL
Field	Robert		Jan. 11, 1833	Sep. 7, 1834	Oh	CEM4
Field	William	D.	Jun. 27, 1797	Oct. 26, 1870	Oh	CEM4
Field	William	T.	Jun. 27, 1834	Oct. 26, 1870	Oh	CEM4
Field	William		Dec. 15, 1850	Sep. 16, 1857	Oh	CEM4
Field	William		Mar. 20, 1797?	Mar. 6, 1876	Oh	CEM4
Field	Wm. Franklin		Mar. 20, 1834	Mar. 5, 1876	Oh	CEM4
Fielden	Foster		Jun. 24, 1790	Nov. 26, 1854	Muh	CEM2
Fields	Levy		1884ca		Grn	Marr1
Fields	Mildred		1771ca	Nov. 28, 1853	Dav	C1
Fields	Rodger	E.	1930	Dec. 1, 1950	KY	KMIL
Fielinger	Peter		1851ca	Jun. 4, 1853	Grn	C1
Fife	Cassie		1875	1949	Hdn	CEM2
Fife	Clara	R.	Jan. 7, 1877	Jul. 30, 1911	Hdn	CEM2
Fife	Dr. Clay Danl.		Apr. 24, 1901	Dec. 3, 1977	Hdn	CEM2
Fife	Female		May 5, 1899	May 5, 1899	Hdn	CEM2
Fife	L.	H.	1865	1928	Hdn	CEM2
Fife	Lura	D.	Mar. 10, 1879	Nov. 10, 1897	Hdn	CEM2
Fife	Mary Lula		Nov. 13, 1882	Apr. 6, 1900	Hdn	CEM2
Fife	Mitchell Lee		Sep. 1, 1861	Sep. 30, 1915	Hdn	CEM2
Fife	Nellie	B.	Nov. 10, 1892	Apr. 6, 1900	Hdn	CEM2
Fife	Priscilla		Jul. 23, 1837	Jun. 14, 1923	Hdn	CEM2
Fife	Washington	L.	Jun. 24, 1828	Jul. 30, 1898	Hdn	CEM2
Fink	Elizabeth	A.	1835ca	May 5, 1856	Dav	C1
Finley	Samuel		1796ca	Feb. 24, 1836	NWS4	BK1
Finnell	Mary Wall			Nov. 1, 1845	NWS1	11/15/1845
Fisher	George	T.	1918	Dec. 1, 1950	KY	KMIL
Fisher	Levenia		1813ca	Oct. ??, 1853	Grn	C1
Fisher	Margaret	E.		Sep. 15, 1852	Brk	C1
Fisher	Sandford	C.	1825ca	Aug. 29, 1852	Brk	C1
Fisher (Linell)	Elizabeth		1828ca	Aug. 29, 1852	Brk	C1
Fitt	Henry		1818ca	Jun. 25, 1856	Dav	C1
Flanagan	Webster		Jan. 9, 1832		Ful	Bk1(P405)T
Flatt	Florence		Feb. 26, 1887	Jan. 25, 1904	Ful	CEM7
Flatt	J.	J.	1856	1930	Ful	CEM7
Flatt	John Melton		Jan. 14, 1885	May 6, 1898	Ful	CEM7
Flatt	M.	I.	Jan. 26, 1832		Ful	CEM7
Flatt	Rev. J.	M.	Aug. 8, 1825	Jul. 6, 1903	Ful	CEM7
Flaughen	James Polk		Aug. 29, 1907		Car	C1
Fleins	Edna		Aug. 15, 1907		Car	C1

Last Name	First Name	I	Birth	Death	Co	Source
Fleming	Gerald		Jan. 17, 1907		Car	C1
Fleming	Russell		Dec. 10, 1906		Car	C1
Fleming	Unknown		1830ca	Dec. 15, 1853	Dav	C1
Flener	Bluit		1848		But	Bk1
Flener	Napoleon		1837		But	Bk1
Flener	Veachel		1847		But	Bk1
Flener	William	H.	1836		But	Bk1
Flener	Worth		1848		But	Bk1
Flinchum	Elizabeth		1818ca	Mar. 3, 1874	Bre	C1
Flinchum	Jacob		1778ca	Dec. 20, 1858	Bre	C1
Flinchum	John	J.	1842ca	Oct. 1, 1876	Bre	C1
Flinchum	Polly		1797ca	Apr. 2, 1874	Bre	C1
Flint	Hezekiah			Sep. ??, 1843	NWS1	9/30/1843
Flippin	Ed. L.		1884	1939	Ful	CEM7
Flowers	Kenneth	R.	1928	Nov. 24, 1951	KY	KMIL
Floyd	Ephraim			1844	NWS1	8/3/1844
Fonch (Robinson)	Malisa		1838ca	Aug. 7, 1878	Bre	C1
Fonow	George	P.		Jun. 12, 1861	Brk	C1
Fontross	H.	E.	Aug. 17, 1833		Gray	C2
Fontz	James		1854ca	Nov. 5, 1855	Bre	C1
Fontz (Walker)	Rachel		1817ca	Oct. 9, 1855	Bre	C1
Fonville	Josephine		Jul. 30, 1842	May 7, 1842	Sim	CEM1
Ford	Burrell		1829ca		Gray	C1
Ford	Elizabeth J.	P.	1815ca	Sep. 3, 1835	NWS4	9/11/1835
Ford	Joel	D.	1835ca	Aug. 24, 1852	Brk	C1
Ford	John	K.	1834ca	Sep. 6, 1852	Dav	MCDR
Ford	Reuben		1816ca	Apr. 18, 1878	Brk	C1
Ford	Virginia		Jun. 11, 1862	Jan. 14, 1889	Muh	Ch1
Ford (Knott)	Catherine		1823ca	Mar. 18, 1878	Brk	C1
Ford (Smith)	Mrs. J.	A.	1859ca	Feb. 24, 1904	Brk	C1
Ford, Jr.	Patrick		1928	Jul. 8, 1951	KY	KMIL
Foreman	Tucker		Mar. 10, 1826		Gray	C2
Forgy	James Monroe		1820		But	Bk1
Forrest	Manford		Mar. 22, 1904		Car	C1
Fortner	Alevilda		1798ca	Dec. 15, 1875	Bre	C1
Fot	Wong	K.	1906ca	Dec. 15, 1949	Fay	MCDR
Fowler	B.	T.	1828ca	May 26, 1894	Brk	C1
Fowler	Dinah			Feb. 4, 1853	Grn	C1
Fowler	John	D.		Jul. 19, 1853	Grn	C1
Fowler	Margaret		Apr. 12, 1850	Jul. 12, 1915	Har	CEM1
Fowler	Robert		Sep. 22, 1851	Aug. 12, 1913	Har	CEM1
Fowler	Thomas	O.	1928	Oct. 15, 1951	KY	KMIL
Fox	Henry	G.	Oct. 4, 1863	Jun. 18, 1892	Muh	CEM3
Fox	Infant		Feb. 5, 1870	Dec. 16, 1870	Muh	CEM3
Fox	Joseph		Jun. 19, 1835	Nov. 18, 1890	Muh	CEM3
Fox	Mildred	P.	Aug. 29, 1837	Nov. 5, 1894	Muh	CEM3
Fox	Nellie		Dec. 16, 1878	Feb. 6, 1906	Muh	CEM3

Last Name	First Name	I	Birth	Death	Co	Source
Fox	Unknown		Apr. 29, 1966	Sep. 11, 1911	Muh	CEM3
Fox	Unknown			Oct. 25, 1853	Grn	C1
Fox, Jr.	Joseph		Oct. 31, 1868	Feb. 6, 1906	Muh	CEM3
Fraize	Bettie		1846ca	May 22, 1852	Brk	C1
Fraize	Susan		1800ca	Sep. 20, 1854	Brk	C1
Fraley	Anna	M.	1931	1987	Row	CEM1
Fraley	Arthur	L.	1926	1985	Row	CEM1
Fraley	Carolyn	S.	1951	1963	Row	CEM1
Fraley	David Ray		Aug. 26, 1970	Aug. 27, 1970	Row	CEM1
Fraley	Jesse		Mar. 15, 1907		Car	C1
Fraley	Mary		1832ca	Nov. 5, 1858	Bre	C1
Fraley	Patricia	J.	Aug. 8, 1954	Oct. 25, 1984	Row	CEM1
Fraley	Thomas		1865ca	Apr. 23, 1878	Bre	C1
Fraly	Unknown Male			Nov. 25, 1875	Bre	C1
Francis	Nancy		1851ca	Dec. 8, 1852	Bre	C1
Francis (Casidy)	Polly		1827ca	Dec. 16, 1852	Bre	C1
Franco	Joseph		1910ca	Nov. 7, 1974	Jef	MCDR
Frank	Elizabeth		1872ca	Nov. 5, 1878	Brk	C1
Frank	Ezra			Dec, 5, 1878	Brk	C1
Franklin	James	W.	Jun. 19, 1854		Cam	MCDR
Franklin	Mary		Nov. 8, 1844	Feb. 1, 1922	Ful	CEM7
Franklin	William	C.	Feb. 6, 1893	Aug. 25, 1894	Ful	CEM7
Frasure	Adam	D.	1930	Aug. 8, 1951	KY	KMIL
Frazier	Andrew	J.		Dec. 10, 1876	Bre	C1
Frazier	Glen Elsworth		Dec. 31, 1929	Sep. 19, 1950	KY	KMIL
Frazier	John		1804ca	Apr. 3, 1874	Bre	C1
Frazier	Nancy Jane			Oct. 15, 1877	Bre	C1
Frazier	Rebecca		1894ca		Grn	Marr1
Frazier	Unknown		1813ca	Nov. 30, 1853	Dav	C1
Frazier (Haddix)	Hariah		1807ca	Jun. 7, 1877	Bre	C1
Frederick	William		1920	Jan. 14, 1950	KY	KMIL
Freeman	James		Jan. 23, 1842		Han	Bk1
Freeman	Nathan		Jul. 12, 1811		Han	Bk1
Freeman	Ray			Jul. 30, 1862	KY	CMIL2
Freeman	Tammie	R.	1907ca	Jan. 10, 1978	Bal	MCDR
Freeman	Unknown Male			Apr. 10, 1882	Ful	CEM7
Freeman (Bennett)	Elizabeth		1816	1860	Han	Bk1
French	Jennigs		1931	Sep. 27, 1952	KY	KMIL
French	Mrs. Deborah		1806ca	Jul. 21, 1835	NWS4	7/31/1835
French	Phebe		1810ca	Aug. 9, 1855	Brk	C1
Frey	Harvey	L.	1929	Aug. 27, 1951	KY	KMIL
Friend	Charles		Jan. 20, 1841	Oct. 15, 1922	Hdn	CEM2
Friend	Edward	T.	Jan. 18, 1893		Hdn	CEM2
Friend	Iva	V.	Sep. 20, 1900		Hdn	CEM2
Friend (Coleman)	Margaret		Apr. 20, 1847	Apr. 2, 1912	Hdn	CEM2
Friley	Sarah		1833ca	Aug. 12, 1856	Bre	C1
Fritz	Addie		1890ca		Grn	Marr1

Last Name	First Name	I	Birth	Death	Co	Source
Frizzell	Georgia		Sep. 13, 1904		Car	C1
Frost	William	R.	1924	Aug. 21, 1950	KY	KMIL
Fry	Susie	E.	Sep. 15, 1849	Nov. 28, 1903	Ful	CEM7
Fu	Elmer			Nov. 6, 1916	Ken	MCDR
Fugate	Benjamin		1852ca	Apr. 19, 1855	Bre	C1
Fugate	Elizabeth			Dec. 24, 1877	Bre	C1
Fugate	Hannah		1753ca	Aug. 10, 1853	Bre	C1
Fugate	Henchel		1863ca	Nov. 30, 1875	Bre	C1
Fugate	Jonathan		1755ca	Sep. 21, 1859	Bre	C1
Fugate	Lariny		1850ca	Oct. 19, 1852	Bre	C1
Fugate	Mary		1872ca	May 15, 1877	Bre	C1
Fugate	Norris		1931	May 18, 1951	KY	KMIL
Fugate	Samuel		1854ca	Jan. 18, 1855	Bre	C1
Fuguate	Robert		1875ca	Feb. ??, 1878	Bre	C1
Fuguate	Unknown Female			Jan. 2, 1877	Bre	C1
Fuhrman	Frederick		1928	Oct. 24, 1951	KY	KMIL
Fulkerson	John		1826ca		Gray	C1
Fulkerson	Samuel		1831ca		Gray	C1
Fuller	I.	D.	1854	1904	Hdn	CEM1
Fultz	John		1918	Mar. 9, 1951	KY	KMIL
Fultz	Sarah		1887ca		Grn	Marr1
Fuqua	Dr. Moses	H.	1831		But	Bk1
Fuqua	Samuel		1813ca	Oct. ??, 1861	Dav	C1
Furrow	Ella		1876ca	Nov. 19, 1878	Brk	C1
Furrow	Israel			Jul. 23, 1904	Brk	C1
Fuson	Herschel	E.	1925	Jun. 14, 1951	KY	KMIL
Fuson	Herschel	E.	1925	Jun. 14, 1951	KY	KMIL
Gabbard (Peters)	Mary		1792ca	Sep. 16, 1875	Bre	C1
Gabbert	Judith		1832ca	Jul. ??, 1853	Dav	C1
Gahan	John William		Apr. 28, 1928	Mar. 31, 1954	KY	KMIL
Gallaway	John	W.	1792ca	May 6, 1878	Brk	C1
Galloway	Annie Mary		Jul. 7, 1876	Nov. 25, 1883	Dav	CEM3
Galloway	B.	F.	1908	1963	Har	Cem1
Galloway	Belle		Mar. 28, 1865	Jun. 3, 1939	Dav	CEM3
Galloway	Bettie	B.	Nov. 6, 1893	Nov. 29, 1895	Dav	CEM3
Galloway	Bishop	T.	Jun. 21, 1872	Aug. 23, 1917	Dav	CEM3
Galloway	Effie	B.	Feb. 23, 1883	Nov. 29, 1896	Dav	CEM3
Galloway	Elizabeth		Mar. 21, 1852	Nov. 9, 1932	Dav	CEM3
Galloway	Elmore		Dec. 21, 1895	De. 25, 1897	Dav	CEM3
Galloway	Etta		1868	1906	Dav	CEM3
Galloway	Florence		Dec. 29, 1888	May 20, 1889	Dav	CEM3
Galloway	Freddie	R.	Nov. 7, 1898	Nov. 25, 1900	Dav	CEM3
Galloway	Henry		Jul. 1, 1871	May 25, 1892	Dav	CEM3
Galloway	James		Oct. 15, 1849	May 13, 1904	Dav	CEM3
Galloway	Jesse	T.	Jul. 28, 1896	Mar. 17, 1903	Dav	CEM3
Galloway	Lula		Dec. 8, 1870	May 5, 1890	Dav	CEM3
Galloway	Lydia	G.	Jun. 9, 1865	Jan. 16, 1932	Dav	CEM3

Last Name	First Name	I	Birth	Death	Co	Source
Galloway	Minnie Burch		Nov. 11, 1873	Oct. 19, 1895	Dav	CEM3
Galloway	Nellie May		May 7, 1893	Dec. 1, 1895	Dav	CEM3
Galloway	Robert		Mar. 12, 1858	Jan. 6, 1897	Dav	CEM3
Galloway	Sallie	E.	Apr. 27, 1860	Sep. 6, 1921	Dav	CEM3
Galloway	Samuel Osborne		Oct. 20, 1860	Mar. 15, 1935	Dav	CEM3
Galloway	Scott		1848		But	Bk1
Galloway	Sophia		Jul. 17, 1829	Apr. 1, 1900	Dav	CEM3
Galloway	Stephen	O.	Oct. 25, 1904	Mar. 5, 1909	Dav	CEM3
Galloway	Virginia Susan		Feb. 26, 1833	Feb. 19, 1905	Dav	CEM3
Galloway	Walter	T.	Aug. 3, 1886	Oct. 31, 1889	Dav	CEM3
Galloway	Z.	M.	Aug. 31, 1856	Feb. 12, 1891	Dav	CEM3
Galloway	Zachariah		Jun. 4, 1825	Jan. 21, 1903	Dav	CEM3
Gallup	Maria Emma		1844ca	May 20, 1845	NWS1	5/24/1845
Gallup	Mrs. Maria	A		Sep. 9, 1844	NWS1	9/14/1844
Gamble	Henry	C.	1914	Sep. 22, 1950	KY	KMIL
Gammon	Irma	A.	1888ca		Grn	Marr1
Ganany	Sarah	E.	1818ca	Apr. 25, 1855	Brk	C1
Gannaway	Rev. John		1811ca	Nov. 2, 1878	Brk	C1
Gano	Eliza		1833ca	June 17, 1845	NWS1	7/5/1845
Gardner	Ava	M.	Oct. 27, 1879	Jan. 1, 1928	Hdn	CEM2
Gardner	Bertha Bishop		Jul. 4, 1883	May 27, 1958	Hdn	CEM2
Gardner	James	G.	1847	1932	Hdn	CEM2
Gardner	Koeling	B.	1919	Oct. 25, 1951	KY	KMIL
Gardner	Margaret		Nov. 29, 1876	Jun. 18, 1901	Hdn	CEM2
Gardner	Mary Jane		1847	1933	Hdn	CEM2
Gardner	Virgil		Jul. 15, 1874	Jan. 4, 1942	Hdn	CEM2
Gardner	Wm.	H.	1845ca	May 6, 1878	Brk	C1
Gardner (Roper)	Rosie Belle		1923	1951	Ful	CEM7
Garnett	Edward Lynch		Jul. 28, 1807	Jan. 25, 1884	Har	CEM1
Garnett	Eliza Ann			Dec. 20, 1861	Har	CEM1
Garnett	Elizabeth	H.	May 6, 1807	Oct. 18, 1855	Har	CEM1
Garnett	Merva	S.	Aug. 19, 1851	Apr. 8, 1890	Har	CEM1
Garnett	Robert	E.	Feb. 5, 1863	Jan. 9, 1864	Har	CEM1
Garrett	Albert	A.	Nov. 5, 1873	Aug. 15, 1944	Har	CEM1
Garrett	George			Jul. 5, 1874	Brk	C1
Garrett	J.	L.	Mar. 26, 1850		Har	CEM1
Garrett	Jerusha	E.	Feb. 22, 1841	Feb. 16, 1906	Har	CEM1
Garrett	Martha			Aug. ??, 1874	Brk	C1
Garrett	Mary	A.	1840ca	Sep. 12, 1853	Grn	C1
Garrett	Robert	E.	Feb. 5, 1863	Jan. 9, 1864	Har	CEM1
Garrett	Robert		1834ca	Sep. 5, 1852	Brk	C1
Garrett	Sally		1889ca		Grn	Marr1
Garrett	Tinsie		Aug. 19, 1882	Mar. 2, 1961	Har	CEM1
Garrison	Fred Herren		Jul. 22, 1917	Nov. 9, 1953	KY	KMIL
Garver	Elizabeth		1803ca	Apr. 3, 1853	Dav	C1
Garvey	Stella		1889ca		Grn	Marr1
Garvin	Murrel		1922	Nov. 28, 1950	KY	KMIL

Last Name	First Name	I	Birth	Death	Co	Source
Gatewood	John		1759		All	RP1
Gayhart	James	D.	1931	Feb. 12, 1950	KY	KMIL
Gayheart	Albert		1868ca	Jun. 21, 1930	Jef	MCDR
Gayheart	Amanda	T.	1923ca	Nov. 25, 1969	Fay	MCDR
Gayheart	Arnold		1927ca	Sep. 28, 1972	Boy	MCDR
Gearhart	Martha		1894ca		Grn	Marr1
Gearhart	William		1795ca	Jul. 25, 1854	Bre	C1
Geary	Billy	L.	1930	Sep. 7, 1950	KY	KMIL
Geary	Marin		Mar. 29, 1837		Gray	C2
Gedge	Frederick George		1845ca	Dec. 24, 1845	NWS1	12/27/1845
Gedge	Harriet	A	1814ca	June 14, 1845	NWS1	6/21/1845
Gehue (Kelly)	Melvina		1837ca	1857	Dav	C1
Gennott	James		1828ca		Gray	C1
George (Slave)			1842ca	May 20, 1857	Brk	C1
George (Slave)				Apr. ??, 1861	Brk	C1
Gerlach	Bertha	F.	1890ca	Dec. 15, 1966	Byl	MCDR
Gerlach	Florence	L.	1909ca	Oct. 17, 1965	Fay	MCDR
Gerlach	Franck		1923ca	Apr. 26, 1967	Byl	MCDR
Gerlach	Fritz	L.	1915ca	Feb. 14, 1981	Byl	MCDR
Gibbs	Billy	H.	1932	Dec. 26, 1952	KY	KMIL
Gibson	Allen			Sep. 4, 1835	NWS4	9/18/1835
Gibson	Eliza	J.	1845ca	Aug. 18, 1852	Brk	C1
Gibson	Henry	E.	1930	Oct. 14, 1952	KY	KMIL
Gibson	James	W.	Oct. 6, 1867	Aug. 30, 1897	Dav	CEM3
Gibson	Jonathan		1760		All	RP1
Gidron	James		1927	Sep. 17, 1950	KY	KMIL
Gilbert	Adam		1842ca	Aug. 7, 1876	Bre	C1
Gilbert	Edney		1828ca	Sep. 15, 1904	Brk	C1
Gilbert	Elijah			Dec. 18, 1821	Way	C1
Gilbert	Jacob		1789ca	Oct. 13, 1861	Brk	C1
Gilfrin	Catherine			Aug. ??, 1861	Brk	C1
Gill	Louis	M.	1928	Aug. 7, 1950	KY	KMIL
Gillaspy	Anna		Oct. ??. 1826	Jan. 7, 1852	Oh	Cem2
Gillaspy	Dr. S.	A.	Aug. 3, 1822	Mar. 5, 1900	Oh	Cem2
Gillran	Willie		1868ca	Jan. 1, 1904	Brk	C1
Gillum	Bertha		1887ca		Grn	Marr1
Gilmore	William		1838ca	Jan. 4, 1862	Brk	C1
Gilpin	Anna May		1891ca		Grn	Marr1
Gilvin	Marvin	C.	1927	Sep. 20, 1950	KY	KMIL
Gipson	Ese Myrtle		1887ca		Grn	Marr1
Gipson	Glenn	H.	1929	Mar. 11, 1951	KY	KMIL
Girdley	Vernon	E.	1935	Jun. 18, 1953	KY	KMIL
Given	Nancy		1841ca	May 11, 1854	Bre	C1
Givens	Jas.		Feb. 23, 1837		Gray	C2
Givens	John	W.	Feb. 4, 1830		Cam	MCDR
Givens	Thomas	K.	Jan. 24, 1819		Cam	MCDR
Glasscock (Haynes)	Francis Jane		1798ca	Sep. 1, 1878	Brk	C1

Last Name	First Name	I	Birth	Death	Co	Source
Glenn	Andrew	G.	Sep. 25, 1827	17-May-05	Muh	CEM3
Glenn	Hattie	N.	Sep. 5, 1848	Feb. 12, 1908	Muh	CEM3
Glenn	Infant		Dec. 29, 1911	Dec. 29, 1911	Dav	CEM3
Glenn	Infant		Oct. 7, 1894	Sep. 24, 1895	Dav	CEM3
Glenn	Lucy	E.	Oct. 1, 1898	May 4, 1903	Dav	CEM3
Glenn	Lula		Feb. 2, 1870	Apr. 7, 1893	Muh	CEM3
Glenn	Mary	A.	Feb. 22, 1825	Dec. 27, 1899	Muh	CEM3
Glenn	Mary	L.	Apr. 30, 1843	Apr. 3, 1871	Muh	CEM3
Glenn	Moses	F.	Jul. 5, 1791	Mar. 8, 1869	Muh	CEM3
Glenn	Rudy		Apr. 27, 1892	Sep. 1, 1893	Dav	CEM3
Glenn	Sallie	A.	Feb. 22, 1832	Jul. 21, 1882	Muh	CEM3
Glenn	William	M.	Nov. 2, 1866	May 18, 1869	Muh	CEM3
Godwin	Mary	W.	Sep. 19, 1853			Bk1(P208)T
Goff	Calvin		1832ca		Gray	C1
Goff	Charles	C.	Nov. 16, 1931	Jun. 24, 1952	KY	KMIL
Goff	Jno.	B.	1868ca	Jul. 25, 1876	Brk	C1
Goff	Phoebe		Mar. 18, 1838		Gray	C2
Goings	Thomas		1761ca		NWS5	7/23/1791
Goldsmith	Melvin Eugene		Aug. 13, 1932	Oct. 27, 1952	KY	KMIL
Goodman	Chas.	E.		Mar. 12, 1877	Brk	C1
Goodman	J. Welsey		1839		But	Bk1
Goodnight	Thomas		Feb. 7, 1863	Jun. 19, 1864	Sim	CEM1
Goodrum	Cammie	G.	1895ca	Jan. 18, 1975	All	MCDR
Goodrum	Ellen		Oct. 1, 1850	May 26, 1904	Sim	CEM1
Goodrum	Emma	D.	Sep. 2, 1875	Apr. 19, 1903	Sim	CEM1
Goodrum	Laura		1874	1907	Sim	CEM1
Goodrum	Minnie	G.	Jan. 6, 1876	Oct. 28, 1897	Sim	CEM1
Goodrum	Mrs. Elvira		1819ca	Feb. 13, 1875	Dav	MCDR
Goodrum	W.	J.	Nov. 26, 1846	Jan. 4, 1910	Sim	CEM1
Goodwin	A.	H.	1804ca	Apr. 22, 1856	Dav	C1
Goodwine	P.		Sep. 4, 1835		Gray	C2
Gore	Claude	C.	Dec. 16, 1867	Jan. 31, 1887	Ful	CEM7
Gore	Elizabeth		1842ca	Sep. 3, 1857	Dav	C1
Gore	Inez	H.	1882	1908	Ful	CEM7
Gorman	Amelia	H.	1906ca	Jun. 10, 1936	Jef	MCDR
Gorman	Andrew	J.	1862ca	Dec. 18, 1932	Jef	MCDR
Gorman	Angeline		1862ca	May 7, 1926	Jef	MCDR
Gorman	Ann	C.	1920ca	Jul . 9, 1963	Fay	MCDR
Gorman	Annie Ophelia		1872ca	Dec. 4, 1957	Jef	MCDR
Gott	Moses	P.	1824		But	Bk1
Gragsdon	Thomas	E.	1828ca		Gray	C1
Graham	Adam	R.	Mar. 4, 1804	Sep. 19, 1876	Hdn	CEM1
Graham	Fannie	L.	1863		Hdn	CEM1
Graham	Garrett		1836		But	Bk1
Graham	John	W.	Dec. 10, 1842	Apr. 8, 1868	Hdn	CEM1
Graham	Susan	M.	May 4, 1820	Sep. 10, 1891	Hdn	CEM1
Graham	Thomas	A.	1858	1921	Hdn	CEM1

Last Name	First Name	I	Birth	Death	Co	Source
Grant	America Letcher		1798ca	Mar. 31, 1843	NWS1	8/5/1843
Grant	Billy		1836ca	Oct. ??, 1853	Brk	C1
Grary	Amanda		May 14, 1832		Gray	C2
Grause	Joseph	W.	1929	Nov. 26, 1950	KY	KMIL
Graves	Thomas	C.	1819ca	Aug. 18, 1845	NWS1	8/30/1845
Graves	Thomas	G.	1822ca	Aug. 18, 1845	NWS1	8/23/1845
Graves (Clark)	Sarah	E.	1836ca	Nov. 7, 1861	Dav	C1
Gray	Adnia	C.	1894ca	Dec. 14, 1979	Dav	MCDR
Gray	Curtis	A.	Oct. 10, 1904	Oct.. 13, 1968	Hdn	CEM2
Gray	Eula Lewis		Oct. 5, 1874	Oct. 10, 1959	Hdn	CEM2
Gray	Fannie	M.	Oct. 6, 1882	Sep. 28, 1969	Hdn	CEM2
Gray	Felix		1818		But	Bk1
Gray	Frank	M.	Jan. 17, 1867	Apr. 12, 1956	Hdn	CEM2
Gray	James	A.	May 7, 1841	Aug. 11, 1904	Ful	CEM4
Gray	Katherine		Sep. 15, 1838	Jan. 25, 1921	Hdn	CEM2
Gray	Lena		1890ca		Grn	Marr1
Gray	Louisa		Nov. 27, 1844	Jan. 26, 1917	Ful	CEM4
Gray	Martha		1837ca	Jul. 18, 1853	Grn	C1
Gray	Mary	E.	Aug. 24, 1828	Feb. 8, 1885	Dav	CEM2
Gray	Perry Dempsey			Sep. 1, 1877	Brk	C1
Gray	Susannah		1826ca	Apr. 7, 1853	Grn	C1
Gray	Thomas		1834ca	Aug. 25, 1853	Grn	C1
Gray	William	C.	1931	Aug. 16, 1950	KY	KMIL
Gray	William	M.	Dec. 11, 1835	Jun. 3, 1921	Hdn	CEM2
Gray	Isaac		1763ca		NWS5	1/12/1793
Grayson	Dr.			1791ca	NWS5	11/12/1791
Greathouse	Dr. Isaac	N.	1792	1832	Han	Bk1
Greathouse	Harmon	B.	May 2, 1822		Han	Bk1
Greathouse (Haywood)	Martha	E.	1830	Sep. ??, 1878	Han	Bk1
Greathouse (Haywood)	Martha	R.	1827		Han	Bk1
Greathouse (Smith)	S.	C.	1836		Han	Bk1
Green	A.	G.	Mar. 2, 1840		Gray	C2
Green	Cammie		1874ca	Feb. 7, 1929	Jef	MCDR
Green	Ida Elizabeth		Nov. 1, 1876	Sep. 12, 1877	Dav	CEM2
Green	J.	P.	Apr. 27, 1841		Gray	C2
Green	Robert	L.	1928	Sep. 28, 1951	KY	KMIL
Green	Unknown Male			Jun. 15, 1878	Bre	C1
Green	Widow Mary		1879ca		Grn	Marr1
Green (Butler)	Nannie			Apr. 24, 1860		BK2(P270)
Greenlee	Elijah		1772		KY	BK2(P10)
Greenlee	James		1769		KY	BK2(P11)
Greenlee	James		1740		KY	BK2(P11)
Greenwade	Sadie		1881ca		Grn	Marr1
Greenwalt	Minnie		1876ca	Oct. 12, 1878	Brk	C1
Greenwalt	Sarah	F.	1850	1852	Hdn	CEM1
Greenwalt	Sarah		1781	1852	Hdn	CEM1
Greenwell	Elizabeth		Aug. 1, 1900	Jan. 15, 1901	Hdn	CEM2

Last Name	First Name	I	Birth	Death	Co	Source
Greenwell	Gladdys		1906	1911	Hdn	CEM2
Greenwell	H. Clay		Mar. 10, 1859	May 4, 1927	Hdn	CEM2
Greenwell	Kate Richards		Dec. 16, 1873	Feb. 24, 1909	Hdn	CEM2
Greenwell	Mamie	L.	Sep. 11, 1904	May 23, 1905	Hdn	CEM2
Greer	B.	T.	Nov. 26, 1862		Oh	CEM1
Greer	Henry		1807ca	Jan. 28, 1854	Brk	C1
Greer	Herman		Feb. 28, 1880	Mar. 2, 1889	Oh	Cem2
Greer	Infant		Feb. 27, 1883	Mar. 2, 1883	Oh	CEM1
Greer	John		Dec. 14, 1854	Dec. 7, 1886	Oh	CEM1
Greer	Lucy Jane			Oct. 26, 1845	NWS1	11/8/1845
Greer	Mary		May 8, 1829		Oh	CEM1
Greer	Millie		Dec. 29, 1855	Aug. 3, 1889	Oh	CEM1
Greer	Murtie		May 26, 1884	Sep. 8, 1885	Oh	CEM1
Greer	Rosie		Apr. 1, 1884	Dec. 31, 1884	Oh	Cem2
Greer	Samuel	H.	Jun. 15, 1828	Sep. 18, 1903	Oh	CEM1
Greer	Viola		Oct. 21, 1879	Jun. 25, 1925	Oh	CEM1
Gregg	Thomas	M		Oct. 30, 1843	NWS1	11/11/1843
Gregory	Ben		1884	1960	Muh	CEM3
Gregory	Catherine		Oct. ??, 1918	Jun. ??, 1932	Muh	CEM3
Gregory	Count	P.	Apr. 13, 1893	Jul. 10, 1917	Muh	CEM3
Gregory	Edward		Mar. 31, 1841		Han	Bk1
Gregory	Elizabeth	L.		Nov. 12, 1855	Brk	C1
Gregory	Emma		1866	1937	Muh	CEM3
Gregory	Hubeert		Dec. ??, 1921	Jan. ??, 1923	Muh	CEM3
Gregory	James Allen		Jan. 26, 1928	Mar. 12, 1951	KY	KMIL
Gregory	John	A.	1818		Han	Bk1
Gregory	John	E.	1859ca	Mar. 17, 1874	Brk	C1
Gregory	Marquis	D.	Jul. 4, 1838	Sep. 1, 1923	Muh	CEM3
Gregory	Mildred		1696		KY	BK2(P156)
Gregory	Rev. I.	V.	1858	1897	Hdn	CEM1
Gregory (Board)	Cindrella		1822ca	May 24, 1904	Brk	C1
Gregory (Holder)	Elizabeth			1845	Han	Bk1
Gregory (Pate)			Apr. 23, 1847		Han	Bk1
Gregory (Wood)	Elizabeth	L.	1812ca	Sep. 30, 1855	Brk	C1
Gribbins	Homer	F.	Dec. 31, 1930	Jul. 25, 1953	KY	KMIL
Grider	Stout		1897ca	Jun. 13, 1929	Byl	MCDR
Griffin	Dr. P.	H.	1856		Cam	MCDR
Griffin	George		1837ca	Sep. 24, 1852	Brk	C1
Griffith	Elizabeth Jane		1891ca		Grn	Marr1
Griffith	Lila		1880ca		Grn	Marr1
Griffith	Mary Ann		1846ca	Sep. 22, 1852	Bre	C1
Griffith	Virgie	D.	1885ca		Grn	Marr1
Griffith	William	H.	1848		Cam	MCDR
Grimes	Carl	D.	1932	Jan. 31, 1951	KY	KMIL
Grimes	Ephraim			Oct. 7, 1845	NWS1	10/11/1845
Grizzle	Frances		1891ca		Grn	Marr1
Grogan	Clarence	R.	1928	Apr. 21, 1951	KY	KMIL

Last Name	First Name	I	Birth	Death	Co	Source
Gross	Whitney	A.	1925ca	Jul. 28, 1975	Ken	MCDR
Gross	Whitney		1895ca	Sep. 9, 1925	Ken	MCDR
Guest	Ebeneezer	C.	1815		But	Bk1
Guffey	Herbert	E.	1929	Dec. 28, 1951	KY	KMIL
Guffy	B. L.	D.	1832		But	Bk1
Guffy	James	H.	1828		But	Bk1
Guill, Jr.	Leslie		1923	Dec. 10, 1950	KY	KMIL
Guthrie	Capt.			1791ca	NWS5	11/12/1791
Guthrie	Mary			Jan. 4, 1876	Brk	C1
Guthrie	Milly		1850ca	Jan. 29, 1874	Brk	C1
Guthrie (Stone)	Elizabeth		1823ca	Sep. 10, 1856	Dav	C1
Haag	Douglas	H.	1923	Jul. 12, 1950	KY	KMIL
Hackney	Jacob		1832ca	Oct. 14, 1832	Bre	C1
Hackworth	Joseph		1844ca	Aug. 15, 1853	Grn	C1
Haddix	James	U.	1874ca	Oct. 15, 1877	Bre	C1
Haddix	Mariarette			Oct. 5, 1875	Bre	C1
Haddix	Nannie		1877ca	Apr. 16, 1878	Bre	C1
Haddix	Pearl		1848ca	Nov. 8, 1875	Bre	C1
Haddix	Sally		1788ca	Oct. 30, 1858	Bre	C1
Haddix	Silva	B.	1831ca	Sep. 22, 1878	Bre	C1
Haddix	Ursula		1850ca	Sep. 11, 1852	Bre	C1
Haddix	America		1829ca	Nov. 5, 1854	Bre	C1
Haddix (Muller)	Amelia		1815ca	Oct. 10, 1854	Bre	C1
Haddox	Elias			1835	NWS4	8/14/1835
Hadley	Margaret		1779ca	Aug. 31, 1854	Dav	C1
Hagan	Abblie	L.	1910ca	Apr. 8, 1970	Dav	MCDR
Hagan	Ada	M.	1906ca	Jul. 28, 1972	Fay	MCDR
Hagan	Morgan		1828ca	Mar. 27, 1861	Dav	C1
Hagans	Daniel			Oct. 22, 1875	Bre	C1
Hagans	Sourana			Jul. 15, 1858	Bre	C1
Haggard	John			1793ca	NWS5	2/9/1793
Haggard	Mrs. John			1792ca	NWS5	2/9/1793
Haggin	James			Aug. 31, 1835	NWS4	9/18/1835
Hagins	Thomas		1787ca	Oct. 11, 1852	Bre	C1
Haines	Christopher		1759		All	RP1
Haire	Ova	L.	1932	Dec. 12, 1950	KY	KMIL
Hale	Henry		1834ca	Dec. 1, 1878	Bre	C1
Haley	Daniel			Sep. ??, 1861	Dav	C1
Haley	James		1853ca	Jan. 8, 1875	Dav	MCDR
Hall	Betty		Mar. 30, 1881	Mar. 6, 1888	Dav	CEM3
Hall	Charlotte		Jun. ??, 1808	Mar. 25, 1882	Dav	CEM3
Hall	Christopher		Sep. 12, 1835		Gray	C2
Hall	Dwaine		1932	Nov. 6, 195	KY	KMIL
Hall	Elizabeth	A.	1839	1894	Dav	CEM3
Hall	Etna		1885ca		Grn	Marr1
Hall	Garland		1931	Aug. 16, 1950	KY	KMIL
Hall	George	W.	1869	1939	Ful	CEM7

Last Name	First Name	I	Birth	Death	Co	Source
Hall	George Wash.		1832	1899	Dav	CEM3
Hall	Judge L.	B.	1842		Cam	MCDR
Hall	Martin		1912	1936	Ful	CEM7
Hall	Millie		1888ca		Grn	Marr1
Hall	Minnie	E.	Dec. 5, 1884	Jul. 10, 1961	Ful	CEM7
Hall	Napoleon	B.	1851ca	Aug. 9, 1852	Brk	C1
Hall	Nora		Jul. 12, 1865	May 24, 1889	Dav	CEM3
Hall	Quinton	V.	Jun. 6, 1931	Mar. 26, 1953	KY	KMIL
Hall	Theodoric		Feb. 8, 1828	May ??, 1851	Dav	CEM3
Hall	Theodoric		Mar. 9, 1870	Jun. 26, 1871	Dav	CEM3
Hall	Thomas	T.	1849ca	Jan. 15, 1852	Brk	C1
Hall	Unknown Male			Sep. 21, 1861	Brk	C1
Hall	William		Sep. 2, 1804	Jan. 23, 1887	Dav	CEM3
Hall (Day)	Lydia Ann	G.	Jan. 10, 1841		Gray	C2
Halley	Frances		1887ca		Grn	Marr1
Halley (Gibson)	Sarah	N.	1818ca	Feb. 13, 1852	Brk	C1
Halloway	W.		Jun. 6, 1839		Gray	C2
Hamilton	George		1801ca	Sep. 15, 1861	Dav	C1
Hamilton	Jerema		1838ca	Dec. 3, 1852	Grn	C1
Hamilton	William		1750ca	Oct. 25, 1800	Cal	CEM1
Hamlin	Billy	R.	1931	Jul. 27, 1950	KY	KMIL
Hammer	Elias		May 29, 1852		Sim	C1
Hammer	Julia	A.	May 16, 1854		Sim	C1
Hammer	Morris	G.	1827		But	Bk1
Hammond	J.	N.	1860	1925	Muh	CEM2
Hammond	Sarah	E.	1860	1925	Muh	CEM2
Hammond	Susan		Nov. 15, 1828	Jun. 15, 1908	Muh	CEM2
Hancock	Effie	J.	Apr. 7, 1839	Jan. 7, 1926	Sim	CEM1
Hancock	H.	C.	May 10, 1822	Jan. 30, 1882	Sim	CEM1
Hancock	J.	H.	Sep. 27, 1870	Mar. 20, 1900	Sim	CEM1
Hancock	Jane	P.	Aug. 25, 1818	May 16. 1852	Muh	CEM2
Hancock	Lewis	T.	Oct. 18, 1829	Jul. 3, 1890	Web	CEM1
Hancock	Lucien		May 11, 1861	May 11, 1861	Web	CEM1
Hancock	Norman		Feb. 20, 1873	Mar. 5, 1873	Web	CEM1
Hancock	Sally		Sep. 10, 1798	May 5, 1872	Web	CEM1
Hancock	Sarah		Aug. 2, 1833		Web	CEM1
Hancock	William Lewis		Nov. 7, 1792	Feb. 2, 1883	Web	CEM1
Handley	Lollie		1886ca		Grn	Marr1
Hanes	David	E.	1844ca	Aug. 3, 1853	Grn	C1
Hanes	John	K.	1838ca	Feb. 17, 1853	Grn	C1
Haney	Robert		1832ca	Feb. 10, 1853	Dav	C1
Hankins	Jonathan			1793ca	NWS5	2/9/1793
Hankla	Mary	A.	Mar. 17, 1829	Sep. 13, 1916	Hdn	CEM2
Hanks	Dinah		1850ca	Sep. 10, 1878	Brk	C1
Hanks	Elizabeth		1882ca		Grn	Marr1
Hanks	Mary Lee			Jan. 13, 1878	Brk	C1
Hanna	Isaac	A	1842ca	Sep. 11, 1842	Lew	CEM1

Last Name	First Name	I	Birth	Death	Co	Source
Hanna	John	E		Aug. 9, ????	Lew	CEM1
Hanna	John	M.	1832ca	Sep. ??, 1852	Grn	C1
Hanna	Mary	J	1837ca	Jan. 13, 1844	Lew	CEM1
Hanna	Martha	A		Oct. 21, 1852	Lew	CEM1
Hannah	Amanda	M	1818ca	Dec. 25, 1833	Lew	CEM1
Hannah	Elizabeth	J	1817ca	Feb. 28, 1854	Lew	CEM1
Hannah	Hoch		Jan. 6, 1827	May 13, 1866	Lew	CEM1
Hannah	John		1788ca	Mar. 27, 1859	Lew	CEM1
Hannah	Nancy	E	1822ca	Mar. 3, 1855	Lew	CEM1
Hannah (Black)				Feb. 10, 1856	Bre	C1
Hannahs	Cordelia			Dec. 25, 1877	Grn	C2
Hannahs	Elizabeth		1853ca	Apr. 15, 1877	Grn	C2
Hanner	Emma		1848ca	Sep. ??, 1852	Grn	C1
Hanner	Nannie	B.	1887ca		Grn	Marr1
Hansborough	Permelia		1815ca	Dec. 23, 1880	Hen	CEM1
Harcourt	Alexander			1862		Bk1(P156)T
Harcourt	Frances Marion			Jan, 3, 1845	NWS1	1/11/1845
Harcourt	John	T.	Jun. 9, 1825			Bk1(P156)T
Hardawaay	Jas.		1871ca	Apr. 20, 1878	Brk	C1
Hardaway	Adaline			Sep. 29, 1852	Brk	C1
Harden	Lena			Nov. 8, 1878	Brk	C1
Harden	Semen	W.	1846ca	Mar. 18, 1853	Grn	C1
Hardin	Ben		Apr. 28, 1825	May 24, 1890	Hdn	CEM2
Hardin	John		1753		KY	BK2(P177)
Hardin	Martin	D.		1823	KY	BK2(P179)
Hardin (Jolly)	Nancy		1817ca	Sep. 20, 1894	Brk	C1
Harding	William	R.		1835	NWS4	8/14/1835
Hardwick	C.	C.	Mar. 31, 1829		Cam	MCDR
Hardy	Solomon			1835	NWS4	8/14/1835
Hargis	William		1849ca	Aug. 18, 1874	Bre	C1
Hargis (Davis)	Eveline		1836ca	Jun. 15, 1859	Bre	C1
Harlow	Emma		1888ca		Grn	Marr1
Harlow	Martha		1870ca		Grn	Marr1
Harned	Nathaniel		1777ca	Apr. 23, 1855	Brk	C1
Harp	Mearl	L.	1931	Oct. 13, 1952	KY	KMIL
Harper	Edward		Aug. 11, 1930	Sep. 9, 1952	KY	KMIL
Harper	McHenry			Sep. 29, 1875	Brk	C1
Harrel (Rose)	Nancy		1804ca	Apr. 27, 1853	Dav	C1
Harreld	J.	E.	1846		But	Bk1
Harreld (Gray)	Sally		1839		But	Bk1
Harrell	Moses		1802ca	1852	Brk	C1
Harris	B.	F.	Dec. ??, 1854		Sim	C1
Harris	Benj.	P.	Feb. 20, 1853		Sim	C1
Harris	Bettie	A.	Oct. 27, 1861		Sim	C1
Harris	Bobby	R.	1931	Sep. 12, 1950	KY	KMIL
Harris	Donald	W.	1932	Apr. 22, 1953	KY	KMIL
Harris	Eunice	J.	Jul. 17, 1854		Sim	C1

Last Name	First Name	I	Birth	Death	Co	Source
Harris	Female		Dec. ??, 1859		Sim	C1
Harris	Franklin	J.	Mar. 6, 1853		Sim	C1
Harris	G.	M.	Nov. ??, 1854		Sim	C1
Harris	H.	G.	Jul. ??, 1857		Sim	C1
Harris	J.	W.	Oct. 30, 1859		Sim	C1
Harris	Jesse	B.	Jan. ??, 1854		Sim	C1
Harris	Jesse Edward		Sep. 4, 1905	Jul. 29, 1934	Row	CEM1
Harris	John			May 5, 1865	KY	CMIL2
Harris	Johnson	S.	1928	Oct. 14, 1951	KY	KMIL
Harris	Male		Dec. 1, 1857		Sim	C1
Harris	Marietta		1885ca		Grn	Marr1
Harris	N.	G.	Feb. ??, 1857		Sim	C1
Harris	Sarah Vilet		Nov. 20, 1853		Sim	C1
Harris	Stella		1885ca		Grn	Marr1
Harris	William	F.	Mar. 6, 1918	Dec. 7, 1950	KY	KMIL
Harris (Sympkins)	Lucinda		1836ca	May 11, 1875	Bre	C1
Harris (twin)	James	W.	May 1, 1861		Sim	C1
Harris (twin)	John	H.	May 1, 1861		Sim	C1
Harrison	Jack Ray		7-May-31	May 24, 1950	KY	KMIL
Harrison	Richard		1763		All	RP1
Harrison	Robert		1831ca	Jun. 22, 1853	Dav	C1
Harry (Slave)			1788ca	Feb. 24, 1854	Brk	C1
Hart	Catherine	A.	1824	1913	Hdn	CEM1
Hart	Ester		Nov. 2, 1876	Jan. 23, 1877	Hdn	CEM1
Hart	Maj.			1791ca	NWS5	11/12/1791
Hart	William	K.	Oct. 11, 1818	Apr. 7, 1874	Hdn	CEM1
Hartley	Green			Aug. 7, 1864	KY	CMIL2
Hartley	Kenneth Dwight		Oct. 1, 1932	Oct. 6, 1952	KY	KMIL
Hartsock	Elizabeth		1829ca	Jun. 26, 1853	Grn	C1
Harvey	William	H.		May 1, 1857	Bre	C1
Harwood	Sarah	A.		Nov. 14, 1852	Grn	C1
Hash	Billie	J.	1932	Dec. 6, 1950	KY	KMIL
Hasley	James		1757ca	Jul. 30, 1853	Gm	C1
Hastings	C.	J.	Aug. 2, 1841	Mar. 31, 1908	Hdn	CEM1
Hastings	Elizabeth		Jan. 1, 1854	Jul. 15, 1945	Hdn	CEM1
Hastings	Joseph		Jun. 16, 1848	Oct. 27, 1917	Hdn	CEM1
Hastings	Nellie		Sep. 13, 1880	Apr. 4, 1901	Hdn	CEM1
Hastings	S.	E.	Dec. 19, 1845	Apr. 1, 1933	Hdn	CEM1
Haswell	Johnie			Oct. 31, 1874	Brk	C1
Hatfield	Bettie		Dec. 25, 1868	Jul. 14, 1957	Hdn	CEM1
Hatfield	Bettie		1852	1902	Hdn	CEM1
Hatfield	Bryant	F.	Jul. 10, 1875	Nov. 5, 1888	Hdn	CEM2
Hatfield	Frances	A.	1876	1969	Hdn	CEM2
Hatfield	Harland	M.	1872	1937	Hdn	CEM2
Hatfield	J.	N.	Apr. 17, 1863	Sep. 9, 1913	Hdn	CEM1
Hatfield	Lena		Oct. 7, 1871	Jun. 24, 1896	Hdn	CEM1
Hatfield	Lully	B.	Jun. 10, 1874	Jul. 22, 1874	Hdn	CEM2

Last Name	First Name	I	Birth	Death	Co	Source
Hatfield	Malem		Jan. 31, 1819	May 29, 1890	Hdn	CEM1
Hatfield	Mary Ellen		1857ca	Sep. 11, 1875	Dav	MCDR
Hatfield	Oscar	B.	Feb. 19, 1900	May 16, 1974	Hdn	CEM2
Hatfield	R.	J.	1849	1926	Hdn	CEM1
Hatfield	Sarah	E.	Dec. 20, 1835	Jun. 25, 1903	Hdn	CEM2
Hatfield	W.	H.	Mar. 1, 1846	Apr. 19, 1916	Hdn	CEM2
Hatfield	Willie Bell		Feb. 1, 1904		Hdn	CEM2
Hathway (Hawes)	Martha		1801ca	Jul. 29, 1861	Dav	C1
Hatler	Michael		1758		All	RP1
Hatter	Jonathan		1783ca		NWS5	1/16/1799
Hawes	Marion	W.	1844		But	Bk1
Hawes	William	H.	1839		But	Bk1
Hawkins	Allie	F.		Apr. 27, 1904	Brk	C1
Hawkins	Littlebery		1809ca	Jun. 5, 1854	Dav	C1
Hawkins (Hewill)	Sarah		1788ca	Apr. 6, 1861	Brk	C1
Hawley	Sythe		1775ca	May 30, 1845	NWS1	6/7/1845
Hay	Vergia		1895ca		Grn	Marr1
Hay (Mercer)	Nancy	C.	1842ca	Jan. 12, 1878	Brk	C1
Haycraft	C.		1886ca	May 20, 1894	Brk	C1
Hayden	Annie Ophelia		1882ca		Grn	Marr1
Hayden	Benjamin		1836ca	Dec. 17, 1855	Brk	C1
Hayden	F.	R.		Oct. 22, 1861	Dav	C1
Hayden	Susannah			185?	Hdn	CEM1
Haydin	Lula	B.		Mar. 16, 1912	Dav	MCDR
Haydon	Raymond		1818ca	Feb. 12, 1856	Dav	C1
Hayes	Arvin	T.	Jan. 1, 1896	Apr. 10, 1975	Hdn	CEM2
Hayes	Eva	C.	1858	1923	Har	CEM1
Hayes	Julian	J.	Jul. 9, 1850	Dec. ??, 1879	Har	CEM1
Hayes	Lillie		1869ca	Nov. 6, 1875	Brk	C1
Hayes	Mary		Jul. 1, 1856	Nov. 2, 1878	Har	CEM1
Hayes	Mary Opha		Dec. 28, 1897		Hdn	CEM2
Hayes	Mollie	E.	Oct. 17, 1861	Sep. 22, 1879	Har	CEM1
Haynes	B.	M.	Mar. 3, 1834	Aug. 22, 1902	Ful	CEM7
Haynes	Charles		1834		But	Bk1
Haynes	H.	E	Nov. 8, 1822		Han	Bk1
Haynes	H.	E.	Mar. ??, 1843	Jan. 11, 1898	Ful	CEM7
Haynes	Hardin			May 20, 1822	Han	Bk1
Haynes	James	P.		Jul. 17, 1953	KY	KMIL
Haynes	Martha		1847ca	Jun. 10, 1859	Brk	C1
Haynes	Miss		Jan. 13, 1800		Han	Bk1
Haynes (Nicholson)	Lucinda		1860ca	Sep. 4, 1878	Brk	C1
Haynes (Powers)	Margaret	C.	Aug. 2, 1846		Han	Bk1
Hays	Armina		1855ca	Oct. 18, 1874	Bre	C1
Hays	Baby of Henry			Jan. 20, 1886	Muh	Ch1
Hays	Gwendolyn		Sep. 2, 1931	Jul. 1, 1932	Hdn	CEM2
Hays	James			Jul. 30, 1875	Bre	C1
Hays	Lucius		1846	1925	Har	CEM1

Last Name	First Name	I	Birth	Death	Co	Source
Hays	Mary	H.	1856	1878	Har	CEM1
Hays	Mary Jane			Dec. 7, 1874	Bre	C1
Hays	R.	B.		Aug. 20, 1877	Bre	C1
Hays	Rachel	C.	1815	1904	Har	CEM1
Hays	Thomas	G.	1811	1881	Har	CEM1
Hays	Unknown Male			May 14, 1876	Bre	C1
Hayse	Henry	J.	1823ca		Gray	C1
Hayse	J.	H.	Jul. 1, 1836		Gray	C2
Hayse	N.	A.	Jan. 29, 1836		Gray	C2
Hayse (Skaggs)	Em	L.	Feb. 3, 1838		Gray	C2
Hazel	Caleb	W.	1931	Sep. 1, 1950	KY	KMIL
Hazelip	Carrie	E.	Jun. 23, 1878	??? 27, 1897	Sim	CEM1
Hazelip	Edward		Mar. 12, 1903	Nov. 19, 1908	Sim	CEM1
Hazelip	Jewell Puckett		Sep. 9, 1900	Jul. 7, 1971	Hdn	CEM2
Hazelip	Lector		Oct. 25, 1876	Aug. 18, 1899	Sim	CEM1
Hazelip	Male		Oct. 13, 1901		Sim	CEM1
Hazelip	Sarah	M.	Aug. 31, 1854	Jun. 22, 1900	Sim	CEM1
Hazelip	W.	A.	Sep. 18, 1878	Jan. 3, 1909	Sim	CEM1
Heaberlin	May	L.	1890ca		Grn	Marr1
Hearin	Ellis		Jul. 23, 1839		Cam	MCDR
Heath	Fredric		Oct. 24, 1839		Gray	C2
Hebard	Harriett		1827ca	Oct. 23, 1856	Dav	C1
Hebbard	Charles		1796ca	Oct. 10, 1861	Dav	C1
Hector	George		1751		All	RP1
Hedges	Lucinda		1812ca	Feb. 24, 1857	Dav	C1
Hedgespeth	Clifton		1927	Jun. 12, 1953	KY	KMIL
Hedson	Lucy	A.	1849ca	Nov. 4, 1853	Grn	C1
Heer	David Thames		Feb. 18, 1929	Dec. 31, 1953	KY	KMIL
Helm	Ben. Hardin		Jun. 2, 1831			BK2(P219)
Helm	John	B.	1815		But	Bk1
Helsley	Belle		1860	1925	Muh	CEM3
Helsley	Elizabeth		Dec. 13, 1825	Jun. 22, 1903	Muh	CEM3
Helsley	Etta		Dec. 15, 1897	Jul. 8, 1915	Muh	CEM3
Helsley	M. Noruse		Sep. 3, 1843	Oct. 2, 1906	Muh	CEM3
Helsley	Mary	W.	Jul. 29, 1864	Jan. 18, 1934	Muh	CEM3
Helsley	P.	G.	1855	1938	Muh	CEM3
Helsley	Phillip	W.	Dec. 7, 1825	Sep. 9, 1864	Muh	CEM3
Helsley	Sarah	E.	Jun. 16, 1855	Jun. 18, 1908	Muh	CEM3
Helsley	Sarah Ann		1879	1951	Muh	CEM3
Helsley	William	H.	Jul. 8, 1863	Dec. 27, 1908	Muh	CEM3
Helton	Wilburn		1925	Apr. 3, 1952	KY	KMIL
Helwig	Mattie	R.	May 4, 1868	Jul. 4, 1907	Men	CEM1
Hemingway	M.		1809ca	Nov. 3, 1855	Dav	C1
Hemingway	W.	K.	1885ca	Dec. 4, 1963	Dav	MCDR
Hemmingway	Samuel		1773ca	Oct. ??, 1855	Dav	C1
Henderson (Slave)				Oct. 30, 1858	Bre	C1
Hendrick	Laurance		1869ca	Sep. 6, 1875	Brk	C1

Last Name	First Name	I	Birth	Death	Co	Source
Hendrick	Obadiah		Apr. 30, 1814		KY	Bk1(P268)T
Hendricks	Donald	E.	Apr. 21, 1932	Mar. 28, 1953	KY	KMIL
Hendrix	E.	S.	Nov. 17, 1863	Jun. 9, 1885	Muh	CEM2
Hening	Harriett		1831ca	May 13, 1857	Dav	C1
Henlsey	Elizabeth		1848ca		Grn	Marr1
Henning	Charles		1830ca	Dec. 13, 1852	Dav	MCDR
Henry	Ethel	M.	1885ca		Grn	Marr1
Henry	James		1788ca	Oct. 31, 1866	Har	CEM2
Henry	John Wesley		Jul. 31, 1820		KY	Bk1(P39)C
Henry	Junietta			1854	Har	CEM2
Henry	Kate		1858	1858	Har	CEM2
Henry	Mary		Jan. 16, 17??	Jul. 20, ??	Har	CEM2
Henry	Mary	F.	Feb. 18, 1850	Sep. 9, 1869	Har	CEM2
Henry	Mary	H.	Jul. 22, 1821	Aug. 29, 1890	Har	CEM2
Henry	Roper		May 19, 1919	Dec. 11, 1950	KY	KMIL
Henry	Susannah		1806ca	Sep. 9, 1866	Har	CEM2
Henry	William	J.	Nov. 11, 1832	Aug. 21, 1879	Har	CEM2
Henry C. (Slave)			1814ca	Jan. 10, 1854	Brk	C1
Henshorn	Robert		1832ca	1853	Grn	C1
Hensley	Polly		1854ca	Oct. 10, 1856	Bre	C1
Hensley, Jr.	Bird		Jun. 9, 1919	Oct. 31, 1950	KY	KMIL
Henson	Darthula		May 24. 1860	Feb. 28, 1906	Sim	CEM1
Henson	James T.	M.	Nov. 25, 1844	Jan. 3, 1864	Sim	CEM1
Henson	R.	S.	Feb. 2, 1899	Jan. 9, 1900	Sim	CEM1
Hepplen	Mary		1808ca	Dec. 15, 1857	Dav	C1
Herald	Paschal		1847ca	May ??, 1853	Bre	C1
Hereson	Beda Ann		1890	1949	Har	CEM1
Hereson	Herman		1886	1962	Har	CEM1
Herington	Stella		1890ca		Grn	Marr1
Hern	Maude		1889ca		Grn	Marr1
Hern	Ona		1868ca		Grn	Marr1
Herrald	Alexander		1839ca	Aug. 14, 1852	Bre	C1
Herrald	Unknown Female			Aug. 15, 1857	Bre	C1
Herrald (Tuson)	Pinder		1822ca	Jan. 22, 1875	Bre	C1
Heston	Daniel	P.	1814ca	Sep. 2, 1874	Brk	C1
Hewit	Sydney		1836ca	Nov. 4, 1854	Dav	C1
Hewlett	James		1838ca	Dec. 24, 1855	Dav	C1
Hichman	Unknown Male		Jan. 10, 1907		Car	C1
Hick	Lewis			Apr. ??. 1845	NWS1	4/5/1845
Hickerson	Damon	W.	1932	Mar. 28, 1951	KY	KMIL
Hickman	Charles		Jul. 29, 1870	Oct. 28, 1936	Har	CEM1
Hickman	Mildred Catherine		Sep. 21, 1892		Har	CEM1
Hickman	Mrs. Sarenia			Sep. 10, 1885	Muh	Ch1
Hickman	Sidney	H.	1902	1925	Har	CEM1
Hicks	Arvil		1932	Jul. 10, 1953	KY	KMIL
Hicks	Edith		1887ca		Grn	Marr1
Hicks	James	J.	Sep. 2, 1820		Cam	MCDR

Last Name	First Name	I	Birth	Death	Co	Source
Hicks	James	M.	1819ca		Gray	C1
Hicks	Maggie		1888ca		Grn	Marr1
Hicks	Pearlie		1890ca		Grn	Marr1
Hicks	Shelby		Jan. 15, 1854		Cam	MCDR
Higdon	Arthur		1877ca	Oct. 22, 1878	Brk	C1
Higdon	Henry		1804ca	Sep. 1, 1854	Dav	C1
Higdon	Ida		1872ca	Oct. 25, 1878	Brk	C1
Higdon	Ignatius		1832ca		Gray	C1
Higdon	Jean		1825ca	Dec. 23, 1853	Dav	MCDR
Higdon	Jno.	W.	1874ca	Oct. 25, 1878	Brk	C1
Higgs, Jr.	Allen		1928	Mar. 8, 1951	KY	KMIL
High	Carlis	E.	1929	Aug. 12, 1950	KY	KMIL
Hildreth	John		1829ca	Jan. 6, 1852	Grn	C1
Hildreth	Uriah		1802ca	Sep. 28, 1852	Grn	C1
Hill	Charlotte	G.	Jun. 2, 1843	Jan. 3, 1872	Muh	CEM3
Hill	James	A.	1827ca	Jan. 17, 1852	Dav	MCDR
Hill	Thomas		1831ca		Gray	C1
Hill	W.	O.	1836ca	Apr. 6, 1856	Dav	C1
Hill	William		1771ca		NWS5	7/2/1791
Hill (Hagan)	Ann	S.	1798ca	Aug. ??, 1855	Dav	C1
Hilmore	Richard	J.	1848ca	Jul. 5, 1852	Grn	C1
Hilton	Hargis		Jan. 28, 1907		Car	C1
Hilton	Mr.			1835	NWS4	8/14/1835
Hinant	G.	A.	1858		But	Bk1
Hindman	Henry	H.	Mar. 22, 1878			Bk1(P394)T
Hindman	Polly		1812			Bk1(P394)T
Hines (Lawerence)	Elizabeth		1833ca	Jul. 22, 1855	Dav	C1
Hinson	Martha		1819ca	May 1, 1855	Dav	C1
Hinton	Charles		1855ca	Sep. 17, 1875	Brk	C1
Hinton	Elizabeth			1852	Brk	C1
Hinton	John		1807ca	Jul. 20, 1854	Brk	C1
Hinton	Peny	C.	1865ca	Apr. 25, 1878	Brk	C1
Hite	Artie		Jul. 16, 1884	Dec. 23, 1884	Dav	CEM2
Hite	Beaulah		Apr. 23, 1887	Feb. 16, 1889	Dav	CEM2
Hite	Courtney	T.	Nov. 6, 1806	Jan. 2, 1876	Dav	CEM2
Hite	James		Oct. 15, 1867	Dec. 5, 1894	Dav	CEM2
Hite	Joan		Sep. 12, 1842	Nov. 17, 1904	Dav	CEM2
Hite	John	J.	Oct. 16, 1836	Jan. 23, 1889	Dav	CEM2
Hite	Mary	S.	Feb. 25, 1866	Aug. 27, 1893	Dav	CEM2
Hite	Sarah	E.	Sep. 2, 1877	Oct. 16, 1894	Dav	CEM2
Hite	Zarilda		Mar. 30, 1816	Jan. 23, 1889	Dav	CEM2
Hoak	George	W.	1824ca		Gray	C1
Hoak	John	W.	1832ca		Gray	C1
Hockaday	Juliett		1880ca		Grn	Marr1
Hodge	Allye Victoria		1888	1951	Dav	CEM3
Hodge	Orville	R.	1885	1937	Dav	CEM3
Hodges	Thomas	P.	1828ca	Jan. 14, 1856	Dav	C1

Last Name	First Name	I	Birth	Death	Co	Source
Hodgin	Eliza	J.	Sep. 17, 1827	Jul. 25, 1901	Dav	CEM3
Hodgkins	Anna		1832ca	Sep. 7, 1853	Dav	C1
Hoelscher	James	A.	1930	Sep. 24, 1951	KY	KMIL
Hogan	William		Jul. 21, 1814	Apr. 23, 1856	Hdn	CEM1
Hogg	Stephen		1839ca	Oct. 15, 1852	Bre	C1
Hogsten	Bessie	E.	1885ca		Grn	Marr1
Holand	Unknown Female			Jun. 25, 1875	Bre	C1
Holbert	Ollie		1894ca		Grn	Marr1
Holbrook	Essie		1885ca		Grn	Marr1
Holbrook	Ethel		Apr. 12, 1907		Car	C1
Holbrook	John		1806ca	Aug. 21, 1876	Bre	C1
Holbrook	Morgan		1833ca	Oct. 24, 1853	Grn	C1
Holbrook	William	C.	1823ca	Aug. 21, 1875	Bre	C1
Holbrooks	Dianner Bell		1877ca	Feb. 19, 1879	Bre	C1
Holbrooks	Hargis		1838ca	Sep. 18, 1878	Bre	C1
Holcomb	Manervia	J.	1877ca		Grn	Marr1
Holder	Mary	E.	1856ca	May 1, 1861	Brk	C1
Holder	Unknown Male			Jun. 8, 1861	Brk	C1
Hollan	Simon		1830ca	Jan. 23, 1875	Bre	C1
Holland	Lydia		1852ca	Sep. 26, 1859	Bre	C1
Holland	Thos.	A.	1853ca	Aug. 28, 1854	Brk	C1
Holland	Unknown Male			Apr. 15, 1859	Bre	C1
Hollen	Ambrose		1853ca	Oct. ??, 1854	Bre	C1
Hollen	John		1776ca	Nov. 25, 1854	Bre	C1
Holloman	Harvey	B.	Nov. 18, 1840		Cam	MCDR
Holloway	William	G.	1931	Jul. 11, 1950	KY	KMIL
Holmes	John	L.	1836ca	May 17, 1861	Brk	C1
Holmes	Mabel		1888ca		Grn	Marr1
Holmes	Mary	E.	1863ca	Apr. 28, 1878	Brk	C1
Holmes	Peter		1806ca	May 15, 1876	Bre	C1
Holms	John	D.	1836ca	Aug. 15, 1859	Bre	C1
Honaker	Pleasant	M.	1820		But	Bk1
Honey	Josephine		Aug. 30, 1918	Oct. 23, 1918	Hdn	CEM1
Hood	Alice		1885ca		Grn	Marr1
Hood	Newel	T.	1836		But	Bk1
Hood	Phebe			Dec. 11, 1853	Grn	C1
Hood	Stpehen Hobson		1833		But	Bk1
Hoodenpyle	Amanda	R.	1856	1939	Ful	CEM7
Hoodenpyle	Charlie	Y.	1860	1916	Ful	CEM7
Hoodenpyle	Unknown Male		Oct. 25, 1886	Oct. 27, 1887	Ful	CEM7
Hook (Jarbor)	Mrs. Sarah	A.	1840ca	Apr. 23, 1904	Brk	C1
Hooks	Orman	C.	1903ca	Jun. 25, 1946	Jef	MCDR
Hoover	Addie	R.	Dec. 6, 1893	Aug. 10, 1895	Dav	CEM3
Hoover	Infant		Mar. 27, 1909	Mar. 27, 1909	Dav	CEM3
Hoover	Lewis Mortimer		Nov. 13, 1913	Nov. 11, 1915	Dav	CEM3
Hoover	Luella	M.	1898		Hdn	CEM2
Hoover	M. Fred		1895		Hdn	CEM2

Last Name	First Name	I	Birth	Death	Co	Source
Hoover	Marion		1856	1933	Hdn	CEM2
Hoover	Maude		1883	1950	Dav	CEM3
Hoover	Minnie	R.	1870	1955	Hdn	CEM2
Hoover	Samuel		1868	1934	Dav	CEM3
Hoover	Sarah		Aug. 8, 1824	Jul. 10, 1894	Hdn	CEM1
Hopper	John	T.	Apr. 29, 1832		Gray	C2
Hopper	Lieut.			1791ca	NWS5	11/12/1791
Hopson	Nevil			Nov. 15, 1835	NWS4	11/20/1835
Hornback	John		1830ca		Gray	C1
Hornbleton	Francis	W.		Nov. 29, 1903	Brk	C1
Horner	Linda Vina		1890ca		Grn	Marr1
Horsely	Richard			1874	Brk	C1
Horseman	Z.		1839ca	Aug. ??, 1855	Dav	C1
Horsley	Amanda		1854ca	Aug. 5, 1855	Brk	C1
Horsley				Oct. 28, 1861	Brk	C1
Horsley (Adams)	Paulina		1840ca	Oct. 28, 1861	Brk	C1
Horton	Thomas Lyle		Nov. 8, 1931	Jun. 8, 1954	KY	KMIL
Hoskinson	Catherine		Mar. 5, 1809	Sep. 29, 1893	Hdn	CEM3
Hoskinson	Christine	M.	1849	1922	Hdn	CEM3
Hoskinson	Enola			Jul. 13, 1876	Brk	C1
Hoskinson	Rev. W.		Oct. 22, 1810	Jul. 12, 1882	Hdn	CEM3
Hoskinson	Rev. W.	N.	Dec. 25, 1819	Dec. 24, 1907	Hdn	CEM3
Hoslty	Unknown Female		1856ca	Dec. 13, 1859	Brk	C1
Hough	William	G.		Jul. 13, 1835	NWS4	7/17/1835
Houghin	Chas.	M.	1863ca	Aug. 15, 1877	Brk	C1
Hounshell	Andrew		1811ca	Jun. 22, 1875	Bre	C1
Hounshell	Viva		1812ca	May 23, 1878	Bre	C1
House	Benoni		1808	1849	Han	Bk1
House	J.	J.	Dec. 20, 1831		Han	Bk1
House (Lewis)	Hannah	A.	1811	Jul. 31, 1881	Han	Bk1
Hovy	Mrs. Dorothy		1782ca	Mar. 28, 1844	NWS1	4/6/1844
Howard	Charles	H.	1933	Apr. 18, 1953	KY	KMIL
Howard	Charles	M.	1850		But	Bk1
Howard	Daniel		Jul. 6, 1920	Jan. 29, 1981	Row	CEM1
Howard	Dr. John Wood.		1848		But	Bk1
Howard	Dr. Joshua	N.	1827		But	Bk1
Howard	Female		May 6, 18??	Nov. 30, 1876	Dav	CEM2
Howard	Gardner		1849ca	Aug. 15, 1858	Bre	C1
Howard	Hiram		1845ca	Sep. 4, 1856	Bre	C1
Howard	John	W.	1853ca	Dec. 27, 1855	Bre	C1
Howard	John		1830ca	Jul. 12, 1853	Bre	C1
Howard	Larkin		1847ca	Nov. 14, 1852	Bre	C1
Howard	Lewis		1851ca	Jun. 21, 1857	Bre	C1
Howard	Mrs. Mary		1830ca	Dec. 7, 1875	Dav	MCDR
Howard	N.	T.	1860		But	Bk1
Howard	Persis	H.	Jan. 2, 1808	Feb. 16, 1866	Dav	CEM2
Howard	Thomas	J.	Oct. 19, 1806	Mar. 27, 1880	Dav	CEM2

Last Name	First Name	I	Birth	Death	Co	Source
Howard	Thomas Henry		Dec. 11, 1808	Feb. 9, 1869	But	CEM2
Howard	Unknown Female			Dec. 15, 1857	Bre	C1
Howard	Male		Oct. 14, 1885	Nov. 26, 1885	Dav	CEM2
Howard (Green)	Elizabeth		1766va	Jul. 7, 1855	Bre	C1
Howe	Henrietta		1823ca	Apr. 28, 1853	Grn	C1
Howe	Rachel			Mar. 15, 1853	Grn	C1
Howell	Catherine		1799ca	May 15, 1852	Grn	C1
Howell	John		1813ca	1853	Grn	C1
Howell	Mrs. Mary			Mar. 18, 1844	NWS1	3/23/1844
Howerton	Cordelia		Dec. 13, 1871	Apr. 13, 1872	Muh	CEM3
Howerton	Elizabeth	W.	Oct. 20, 1869	Apr. 10, 1874	Muh	CEM3
Howerton	Lucy		1893ca		Grn	Marr1
Howerton	Ollie		1884ca		Grn	Marr1
Howerton	R.		Jul. 13, 1832	Aug. 22, 1855	Muh	CEM3
Hoyden	W.	H.	1833ca	Feb. 16, 1904	Brk	C1
Hubarrd	Emarine		Jan. 25, 1836	Dec. 26, 1904	Hdn	CEM2
Hubbard	Charlotte		Feb. 18, 1784	Oct. 30, 1858	Ful	CEM8
Hubbard	Dr. E.	A.	1828	1857	Ful	CEM8
Hubbard	E.	R.	Nov. 15, 1836		Hdn	CEM2
Hubbard	Geo.	S.	Mar. 18, 1809	Jun. 16, 1848	Ful	CEM8
Hubbard	Ida	P.	1872ca		Grn	Marr1
Hubbard	Rev. E.		Nov. 12, 1793	Sep. 1, 1858	Ful	CEM8
Hubbard (Craig)	Sue		1838	1918	Ful	CEM8
Huddleston	George		1930	Jul. 3, 1952	KY	KMIL
Hudson	Sanford		1833ca	Apr. 23 1854	Brk	C1
Hudson	Squire		1799ca	Nov. 20, 1876	Brk	C1
Hudson	Unknown Female		1873ca	Aug. 20, 1875	Brk	C1
Hudson	William	E.	1838		But	Bk1
Huff	Mary	A.	1879ca		Grn	Marr1
Huffin	Dr.	W.	1876ca	Jul. ??, 1878	Brk	C1
Huffin	Lulu		1872ca	Jul. 16, 1878	Brk	C1
Huffines	Unknown Female		1872ca	Aug. 13, 1875	Brk	C1
Huffines (Lucas)	Ann		1835ca	Nov. 24, 1856	Brk	C1
Huffman	John	W.		Sep. ??, 1877	Grn	C2
Huffman	Roberta		1891ca		Grn	Marr1
Huffman	Victoria		1854ca	1877	Grn	C2
Huggins	Ramon	H.	1931ca	Apr. 8, 1984	Fay	MCDR
Hughes	Dorman	D.	1924	Sep. 19, 1950	KY	KMIL
Hughes	Leonard		Dec. 2, 1923	Aug. 16, 1951	KY	KMIL
Huguley	Barney	M.	1931	Jan. 26, 1953	KY	KMIL
Huley	Allie Bell		1874ca	Aug. 10, 1875	Dav	MCDR
Hull	Infant			1835	NWS4	8/14/1835
Hull	William		Mar. 27, 1829	Jan. 6, 1898	Dav	CEM3
Hulsey	M.	E.	1843ca	Oct. ??, 1861	Dav	C1
Hultz	Joe		1883ca	Aug. 5, 1904	Brk	C1
Hultz (Davidson)	Emily		1875ca	Jul. 15, 1904	Brk	C1
Humphrey	S.		1817ca	Aug. 1857	Dav	C1

Last Name	First Name	I	Birth	Death	Co	Source
Humphreys	Alice	B.	Dec. 2, 1859	Dec. 13, 1928	Ful	CEM7
Humphreys	John	R.	Jun. 23, 1855	Mar. 6, 1941	Ful	CEM7
Hunley	Martha	V.	Mar. 10, 1805	Aug. 3, 1883	Muh	CEM3
Hunt	John		1800		But	Bk1
Hunt	Lena		1880ca		Grn	Marr1
Hunt	William	C.	1933	Nov. 26, 1950	KY	KMIL
Hunter	J.	B.	1842ca	Jun. 14, 1894	Brk	C1
Hunter	Madge		1889ca		Grn	Marr1
Hunter	Mrs.			1835	NWS4	8/14/1835
Hunter (Carman)	Polly		1817ca	Aug. 8, 1855	Brk	C1
Hures	Elija			Aug. 22, 1853	Grn	C1
Hures	Mary	A.		May ??, 1853	Grn	C1
Hurst	Donald	L.	1927	Jan. 29, 1951	KY	KMIL
Hurst	Dulany		1855ca	Jan. 10, 1857	Bre	C1
Hurst	Harrison	B.		Nov. 19, 1852	Bre	C1
Hurst	Isabell			Oct. 4, 1874	Bre	C1
Husley	Mary			1852	Brk	C1
Husley	Ralph			1852	Brk	C1
Hutchinson	Grace		1891ca		Grn	Marr1
Hutchinson	John		1777ca		NWS5	9/7/1793
Hyatt	Lester	T.	1927	Nov. 28, 1950	KY	KMIL
Hyson	Minerva		1825ca	Dec. 23, 1853	Dav	C1
Iglehart	Alfred		No Date	No Date	Oh	CEM3
Iglehart	Edgar John		Jun. 21, 1914	May 12, 1926	Oh	CEM3
Iglehart	H.	M.	Jan. 30, 1880	Jun. 30, 1945	Oh	CEM3
Iglehart	Ida Mae		Sep. 7, 1924	Aug. 10, 1925	Oh	CEM3
Iglehart	James	B.	Sep. 28, 1842	1926	Oh	CEM3
Iglehart	John	W.	Oct. 26, 1859	Apr. 19, 1936	Oh	CEM3
Iglehart	Louvga		Jul. 13, 1859	Aug. 20, 1893	Oh	CEM3
Iglehart	Margaret		Oct. 19, 1892	Apr. 25, 1925	Oh	CEM3
Iglehart	Mary	A.		Jan. ??, 1897	McL	CH1
Iglehart	Permelia	J.	Jan. 24, 1847	1928	Oh	Cem3
Iglehart	Rhoda		Aug. 15, 1853	Jul. 23, 1903	Oh	Cem3
Iglehart	Ruth		1840ca	Feb. 20, 1855	Dav	C1
Iglehart	Sylvester		Apr. 4, 1847	Apr. 10, 1916	Oh	Cem3
Iglehart	Thomas		1801ca	Feb. ??, 1855	Dav	C1
Ingle	Anna		Mar. 5, 1893	Jan. 12, 1980	Row	CEM1
Ingle	John	H.	May 6, 1881	Nov. 23, 1969	Row	CEM1
Ingram	James		Nov. 19, 1820	Dec. 24, 1870	Sim	CEM1
Ingram	Simeon	W.	Oct. 28, 1866	Oct. 6, 1872	Sim	CEM1
Innes	Sarah		1776		KY	BK2(P194)
Innes	Whitney	R.	1918ca	May 12, 1980	Fay	MCDR
Ireland	John		Jan. 1, 1827		KY	Bk1(P82)T
Ireland	Joseph	M.	1851ca	Dec. 9, 1853	Grn	C1
Irvin	Theodore	R.	Feb. 7, 1934	Mar. 27, 1953	KY	KMIL
Irwin	E.	H.	1861	1923	Hdn	CEM2
Irwin	Emma	B.	Mar. 11, 1838	Apr. 10, 1924	Hdn	CEM2

Last Name	First Name	I	Birth	Death	Co	Source
Irwin	Eugenia		Jan. 25, 1906	May 7, 1910	Hdn	CEM2
Irwin	Harold		Apr. 26, 1910	Mar. 6, 1911	Hdn	CEM2
Irwin	John Lacy		Apr. 8, 1867	Mar. 21, 1942	Hdn	CEM2
Irwin	William	S.	Dec. 8, 1833	Mar. 8, 1894	Hdn	CEM2
Isham	Sarah		1869ca		Grn	Marr1
Isom	America		1881ca		Grn	Marr1
Isom	Bessie		1891ca		Grn	Marr1
Ison	Wm. Lee		May 1, 1907		Car	C1
Jaboe	I.	A.	1845ca	Sep. 11, 1861	Dav	C1
Jacke	Anna Lee		Oct. 13, 1893	Dec. 9, 1963	Hdn	CEM2
Jacke	Norma Lee		Sep. 10, 1929		Hdn	CEM2
Jackson	Juda		1892ca		Grn	Marr1
Jackson	Laura		1892ca		Grn	Marr1
Jackson	Male		Nov. 9, 1896	Nov. 9, 1896	Oh	Cem3
Jackson	Male		Jul. 19, 1906	Jul. 19, 1906	Oh	Cem3
Jackson	Mattie		1885ca		Grn	Marr1
Jackson	Ruth		1895ca		Grn	Marr1
Jackson	Sarah Ann		1889ca		Grn	Marr1
Jackson	T.	J.	1826		Cam	MCDR
Jackson	Wiley	E.	Apr. 26, 1863	Mar. 29, 1906	Ful	CEM7
Jackson	William	T.	1929	Nov. 24, 1951	KY	KMIL
Jacob (Slave)			1837ca	Feb. 20, 1858	Bre	C1
Jacobs	Arizona		1866ca		Grn	Marr1
Jacobs	Ronald	D.	1934	Oct. 19, 1952	KY	KMIL
Jaggers	Hattie		May ??, 1903		Hdn	CEM2
Jaggers	Tho. Edward		Aug. 29, 1967	Dec. 26, 1973	Hdn	CEM2
Jaggers	Thomas	W.	1905	1954	Hdn	CEM2
James	Chauncey		Apr. 14, 1907		Car	C1
James	Eliza		Feb. 17, 1811	Dec. 27, 1884	Sim	CEM1
James	Morrison		1814		But	Bk1
James	Robert	C.	1865ca	Nov. 13, 1920	Fay	MCDR
James	Robert	L.	1909ca	Sep. 13, 1978	Sim	MCDR
James	Robert	T.		Jun. 25, 1968	Dav	MCDR
James	Robert		1972ca	Nov. 23, 1974	Fay	MCDR
James	Robert			Nov. 4, 1921	Fay	MCDR
James	Thomas		Mar. 9, 1795	Jan. 3, 1869	Sim	CEM1
James (Slave)			1800ca	Dec. 14, 1854	Brk	C1
James, Jr.	Benj.	C.	Nov. 29, 1844		Cam	MCDR
Janett	Clay		1864ca	Sep. 30, 1927	Fay	MCDR
Janett	Female		1831ca	Nov. 23, 1853	Brk	C1
Janett	Lavaughn		1927ca	Dec. 29, 1980	Fay	MCDR
Janett	William		1836ca	Aug. 28, 1855	Dav	C1
Jarbo	Philip			Mar. 31, ????	Dav	MCDR
Jarboe	Samuel		1789ca	Oct. 11, 1861	Brk	C1
Jarrell	Manda		1886ca		Grn	Marr1
Jarrett	Charles Edward		Aug. 16, 1930	Nov. 29, 1950	KY	KMIL
Jarvis	Albert		May 14, 1911	Feb. 11, 1917	Muh	CEM3

Last Name	First Name	I	Birth	Death	Co	Source
Jarvis	James	L.		Aug. 5, 1894	Brk	C1
Jarvis	Annie Ophelia		1901ca	Aug. 4, 1904	Brk	C1
Javred (Wood)	Mary	J.	1854ca	Nov. 18, 1878	Brk	C1
Jayne	Beulah		1884ca		Grn	Marr1
Jeffers	John		1812ca	Mar. 5, 1889	Muh	Ch1
Jeffers	Mrs. Bettie			Jan. 18, 1886	Muh	Ch1
Jefferson	Alexander	A.	1921ca	Nov. 9, 1985	Fay	MCDR
Jefferson	Milton	A.	1909ca	Dec. 29, 1984	Fay	MCDR
Jefferson	Richard	A.		Jun. 12, 1982	Fay	MCDR
Jefferson	Rowena	A.	1887ca	Aug. 16, 1961	Fay	MCDR
Jeffrey	Howard	R.	1909	Nov. 26, 1950	KY	KMIL
Jenkins	Andrew		1844		But	Bk1
Jenkins	C.	C.	1843	1909	Hdn	CEM2
Jenkins	Eliza		1891ca		Grn	Marr1
Jenkins	Harve	P.	May 10, 1875	Aug. 10, 1949	Hdn	CEM2
Jenkins	Harvey		Nov. 11, 1902	Nov. 11, 1902	Hdn	CEM2
Jenkins	Ida Bland		May 29, 1886	Apr. 23, 1957	Hdn	CEM2
Jenkins	James	L.	Sep. 2, 1884	Apr. 10, 1941	Hdn	CEM2
Jenkins	Jas. Woodford		Nov. 15, 1913		Hdn	CEM2
Jenkins	Lenore	L.	1887ca		Grn	Marr1
Jenkins	Lucy		1888ca		Grn	Marr1
Jenkins	Mary	A.	1847	1940	Hdn	CEM2
Jenkins	Ruby	M.	Feb. 23, 1872	Apr. 24, 1947	Hdn	CEM2
Jenkins	Sarah	E.	1862		Har	CEM1
Jenkins	Sarah Elizabeth		Jun. 29, 1908		Hdn	CEM2
Jenkins	Sarah Jane		Feb. 11, 1823	Jul. 4, 1902	Hdn	CEM2
Jenkins	William	H.	Sep. 3, 1853	Sep. 14, 1880	Hdn	CEM2
Jenkins	Wm. Hall		1853		Cam	MCDR
Jenkins (Sutzer)	Marjory		Oct. 17, 1915		Hdn	CEM2
Jennings	J.	I.	Jan. 15, 1860	Apr. 12, 1923	Ful	CEM4
Jennings	Maggie		Jun. 2, 1869	1949	Ful	CEM4
Jennings (Colston)	Susan P.	N.	1833ca	Sep. 10, 1855	Brk	C1
Jerro;d	Mintie		1882ca		Grn	Marr1
Jerry (negro)			Sep. 1, 1859		Sim	C1
Jett	Alfred		1868ca	Feb. 27, 1876	Bre	C1
Jett	Curtis		1854ca	Jul. 16, 1874	Bre	C1
Jett	Curtis		1813ca	May 14, 1878	Bre	C1
Jett	Dr. John P.	M.	Jun. 6, 1828		Han	Bk1
Jett	John C. Breck.			Sep. 27, 1857	Bre	C1
Jett	Lucy	M.	1868ca	Dec. 9, 1876	Bre	C1
Jett	Newton		1809ca	Mar. 21, 1874	Bre	C1
Jett	Richard	C.	1785	Mar. ??, 1862	Han	Bk1
Jett (Miller)	Susan	T.	1801	May ??, 1863	Han	Bk1
Jewett	William		1806ca	Aug. 28, 1856	Dav	C1
John	Carlis	E.	1928	Mar. 9, 1951	KY	KMIL
Johnson	Alice		Jan. 30, 1888	Feb. 3, 1888	Log	CEM1
Johnson	Audry Lorean		Oct. 26, 1957	18-May-59	Row	CEM1

Last Name	First Name	I	Birth	Death	Co	Source
Johnson	Benjamin		1787ca	Sep. 5, 1855	Lew	CEM1
Johnson	Betsy		Dec. 6, 1886		McL	Sch1
Johnson	Bill Ed		Oct. 1, 1933	Aug. 13, 1952	KY	KMIL
Johnson	Bobby		1931	Jul. 31, 1950	KY	KMIL
Johnson	Caplton			Mar. 4, 1856	Bre	C1
Johnson	Carl Lee		1897	1919	Hdn	CEM2
Johnson	Charles	D.	1869ca	Oct. 23, 1878	Brk	C1
Johnson	Charles Lee		Jun. 16, 1928	Oct. 2, 1950	KY	KMIL
Johnson	Charley	W.	Jul. 16, 1913	Sep. 18, 1988	Row	CEM1
Johnson	Charlotte		1868ca	Apr. 17, 1878	Brk	C1
Johnson	Christopher	R.	1824		But	Bk1
Johnson	Cora	B.	Apr. 12, 1881	Dec. 14, 1881	Log	CEM1
Johnson	Cora	L.	1886ca		Grn	Marr1
Johnson	Dewey Earl		May 17, 1900		Hdn	CEM2
Johnson	Dollie		1894ca		Grn	Marr1
Johnson	Earl		May 30, 1926	Jul. 31, 1926	Row	CEM1
Johnson	Edmon	M.	Sep. 7, 1787	May 18, 1888	Har	Cem1
Johnson	Elizabeth	A.	1838ca	Apr. 2, 1853	Dav	C1
Johnson	Elizabeth		1789ca	Jul. 11, 1879	Lew	CEM1
Johnson	Elizabeth		Aug. 26, 1871	Aug. 26, 1871	Log	CEM1
Johnson	Elizabeth		1837ca	Jul. 1, 1852	Bre	C1
Johnson	Elizabeth Jane		Feb. 21, 1819	Apr. 9, 1897	Log	CEM1
Johnson	Ella		Jun. 3, 1914	Jun. 6, 1914	Row	CEM1
Johnson	Ellis		Feb. 21, 1916	Aug. 5, 1988	Row	CEM1
Johnson	Ernest	L.	Jun. 6, 1887	Oct. 14, 1918	Muh	CEM3
Johnson	Eula Katherine		1926		Row	CEM1
Johnson	Frances		Jul. 12, 1922		Row	CEM1
Johnson	Grace		Aug. 1, 1865	Sep. 17, 1914	Muh	CEM3
Johnson	Granville		1931	Jul. 2, 1952	KY	KMIL
Johnson	J.	E.	Sep. 11, 1816		Gray	C2
Johnson	J.	P.	Feb. 17, 1889		McL	Sch1
Johnson	James	C.	Nov. 10, 1813	1835	NWS4	11/13/1835
Johnson	James	G.	Feb. 1, 1862	Dec. 20, 1880	Har	Cem1
Johnson	James	H.	Oct. 21, 1861	Mar. 2, 1938	Muh	CEM3
Johnson	James Wash		1842	1914	Hdn	CEM2
Johnson	Jane		Mar. 20, 1878	Mar. 20, 1878	Log	CEM1
Johnson	Jane		Mar. 15, 1782	Dec. 11, 1818	Cal	CEM1
Johnson	Jemina		1783	1856	Log	CEM1
Johnson	Joanathan Thomas		Aug. 13, 1855	Oct. 5, 1880	Log	CEM1
Johnson	John		Sep. 19, 1816	Apr. 18, 1880	Log	CEM1
Johnson	Jonathan		Nov. 18, 1818	Apr. 12, 1864	Log	CEM1
Johnson	Joseph		1782	1851	Log	CEM1
Johnson	Justis	A.		May 14, 1876	Bre	C1
Johnson	Keenis		1920	1992	Row	CEM1
Johnson	Lydia		1847	1933	Log	CEM1
Johnson	M.	E.		Dec. 7, 1893	Brk	C1
Johnson	Malinda Jane		1859ca	Sep. 18, 1861	Brk	C1

Last Name	First Name	I	Birth	Death	Co	Source
Johnson	Maria		1857ca	Mar. 30, 1878	Brk	C1
Johnson	Martha	B.	Nov. 14, 1869	Aug. 14, 1944	Muh	CEM3
Johnson	Mary		1792ca	Aug. 1, 1850	Lew	CEM1
Johnson	Mary Ann		1866	1933	Hdn	CEM2
Johnson	Myrtle		Feb. 1, 1883		McL	Sch1
Johnson	Nancy		Jul. 20, 1829	Jun. 13, 1906	Log	CEM1
Johnson	Oliver	P.	1830		But	Bk1
Johnson	Orman		1912ca	Nov. 15, 1928	Muh	MCDR
Johnson	Orvel	J.	1930	Sep. 4, 1950	KY	KMIL
Johnson	Patrick Henry			Sep. 2, 1835	NWS4	9/4/1835
Johnson	Pearl		Sep. 21, 1881		McL	
Johnson	Phillip			May 14, 1853	Grn	C1
Johnson	Polly		1781ca	Sep. 15, 1853	Bre	C1
Johnson	Rachel		Jul. 13, 1787	Feb. 5, 1863	Har	Cem1
Johnson	Robert	S.		Jun. 24, 1877	Bre	C1
Johnson	Robert		1759		All	RP1
Johnson	Rozennie	C.	1898	1946	Row	CEM1
Johnson	Russell		Apr. 24, 1922	Aug. 19, 1925	Row	CEM1
Johnson	Ruth		Oct. 30, 1883	Oct. 30, 1883	Log	CEM1
Johnson	Saml.	W.	1874ca	Nov. 18, 1878	Brk	C1
Johnson	Sarah		1783ca	Nov. ??, 1853	Dav	C1
Johnson	Seth	M.	Jul. 3, 1859	Jan. 9, 1938	Muh	CEM3
Johnson	Seth		1836	1928	Log	CEM1
Johnson	T.	D.	1826ca	Nov. 12, 1878	Brk	C1
Johnson	Tom		1889	1969	Row	CEM1
Johnson	W.	C.	May 12, 1929	Jun. 3, 1945	Muh	CEM3
Johnson	Willa Myrel		Dec. 12, 1926	May 5, 1928	Muh	CEM3
Johnson	William		1852ca	Jan. 21, 1875	Bre	C1
Johnson (Claycomb)	Lucy		1827ca	Oct. 4, 1903	Brk	C1
Johnston	Albert Addison		Feb. 2, 1835			Bk1(P166)T
Jolly	Layfeyatt			Nov. 10, 1861	Brk	C1
Jolly (Hardin)	Rachel		1819ca	Feb. 10, 1894	Brk	C1
Jolly (Robbins)	M.	E.	1858ca	Jul. 21, 1894	Brk	C1
Jones	A.	B.	1865ca	Nov. 9, 1934	Fay	MCDR
Jones	A.	C.		May 24, 1923	Bat	MCDR
Jones	A.	C.	1876ca	Sep. 24, 1926	Dav	MCDR
Jones	A.	D.	1861ca	Dec. 30, 1945	Jef	MCDR
Jones	A.	J.	1853ca	Dec. 23, 1918	Ada	MCDR
Jones	A.	L.	1840ca	Dec. 4, 1918	Dav	MCDR
Jones	A.	R.	1860ca	Dec. 21, 1927	Jef	MCDR
Jones	Abraham		1830ca	Jan. 5, 1853	Dav	C1
Jones	Adeline		1841ca	Jul. 2, 1877	Grn	C2
Jones	Anna	M.	1870	1954	Ful	CEM7
Jones	Bessie		1892ca		Grn	Marr1
Jones	Billy			Apr. 7, 1949	Ful	CEM7
Jones	Dock Thomas		1879	1943	Ful	CEM7
Jones	Emeline		1847ca	Mar. 15, 1853	Bre	C1

Last Name	First Name	I	Birth	Death	Co	Source
Jones	Emma		1885ca		Grn	Marr1
Jones	Eva		May 23, 1855	Sep. 20, 1930	Ful	CEM7
Jones	Evans			Aug. 19, 1863	KY	CMIL2
Jones	Gilbert		Apr. 17, 1882	Aug. 22, 1903	Ful	CEM7
Jones	Henry		1932	Oct. 5, 1950	KY	KMIL
Jones	Isaac		Oct. 12, 1836		Gray	C2
Jones	J.	J.		Sep. ??, 1863	KY	CMIL2
Jones	J.	M.	Feb. 11, 1881	Mar. 9, 1933	Ful	CEM7
Jones	J.	A.	1828		But	Bk1
Jones	James	L.		May ??, 1853	Dav	C1
Jones	John Willie		Jan. 27, 1932	Jan. 24, 1953	KY	KMIL
Jones	Kitty			Oct. ??, 1907	McL	CH1
Jones	Lewis		1848ca	Aug. 17, 1855	Bre	C1
Jones	Lucinda		Feb. 26, 1875	Feb. 2, 1938	Oh	Cem3
Jones	Margaret		1874ca	Dec. 15, 1875	Bre	C1
Jones	Martha Eliza		1829ca	Apr. 5, 1844	NWS1	4/27/1844
Jones	Mathew		1824ca	Aug. 21, 1859	Bre	C1
Jones	Nance	E.	1855ca	Dec. 14, 1929	Jef	MCDR
Jones	Robert		1851ca	Dec. 11, 1857	Bre	C1
Jones	Ruby		1891ca		Grn	Marr1
Jones	Samuel		1769ca		NWS5	1/12/1793
Jones	Sarah		1808ca	Jun. 15, 1857	Dav	C1
Jones	Thomas Perry		Apr. 19, 1831		KY	RP1
Jones	Unknown Female		1845ca	Mar. 15, 1854	Brk	C1
Jones	W.	H.	Jan. 24, 1852	Aug. 18, 1887	Ful	CEM7
Jones	Walter		Apr. 10, 1885	Jun. 4, 1885	Ful	CEM7
Jones	Whitney		1896ca	Apr., 16, 1980	Fay	MCDR
Jones (Brown)	Lettie	C.	Nov. 26, 1883	Dec. 23, 1920	Ful	CEM7
Jones (May)	Mary	E.	1805ca	Mar. ??, 1855	Dav	C1
Jones, Jr.	Edward		Dec. 21, 1930	Nov. 28, 1950	KY	KMIL
Jordan	Charles	E.	1928	Sep. 10, 1950	KY	KMIL
Jordan	Clara		1885ca		Grn	Marr1
Jordan	Julia		1891ca		Grn	Marr1
Jordan	Mark		Sep. 8, 1904		Car	C1
Jordan	Marvel		1811ca	Apr. 10, 1894	Brk	C1
Jordan	Nellie	M.	31-May-00	Jan. 4, 1951	Dav	CEM3
Jordan	Samuel	L.	Jan. 3, 1882	May 19, 1922	Dav	CEM3
Jorden	William		Sep. 12, 1904		Car	C1
Jordon (Slave)	Mariah		1830ca	Aug. ??, 1858	Brk	C1
Joseph	Arthur		1930	Sep. 15, 1952	KY	KMIL
Josey (Hinton)	Margaret		1834ca	1857	Dav	C1
Jourdan	Thos.		1872ca	Sep. 6, 1878	Brk	C1
Joyce, Jr.	Thomas		1913	Feb. 13, 1951	KY	KMIL
Juett	Elizabeth		Nov. 17, 1806	Oct. 25, 1826	Har	CEM2
Julia (Slave)			1839ca	Oct. 24, 1855	Brk	C1
Julia (Slave)				Jul. 10, 1861	Brk	C1
Jump	Charlie	A.	Aug. 24, 1911	Feb. 25, 1912	Hdn	CEM2

Last Name	First Name	I	Birth	Death	Co	Source
Jump	Cora	N.	Feb. 26, 1882	Mar. 25, 1966	Hdn	CEM2
Jump	Grover	F.	Apr. 26, 1882	Jul. 22, 1959	Hdn	CEM2
Jump	Hayes	O.	Aug. 29, 1913	Nov. 20, 1960	Hdn	CEM2
Jump	Haynes	C.	Aug. 29, 1913	May 22, 1944	Hdn	CEM2
Jump	Mildred Lee		Sep. 19, 1907	Mar. 17, 1966	Hdn	CEM2
Jump	Thomas Lee		May 17, 1871	Aug. 26, 1943	Hdn	CEM2
Jump	Evelyn	L.	Apr. 5, 1921	Sep. 13, 1930	Hdn	CEM2
Justice	J.	A.	1846		Cam	MCDR
Kallam	James	W.	1829ca	May 3, 1853	Dav	C1
Kam (Elwood)	Margaret		1774ca	Sep. 29, 1854	Dav	C1
Karnes (Blakey)	Mary	C.	1834ca	Nov. 17, 1853	Dav	C1
Karr (Crutchfield)	Nancy		1829ca	Aug. 2, 1861	Dav	C1
Kastor	Charles Richard		May 1, 1932	Jan. 13, 1953	KY	KMIL
Kay	James		1778ca	Oct. 7, 1835	NWS4	10/9/1835
Kays	Billy	J.	1932	Feb. 13, 1951	KY	KMIL
Kearns	Albert		1869	1941	Har	CEM1
Kearns	Andrew	M.	Aug. 18, 1862	May 8, 1915	Har	CEM1
Kearns	Anna		Nov. 3, 1878	Jun. 5, 1916	Har	CEM1
Kearns	Clara		1876	1928	Har	CEM1
Kearns	G.	W.	Jan. 18, 1841	Mar. 29, 1904	Har	CEM1
Kearns	Ida		May 31, 1878	25-May-15	Har	CEM1
Kearns	Louisa	H.	Oct. 12, 1865	Oct. 25, 1901	Har	CEM1
Kearns	Martha	J.	Jan. 8, 1848?	Jan. 20, 1891	Har	CEM1
Kearns	Sarah	E.	1847	1928	Har	CEM1
Kearns	Sophrenia Jackson		Apr. 30, 1831	Nov. 17, 1871	Har	CEM1
Kearns	Sue Batson		1883	1948	Har	CEM1
Kearns	Survina	C.	Nov. 29, 1854	Apr. 28, 1874	Har	CEM1
Keaton	Myrtle		1887ca		Grn	Marr1
Keeley	Charles	E.	1931	Sep. 8, 1950	KY	KMIL
Keen	Pheoba		1891ca		Grn	Marr1
Keenan	J.	T.	1852ca	Aug. 2, 1894	Brk	C1
Kegley	Mary	E.	1891ca		Grn	Marr1
Kegley	Ralph	E.	1927	Dec. 1, 1950	KY	KMIL
Keith	Alexander		1750	1824	Hdn	CEM3
Keith	J.	C.	Feb. 23, 1835		Gray	C2
Keith	Lula Mae		1895	1930	Hdn	CEM3
Keith	Richard			Oct. 25, 1861	Brk	C1
Keith	Shellie	G.	1890	1965	Hdn	CEM3
Keller	Unknown Male		Aug. 10, 1907		Car	C1
Kelley	Bertha		1894ca		Grn	Marr1
Kelley	David	J.	1928	Jul. 23, 1952	KY	KMIL
Kelley	John		1774ca		NWS5	5/25/1793
Kelley	William			Aug. 18, 1853	Grn	C1
Kelly	Charley		1819ca	Dec. 5, 1853	Dav	C1
Kelly	D.	P.	Apr. 15, 1836		Gray	C2
Kelly	Elizabeth		Feb. 21, 1841		Gray	C2
Kelly	Joseph		1813ca	Feb. 12, 1853	Dav	C1

Last Name	First Name	I	Birth	Death	Co	Source
Kelly	Lawrence Bertrand		Jan. 22, 1925	Dec. 31, 1953	KY	KMIL
Kelly	Nancy	A.	1830ca	Apr. 16, 1853	Dav	C1
Kelso	Lieut.			1791ca	NWS5	11/12/1791
Kendall	D.	G.	Jul. 17, 1843	Jan. 3, 1907	Har	CEM1
Kendall	James	T.	Nov. 20, 1835	Oct. 17, 1916	Har	CEM1
Kendall	Jane		1864	1945	Har	CEM1
Kendall	Maude		1880	1953	Har	CEM1
Kendall	Noah		1862	1945	Har	CEM1
Kennedy	Bulley Kate		1900ca	Jul. 7, 1903	Brk	C1
Kennedy	Elizabeth		Mar. 1, 1852		Dav	CEM3
Kennedy	J.	W.	Oct. 3, 1833	Oct. 15, 1915	Dav	CEM3
Kennedy	Jacob		1854ca	Aug. 18, 1874	Brk	C1
Kennedy	James		1780ca	Dec. 29, 1856	Dav	C1
Kennedy	Lydia		1813ca	Apr. 9, 1861	Dav	C1
Kennedy	Martha	E.	Sep. 23, 1845	Aug. 8, 1895	Hdn	CEM2
Kennedy	W.	D.	1840	1908	Hdn	CEM2
Kennedy	Woodie		Jul. 7, 1889	Sep. 8, 1898	Dav	CEM3
Kenney	Oma		1894ca		Grn	Marr1
Kenning	Thomas		1772ca		NWS5	6/9/1792
Keown	Elizabeth		Feb. 1, 1849	Dec. 2, 1876	Dav	CEM3
Keown	Sherman		Oct. 17, 1903	Apr. 18, 1904	Dav	CEM3
Kern	Maggie	E.	1888ca		Grn	Marr1
Kerney	William		1779ca	Dec. 6, 1861	Dav	C1
Kerrick	Mary		1808ca	Jan. ??, 1853	Dav	C1
Kerson	William		1784ca		NWS5	2/14/1798
Kesinger	Nicholas	C.	1847		But	Bk1
Ketchum	Unknown Male			May 18, 1859	Bre	C1
Kettrel	Louise		Jan. 12, 1849	Aug. 7, 1879	Ful	CEM7
Kidd	Emma	L.	1885ca		Grn	Marr1
Kidd (Rose)	Perlina		1818ca	Mar. 10, 1854	Bre	C1
Kidwell	William	U.	1859ca	Aug. 22, 1933	Car	MCDR
Kilburn	Johnny		1930	Aug. 12, 1952	KY	KMIL
Kilcrist	Francis		1777ca		NWS5	9/27/1794
Kilgore	Mary jane		1888ca		Grn	Marr1
Killpatrick	William		1782ca		NWS5	12/12/1798
Kimble	John	A.	1830ca		Gray	C1
Kimbler	Eva		Feb. 25, 1904		Car	C1
Kimmel	H.		1876	1946	Muh	CEM3
Kincheloe	Nance	H.	1928ca	Aug. 6, 1985	Jef	MCDR
Kindling	Caroline			Oct. 20, 1853	Grn	C1
King	A. L.	C.		Sep. 11, 1862	KY	CMIL1
King	Denver		1928	Oct. 19, 1951	KY	KMIL
King	Elster	R.	1929	Nov. 28, 1950	KY	KMIL
King	Emry		1866ca	Sep. 12, 1877	Bre	C1
King	Herbert		1927	Mar. 7, 1952	KY	KMIL
King	Jason		1927	Jun. 27, 1951	KY	KMIL
King	Mildred		1891ca		Grn	Marr1

Last Name	First Name	I	Birth	Death	Co	Source
King	Monna Mobely		Feb. 4, 1907		Car	C1
King	Presley		Sep. 18, 1833		Gray	C2
King	Saml. Alexander		Oct. 11, 1834			Bk1(P527)T
King	Slvania		1854	1915	Hen	CEM1
King	Willie		Mar. ??, 1865	Nov. ??, 1865	Hdn	CEM1
King (Hollan)	Polly		1831ca	May 7, 1858	Bre	C1
Kinman	James			Jan. 27, 1862	Har	CEM2
Kinman	Louisa		Aug. 18, 1834	Jan. 16, 1885	Har	CEM2
Kinman	Lucy			Apr. 10, 1875	Har	CEM2
Kinser	August	J.	1872ca	Jul. 21, 1935	Ken	MCDR
Kinsey	Virgie Lee		1882ca		Grn	Marr1
Kiper	John		Oct. 18, 1822		Gray	C2
Kiper	Zoella			Apr. 16, 1878	Brk	C1
Kirbee	Ezekile Thompson		1835ca	Sep. ??, 1853	Dav	C1
Kirk	Sadie		1888ca		Grn	Marr1
Kirk	Susan		1816ca	Jun. 3, 1853	Dav	C1
Kirkwood	Capt.			1791ca	NWS5	11/12/1791
Kiser	Ango (?)		1889ca		Grn	Marr1
Kiser	John	S.	Aug. 20, 1904		Car	C1
Kitchen	Abner		Jul. 28, 1907		Car	C1
Kitchen	Sarah	H.	1897ca		Grn	Marr1
Kitts	Rosa	E.	1888ca		Grn	Marr1
Klinglesmith	Amanda Clater		1883	1963	Hdn	CEM3
Klinglesmith	C.	W.	Sep. 8, 1830	Jan. 8, 1908	Hdn	CEM3
Klinglesmith	Eliza	J.	Aug. 17, 1802	Jun. 24, 1871	Hdn	CEM3
Klinglesmith	Eunice		Apr. 16, 1912	Dec. 13, 1964	Hdn	CEM3
Klinglesmith	Gracie		Jun. 27, 1882		Hdn	CEM3
Klinglesmith	J.	S.	Sep. 29, 1879	Dec. 15, 1947	Hdn	CEM3
Klinglesmith	J. Carl		Aug. 28, 1875	May 21, 1930	Hdn	CEM3
Klinglesmith	Jacob	B.	Jul. 2, 1838	Mar. 6, 1926	Hdn	CEM3
Klinglesmith	John		Jan. 9, 1807	Jan. 12, 1878	Hdn	CEM3
Klinglesmith	S. Frances		1912	1915	Hdn	CEM3
Klinglesmith	Sarah	J.	Jul. 4, 1841	Jul. 27, 1941	Hdn	CEM3
Klinglesmith	Susan Ann		Sep. 10, 1834	Jan. 24, 1886	Hdn	CEM3
Klinglesmith	William	E.	1862	1937	Hdn	CEM3
Kloop	John	L.	Dec. 9, 1930	Dec. 11, 1950	KY	KMIL
Knight	Arty		Jan. 9, 1854		Dav	CEM2
Knight	Charley		Jan. 9, 1852	Sep. 6, 1912	Dav	CEM2
Knight	Female		Jul. 12, 1914	Jul. 12, 1914	Dav	CEM2
Knight	Male		Jul. 12, 1914	Jul. 12, 1914	Dav	CEM2
Knight	Neal	M.	1929	Feb. 12, 1951	KY	KMIL
Knight	Stinson	W.	1889ca	May 8, 1949	Dav	MCDR
Knight	Walter	S.	Sep. 13, 1872	Apr. 25, 1892	Dav	CEM2
Knight	Willie		Oct. 1, 1886	Jul. 18, 1913	Dav	CEM2
Knott	Andrew		1866ca	Jan. 13, 1952	Dav	MCDR
Knott	Ben		1855ca	Jan. 21, 1912	Dav	MCDR
Knott	Betty	A.	1934ca	Jan. 3, 1948	Dav	MCDR

Last Name	First Name	I	Birth	Death	Co	Source
Knott	James		1824ca	Jun. 17, 1854	Dav	C1
Knott	Leonard		1800ca	Apr. 12, 1855	Dav	C1
Knox	John	E.	Mar. 26, 1866	Sep. 20, 1869	Ful	CEM1
Knox	Robert	M.	Nov. 19, 1854	Nov. 21, 1863	Ful	CEM1
Kolb	William	O.	1928	Jul. 21, 1951	KY	KMIL
Korb	Lewis		1837		Cam	MCDR
Kouns	Robert	M.	1930	Sep. 7, 1950	KY	KMIL
Krahan	Alma	E.	Jun. 13, 1929	Mar. 31, 1975	Hdn	CEM2
Krahan	Charles	W.	Aug. 11, 1920		Hdn	CEM2
Krahan	Charlie	W.	Nov. 20, 1890	Jan. 13, 1963	Hdn	CEM2
Krahan	Eva	R.	May 27, 1890	Mar. 10, 1950	Hdn	CEM2
Krahan	Wm. Clifton		Sep. 21, 1922	Mar. 18, 1930	Hdn	CEM2
Kraus	Louis Casper		Oct. 31, 1921	Nov. 28, 1950	KY	KMIL
Kraus	Louis Casper		Oct. 31, 1921	Nov. 28, 1950	KY	KMIL
Kremer	Daniel	L.	1928	Aug. 2, 1951	KY	KMIL
Kresen	Earl	B.	1928	Nov. 29, 1950	KY	KMIL
Krilzer	Aquilla			Sep. 1, 1852	Grn	C1
Kuhl	Arthur	E.	1911ca	Jan. 6, 1976	Cam	MCDR
Kullen	Jane		1800ca	Jul. 26, 1857	Dav	C1
Kully	Theodosia		1787ca	Jun. 20, 1853	Brk	C1
Kuykendall	Robert	B.	1841		But	Bk1
Kyle	James	L.	Oct. 27, 1830	Aug. 3, 1899	Ful	CEM7
Kyle	John	B.	Dec. 9, 1863	Jul. 26, 1935	Ful	CEM7
Kyle	Milanda	G.	Feb. 22, 1865	Jun. 26, 1896	Ful	CEM7
Kyle	Sarah Ann		1856	1939	Ful	CEM7
Lacey	Male			1835	NWS4	8/14/1835
Lacey	William			1835	NWS4	8/14/1835
Lamb (Bryant)	Ann		1798ca	Sep. 7, 1861	Dav	C1
Lamb (Bryant)	Mary		1796ca	Nov. 15, 1861	Dav	C1
Lambert	Danckey		1830ca	Sep. 5, 1855	Dav	C1
Lambert	Infant		Feb. ??, 1889	Feb. ??, 1889	Dav	CEM2
Lambert	Ruth Hackley		May 9, 1861	Apr. 21, 1889	Hdn	CEM1
Lamkins	Clyde	E.	1920	Feb. 4, 1951	KY	KMIL
Lampton	Abba		1821ca	Apr. 24, 1855	Brk	C1
Lampton	Albert		1854ca	Apr. 22, 1855	Brk	C1
Lampton	Marshall	T.	1891ca	Jul. 28, 1904	Brk	C1
Lampton	Martha Ann		1826ca	Jul. 10, 1861	Brk	C1
Lampton (Hall)	Catherine		1789ca	Apr. 21, 1855	Brk	C1
Lampton (Hall)	Christianna		1831ca	Mar. 14, 1855	Brk	C1
Lancaster	Eddie		1874	1940	Har	CEM1
Lancaster	Lucy		Jul. 29, 1818	Dec. 16, 1908	Har	CEM1
Lancaster	Rev. Ransom		Apr. 15, 1818	Sep. 30, 1894	Har	CEM1
Lancaster	Wesley		1856	1927	Har	CEM1
Lancaster (Brown)	W.	A.	1827ca	Aug. ??, 1855	Dav	C1
Lander	William	L.		1835	NWS4	8/14/1835
Landrum	Columbia Wash.		Sep. 10, 1833	Oct. 16, 1859	Ful	CEM1
Landrum	Elizabeth		Sep. 7, 1819	May 24, 1844	Oh	CEM4

Last Name	First Name	I	Birth	Death	Co	Source
Landrum	Thomas		Apr. 2, 1805	Nov. 20, 1877	Oh	CEM4
Landrum	William	J.	Sep. 14, 1839	May 19, 1865	Oh	CEM4
Lane	Barney		Jan. 19, 1818	Jun. 3, 1881	Ful	CEM7
Lane	James	L.	Jul. 26, 1900	Sep. 14, 1900	Ful	CEM7
Lane	Lydia	J.		Sep. 13, 1875	Ful	CEM7
Lane	Mary Jo.		Aug. 12, 1830	Jul. 17, 1881	Ful	CEM7
Lane	Samuel		Apr. 15, 1837	Jul. 20, 1873	Sim	CEM1
Lang	Sarah		1786ca	Jan. 14, 1875	Har	Cem1
Langdon	James			Oct. 3, 1804	NWS1	3/22/1845
Langdon	Richard Chester		Dec. 5, 1789	Mar. 5, 1845	NWS1	3/22/1845
Laningham	Unknown Female			Mar. 10, 1861	Brk	C1
Lannom	Jacob	A.	Nov. 28, 1839	Aug. 15, 1915	Ful	CEM7
Lannom	R. Ellen		Jul. 29, 1849	Mar. 24, 1928	Ful	CEM7
Lannon	W.	S.	Mar. 12, 1867	Dec. 20, 1894	Ful	CEM7
Larkin	Jno.		1775ca	Mar. 22, 1855	Dav	C1
Larkin	John		Feb. 11, 1838		Gray	C2
Lashbrook	Bassell		1832ca	Jul. 20, 1855	Dav	C1
Lashbrook	M.	L.	1824ca	Jun. 28, 1857	Dav	C1
Lashbrook (Sale)	Frances		1811ca	Jun. 20, 1853	Dav	C1
Lashbrook (Stephens)	A.	J.	1832ca	Apr. 15, 1855	Dav	C1
Lashbrooks	Archiles		Jul. 2, 1820	Nov. 20, 1881	Dav	CEM2
Lashbrooks	Female		Jul. 28, 1891	Jul. 28, 1884	Dav	CEM2
Lashbrooks	Flora	M.	Jul. 28,,1891	Feb. 2, 1892	Dav	CEM2
Lashbrooks	Foreman		Sep. 14, 1882	Feb. 12, 1890	Dav	CEM2
Lashbrooks	Martha	A.	Jan. 26, 1824	May 12, 1874	Dav	CEM2
Lashbrooks	Martin	D.	Sep. 14, 1889	Feb. 12, 1890	Dav	CEM2
Laslie (Broadway)	Beatie	A.	1859ca	Aug. ??, 1904	Brk	C1
Laster	John	M.	1837ca	Feb. 14, 1861	Brk	C1
Lavender	Mary Ann		1877ca		Grn	Marr1
Lawhorn	Wid. Lucy		1887ca		Grn	Marr1
Lawhun	Malinda Jane		1889ca		Grn	Marr1
Lawrence	Albert	B.	Mar. 6, 1875	Dec. 9, 1957	Sim	CEM1
Lawrence	Lula		1871ca		Grn	Marr1
Lawrence	Pearlie		Jul. 17, 1883	Feb. 26, 1915	Sim	CEM1
Lawson	Alvis	D.	1929	Aug. 11, 1950	KY	KMIL
Lawson	Ann Maria		1844ca	Sep. 20, 1845	NWS1	10/11/1845
Lawson	Bobby	E.	1929	Aug. 9, 1950	KY	KMIL
Lawson	Horace	B.	Dec. 15, 1859	Mar. 5, 18??	Ful	CEM1
Lawson	Horace		Jun. 4, 1800	Jun. 30, 1883	Ful	CEM1
Lawson	Lucie	B.	Jul. 15, 1837	Nov. 18, 1859	Ful	CEM1
Lawson	Lucy Margarett		1888ca		Grn	Marr1
Lawson	Moses		Jan. 21, 1776	Nov. 30, 1852	Ful	CEM1
Lawson	Myrtle		1889ca		Grn	Marr1
Lawson	T.	J.		Dec. 10, 1877	Bre	C1
Lawson	Taylor		1848ca	Apr. 5, 1852	Grn	C1
Lawson	Walter	T.		Mar. 17, 1836	NWS4	3/19/1836
Lay	Thomas	L.	1856ca	Nov. 10, 1861	Brk	C1

Last Name	First Name	I	Birth	Death	Co	Source
Layman	Alfred		1832ca		Gray	C1
Layman	Anthony		Jan. 7, 1835		Gray	C2
Layne	Roy	L.	1928	Oct. 9, 1951	KY	KMIL
Layson	Olie		1870ca	Oct. 20, 1876	Dav	MCDR
Laytart	J.	W.	Jan. 20, 1855	Aug. 18, 1932	Har	CEM1
Laytart	Lizzie Mae		1909	1942	Har	CEM1
Laytart	Mollie		Dec. 31, 1863		Har	CEM1
Layton	Bertha		Jul. 27, 1883		McL	Sch1
Layton	Charlie	W.	Oct. 26, 1888		McL	Sch1
Layton	Frank	L.	Nov. 21, 1886		McL	Sch1
Layton	John	C.	Mar. 5, 1885		McL	Sch1
Layton	Mollie	H.	Aug. 14, 1890		McL	Sch1
Layton	Sam	H.	Sep. 22, 1892		McL	Sch1
Layton	Willie		Sep. 5, 1893		McL	Sch1
Leach	William	F.	1828		But	Bk1
Lear	????		No Date	No Date	Muh	CEM3
Leavell	Maj. Lewis			Oct. 8, 1835	NWS4	10/16/1835
Ledford	Howard	R.	1931	Aug. 14, 1950	KY	KMIL
Ledford	Vernon	S.	1915	Sep. 1, 1950	KY	KMIL
Lee	Arra		May 5, 1883		McL	Sch1
Lee	Claud		Dec. 14, 1897	Jun. 25, 1926	Muh	CEM2
Lee	Elizabeth	C.	Mar. 29, 1838	Apr. 21, 1860	Dav	CEM2
Lee	Ellen		Jan. ??, 1864	Mar. ??, 1943	Muh	CEM2
Lee	Emily		1830ca	Mar. ??, 1852	Grn	C1
Lee	Female		Jan. 21, 1885	Jun. 19, 1885	Dav	CEM2
Lee	Herbert		Mar. 9, 1891	Nov. 4, 1918	Muh	CEM2
Lee	James	D.	1928	Sep. 1, 1950	KY	KMIL
Lee	John	W		Jul. ??, 1844	NWS1	7/20/1844
Lee	Ruth		Jul. 23. 1892		McL	Sch1
Lee	Samuel		1814ca	Jan. 19, 1898	Muh	CEM2
Lee	William	E.	Oct. 5, 1860	Mar. 15, 1891	Dav	CEM2
Leeze	Charles		1788ca	Oct. 12, 1853	Grn	C1
Legrand	Franklin		1836ca	Feb. 4, 1875	Brk	C1
Legrand	Geo.	C.	1806ca	Mar. 18, 1878	Brk	C1
Leip	Amma		Dec. 1, 1799	Aug. 20, 1883	Ful	CEM7
Leip	Ellen Frances		Oct. 3, 1826	Jan. 25, 1881	Ful	CEM7
Leip	Fritz		1840	Mar. 1, 1893	Ful	CEM7
Leip	George	W.	Oct. 26, 1835	Jun. 19, 1898	Ful	CEM7
Leip	Martha		Sep. 9, 1838	Sep. 26, 1880	Ful	CEM7
Leitner	Ralph	L.	1929	Dec. 17, 1951	KY	KMIL
Leman	Jane		1832ca	1861	Dav	C1
Lemaster	Nellie Mae		1892ca		Grn	Marr1
Lemasters	Malinda Jane		1892ca		Grn	Marr1
Leroy	William		Aug. 24, 1853		Ful	CEM7
Leslie	Florence	A.	1834ca	Aug. 26, 1878	Brk	C1
Leslie	Harry Taylor		1899	1944	Har	CEM1
Leslie	Male		May 30, 1903		Har	CEM1

Last Name	First Name	I	Birth	Death	Co	Source
Leslie	Mary	M.	1871	1944	Har	CEM1
Leslie	Rhoda		1811ca	Nov. 15, 1876	Brk	C1
Leslie	William	H.	1826	1915	Har	CEM1
Letcher	Mrs. Ann	M.		Nov. 16, 1845	NWS1	12/20/1845
Letha	Ida		1900	1992	Row	CEM1
Levers	John	A.	1844ca	1852	Brk	C1
Levers	Maria	E.	1846ca	Jan. ??, 1852	Brk	C1
Lewis	Alfred Grundy		1846	1924	Hdn	CEM2
Lewis	Annie	R.	1887ca		Grn	Marr1
Lewis	Clinton	A.	Jan. 20, 1843	May 2, 1896	Hdn	CEM2
Lewis	David	B.		Mar. 19, 1854	Brk	C1
Lewis	Earl	C.	1930	Jan. 7, 1951	KY	KMIL
Lewis	Elisha		1848ca	Aug. 13, 1852	Bre	C1
Lewis	Emma Perry		1852	1920	Hdn	CEM2
Lewis	Eva	S.	1884	1968	Har	CEM1
Lewis	Frederic		May 13, 1893	Jan. 3, 1894	Hdn	CEM2
Lewis	Gabriel Jones		1775		KY	BK2(P90)
Lewis	George	W.	1824	1895	Har	Cem1
Lewis	James	A.	1885	1971	Hdn	CEM2
Lewis	Joseph		1851ca	Aug. 17, 1852	Bre	C1
Lewis	Karl	D.	1883	1973	Hdn	CEM2
Lewis	M. Elizabeth		1887		Hdn	CEM2
Lewis	Margaret	S.	1889		Hdn	CEM2
Lewis	Maria		1810ca	Aug. 13, 1852	Brk	C1
Lewis	Mary	D.	Jun. 10, 1848	Dec. 20, 1943	Hdn	CEM2
Lewis	Mary	J.	1897	Aug. 24, 1904	Brk	C1
Lewis	Mary Aurelia		1805ca	May 4, 1844	NWS1	5/11/1844
Lewis	Oma	J.	1827	Aug. 1, 1864	Oh	CEM5
Lewis	Paul	R.	Aug. 11, 1904	Jul. 8, 1906	Hdn	CEM2
Lewis	Pruitt		1890ca	Dec. 7, 1911	Fay	MCDR
Lewis	Rebecca		Feb. 20, 1821		Gray	C2
Lewis	Stephen	B.	1870	1955	Har	CEM1
Lewis	Unknown		Mar. 13, 1884	Mar. 13, 1884	Hdn	CEM2
Lewis	Unknown Male			Jun. 10, 1894	Brk	C1
Lewis	W.	F.		Sep. 8, 1863	KY	CMIL2
Lewis	Whitney	C.	1921ca	Mar. 21, 1980	Fay	MCDR
Lewis	William	R.	Jun. 12, 1857	May 20, 1915	Hdn	CEM2
Lewis (Greathouse)	Elizabeth		1799	1879	Han	Bk1
Lewis (Slave)			1818ca	Feb. 28, 1855	Brk	C1
Liford	Charles	E.	1931	Oct. 24, 1952	KY	KMIL
Lightfoot	Ernest Deno		Nov. 25, 1880		McL	Sch1
Lightfoot (Miller)	Fronia		1855ca	Jul. 15, 1877	Brk	C1
Likens	Eliza		Dec. 25, 1871	Apr. 15, 1899	Dav	CEM3
Lilley	Charles		1877	1939	Har	CEM1
Lilley	Hays		1904	1946	Har	CEM1
Lilley	Nannie	K.	Jun. 20, 1917	Apr. 17, 1918	Har	CEM1
Lillie	Sudie		Feb. 24, 1878	Sep. 12, 1898	Har	CEM1

Last Name	First Name	I	Birth	Death	Co	Source
Linden	E.	C.	Aug. 31, 1826	Apr. 1, 1894	Ful	CEM7
Linden	Mrs. E.	C.	1831ca	May 23, 1906	Ful	CEM7
Lindon	Edward			Oct. 8, 1857	Bre	C1
Lindsey	Freeman		1931	Dec. 6, 1950	KY	KMIL
Lindsey	Grealy		1894ca	Jun. 10, 1961	But	CEM1
Lindsey	James		1826va	Jan. 2, 1854	Dav	C1
Lindsey	Silva L.	J.	Dec. 27, 1875	May 10, 1906	But	CEM1
Linebaugh	Samuel	W.		1835	NWS4	8/14/1835
Liner	William	R.	1929	Oct. 15, 1951	KY	KMIL
Liskers	Wm.	W.	1882ca	Aug. 8, 1904	Brk	C1
Little	Coellen			Sep. 15, 1874	Bre	C1
Little	Jere			Nov. 17, 1874	Bre	C1
Little	Jeremiah			Nov. 2, 1875	Bre	C1
Little	Pearl		1856ca	Sep. 15, 1859	Bre	C1
Little	Ranier	A.	1845ca	Jul. 15, 1861	Brk	C1
Little	Sylvania		1839ca	Apr. 8, 1853	Bre	C1
Littrell	Sophronia Cath.		Mar. 9, 1839	May 5, 1904	Hdn	CEM1
Littrell	William		Mar. 18, 1821	Nov. 13, 1905	Hdn	CEM1
Lockard	Josephine		Jan. 6, 1848	Feb. 12, 1932	Hdn	CEM3
Lockard	William	J.	Jan. 30, 1842	Feb. 16, 1897	Hdn	CEM3
Logan	Anne Priscilla		Apr. 26, 1847		KY	BK2(P150)
Logan	Caleb Wallace		Jul. 15, 1819		KY	BK2(P148)
Logan	Carl	D.	1928	Sep. 6, 1951	KY	KMIL
Logan	David		1824		KY	BK2(P203)
Logan	John Allen		Mar. 12, 1812		KY	BK2(P172)
Logan	Rev. Eusebius			1827	KY	BK2(P118)
Logan	Stephen Trigg			Jul. 17, 1780	KY	BK2(P202)
Logston	Jas.	S.	1901ca	Jul. ??, 1904	Brk	C1
London	James	M.	1849		But	Bk1
Long	Henry		1782ca	Sep. 30, 1852	Grn	C1
Long	Jasper Newt.		1840		But	Bk1
Long	Mrs. Mary		1788ca	Jun. 24, 1852	Brk	C1
Long	R.	M.	1844ca	Dec. 23, 1861	Dav	C1
Long	Stewart	W.	Nov. 21, 1931	Mar. 29, 1953	KY	KMIL
Long	V.	C.	1843ca	Sep. 10, 1861	Dav	C1
Longworth	Eliza			Mar. 22, 1845	NWS1	3/29/1845
Looker	James	H		Sep. ??, 1843	NWS1	9/30/1843
Loper	Goldie	E.	1889ca		Grn	Marr1
Loper	Laura		1891ca		Grn	Marr1
Lott	James	E.		Jul. 20, 1852	Brk	C1
Lott	Lillian Bell		1885ca		Grn	Marr1
Love	Archie		Feb. 9, 1887	Mar. 1, 1889	Hdn	CEM1
Lovell	A.	S.	Jul. 8, 1856	Mar. 12, 1882	Muh	CEM2
Lovely	Rex		1930	Jul. 21, 1952	KY	KMIL
Lovely	Tentha		1842ca	May 15, 1855	Bre	C1
Lovely	William		1811ca	Mar. 17, 1876	Bre	C1
Lovett	J.			Oct. 15, 1863	KY	CMIL2

Last Name	First Name	I	Birth	Death	Co	Source
Loving	Warren		1813ca	Jul. 31, 1835	NWS4	8/7/1835
Lovins	Edward		1930	Aug. 22, 1952	KY	KMIL
Lowder	Luverna		1889ca		Grn	Marr1
Lucas	Ben		1811ca	Oct. 22, 1876	Brk	C1
Lucas	Iguatius		1758ca	May 5, 1852	Brk	C1
Lucas	Lucinda		1849ca	Dec. 25, 1854	Brk	C1
Lucas	Trina	C.		Oct. 26, 1878	Brk	C1
Lucas, Jr.	Roy		1928	Nov. 22, 1951	KY	KMIL
Lucus	Delila		1807ca	Nov. 19, 1855	Brk	C1
Lucy (Slave)			1768ca	Mar. 2, 1854	Brk	C1
Lucy Ann (Slave)			1853ca	Jul. 26, 1854	Brk	C1
Lukins	Lieut.		1791ca		NWS5	11/12/1791
Lunce	Elbert	R.	1927	Apr. 16, 1953	KY	KMIL
Lundy, Jr.	Clofton	D.	1925	Aug. 15, 1950	KY	KMIL
Lydia (Slave)			1834ca	Dec. 24, 1859	Bre	C1
Lyles	Ottie	B.	Jun. 5, 1911	Mar. 28, 1932	Har	CEM1
Lyon	Ethel		1874ca	Sep. 16, 1878	Brk	C1
Lyon	John	D.	1853ca	Jul. 15, 1855	Brk	C1
Lyon	Rosa		1835ca	Nov. 8, 1854	Brk	C1
Lyons	Pheba		Mar. 25, 1859	Nov. 20, 1930	Row	CEM1
Lzoier	Laura		1889ca		Grn	Marr1
Maag	Cynthia		1946ca	Oct. 27, 1979	Cam	
Mablett (Horn)	Elizabeth		1829ca	Aug. 10, 1854	Brk	C1
MacGregor	Dr. T.	A.	Dec. 16, 1840		Han	Bk1
MacGregor	George		1809		Han	Bk1
Macy	Blanche		1902ca	May 10, 1904	Brk	C1
Maddix	Dennis		Apr. 11, 1907		Car	C1
Maddix	William	T.	1930	Jul. 7, 1950	KY	KMIL
Maddox	J.	W.	1855ca	Dec. 22, 1878	Brk	C1
Maggard	Belle		1896ca		Grn	Marr1
Maggard	Sena	E.	1892ca		Grn	Marr1
Mahan	Hattie		1869	1906	Ful	CEM7
Mahan	John	B.	186?	1938	Ful	CEM7
Mahan (Roper)	Blanche		Jan. 30, 1876	Nov. 14, 1930	Ful	CEM7
Maher	Anna		1875ca	Nov. 18, 1955	Jef	
Maher	Bernade	C.	1915ca	May 12, 1973	Ken	
Maher	Charles	J.	1913ca	Apr. 23, 1985	Ken	MCDR
Maher	Christine	L.	1880ca	Nov. 25, 1975	Fay	MCDR
Maher	Daisy	F.	1930ca	Mar. 29, 1979	Jef	MCDR
Maher	Dan	F.	1892ca	Oct. 15, 1958	Jef	MCDR
Maher	Della		1874ca	Jan. 14, 1951	Ken	MCDR
Maher	Elizabeth		1883ca	Dec. 5, 1974	Ken	MCDR
Maher	Ella		1836ca	Aug. 20, 1914	Fay	MCDR
Maher	Francis	E.	1879ca	Dec. 8, 1938	Jef	MCDR
Maher	Frank	D.	1881ca	Jul. 26, 1927	Cam	MCDR
Maher	Frank	P.	1878ca	May 28, 1915	Ken	MCDR
Maher	Frank		1886ca	Dec. 20, 1930	Cam	MCDR

Last Name	First Name	I	Birth	Death	Co	Source
Maher	George	E.	1899ca	Nov. 20, 1977	Ken	MCDR
Mahorney	Cecil	T.	1889	1962	Har	Cem1
Mahorney	Donald	R.	Jun. 5, 1913	Jul. 25, 1913	Har	Cem1
Mahorney	Lee Roy		Nov. 26, 1910	Dec. 20, 1929	Har	Cem1
Mahorney	Melissa	H.	1878	1936	Har	Cem1
Maleny	John		1809ca	Mar. 15, 1854	Bre	C1
Mallen	James		Oct. 7, 1838	Mar. 16, 1887	Hdn	CEM1
Mallory	E.	M.	May 24, 1857		Sim	C1
Mallory	J.	C.	Dec. 26, 1859		Sim	C1
Mallory	M.	F.	Jun. 11, 1856		Sim	C1
Mallory	Mary		Oct. 16, 1852		Sim	C1
Mallory	R.	H.	Mar. 30, 1856		Sim	C1
Mallory	S.	R.	Sep. 1, 1859		Sim	C1
malone	John		1849ca	Aug. 17, 1878	Bre	C1
Manfield	Armira			1852	Bre	C1
Mangrum	J.	S.	Sep. 17, 1825	Jan. 10, 1902	Ful	CEM7
Mangrum	Joseph	H.	Jul. 9, 1885	Jul. 30, 1922	Ful	CEM7
Mangrum	Nettie		Jun. 16, 1839	May 7, 1910	Ful	CEM7
Mangrum (Ramer)	Sue		Nov. 7, 1874	Jul. 12, 1950	Ful	CEM7
Mann	John		1852ca	Jan. 25, 1854	Bre	C1
Mann	Unknown Male			Apr. 19, 1855	Bre	C1
Manor	Henry		Feb. 22, 1863	May 18, 1905	Dav	CEM2
Mans	Nathaniel		1856ca	Dec. 18, 1859	Bre	C1
Marcum (Strong)	Joanah		1821ca	Sep. 25, 1875	Bre	C1
Marks	Harry	T.	1927	Oct. 16, 1951	KY	KMIL
Markwell	Beedie	J.	Aug. 17, 1914		Row	CEM1
Markwell	Clyde		Apr. 29, 1925	Jul. 31, 1926	Row	CEM1
Markwell	D.	O.	1879	1969	Row	CEM1
Markwell	Ervin		Aug. 3, 1919	Nov. 2, 1991	Row	CEM1
Markwell	Luanna		1888	1970	Row	CEM1
Markwell	Lyda Marie		Apr. 26, 1930	Oct. 17, 1930	Row	CEM1
Marshall	Alexander	K.	1770		KY	BK2(P104)
Marshall	Anna		1891	1940	Har	CEM1
Marshall	B.	F.	1869	1932	Har	CEM1
Marshall	Charles Thomas		Jul. 14, 1800		KY	BK2(P107)
Marshall	Elizabeth Frances		May 1, 1905		Har	CEM1
Marshall	J.	H.	Apr. 10, 1828	Apr. 30, 1881	Han	Bk1
Marshall	Jane		1808		KY	BK2(P113)
Marshall	Jane			1825	KY	BK2(P114)
Marshall	Je??e	C.	1909	1921	Har	CEM1
Marshall	L.	D.	Jun. 15, 1895	Nov. 22, 1911	Har	CEM1
Marshall	Leon		Jan. 22, 1891	Jan. 22, 1891	Hdn	CEM1
Marshall	Leonard		Feb. 16, 1907		Car	C1
Marshall	Leonie		Feb. 16, 1907		Car	C1
Marshall	Lucy		1796		KY	BK2(P112)
Marshall	Malinda Ann		1874	1919	Har	CEM1
Marshall	Maria		Jul. 20, 1795		KY	BK2(P107)

Last Name	First Name	I	Birth	Death	Co	Source
Martin	Columbus		Aug. 13, 1840	Dec. 19, 1863	Muh	CEM2
Martin	Dora	P.	1891ca		Grn	Marr1
Martin	Elizabeth	J.	1822ca	Dec. ??, 1856	Brk	C1
Martin	Elizabeth		1823ca	Mar. 19, 1861	Dav	C1
Martin	Euclid	C.	1852		But	Bk1
Martin	John Ellliott		Dec. 31, 1850	May 17, 1869	Muh	CEM2
Martin	John Lewis		1806		But	Bk1
Martin	Lillie		1895ca		Grn	Marr1
Martin	Lue Vada		1891ca		Grn	Marr1
Martin	Marion		Apr. 1, 1830		Other	Bk1(P348)T
Martin	Martha	A.	1824ca	Feb. ??, 1861	Dav	C1
Martin	Mary	A.	Mar. 8, 1820	May 21, 1860	Muh	CEM2
Martin	Mary	M.	1891ca		Grn	Marr1
Martin	Robert	R.	1902	Jul. 8, 1950	KY	KMIL
Martin	Thomas		1860ca	Aug. ??, 1877	Grn	C2
Martin	William	W.	Jan. 6, 1812	Aug. 2, 1887	Muh	CEM2
Mary (Slave)			1835ca	Sep. 5, 1855	Brk	C1
Mary (Slave)			1832ca	Jan. 15, 1857	Brk	C1
Masey (Raulings)	Sarah		1817ca	Aug. 9, 1852	Brk	C1
Mason	James	L.	1932	Dec. 6, 1950	KY	KMIL
Massey, Jr.	Anthony		1928	Nov. 28, 1950	KY	KMIL
Massie	Whitney			Aug. 15, 1931	Fay	MCDR
Massie	Whitney		1910ca	Apr. 7, 1962	Fay	MCDR
Masterson	Dora Johnson		1899	1919	Hdn	CEM2
Mathers	Dolly		1865	1932	Har	CEM1
Mathers	Joe	G.	1867	1939	Har	CEM1
Mathers	Suda	P.	1839	1920	Har	CEM1
Mathers	Thomas	R.	1863	1946	Har	CEM1
Mathers	W.	H.	1836	1909	Har	CEM1
Mathes	Baby of Nat.			Sep. 13, 1887	Muh	Ch1
Mathews	Dellie		1890ca		Grn	Marr1
Mathews	Ellen		1888ca		Grn	Marr1
Mathews	John			1814	KY	BK2(P23)
Mathews	Joseph	J.		Feb. 24, 1858	Brk	C1
Mathews	Mrs. Eliza		1828ca	Apr. 9, 1904	Brk	C1
Mathis	E.			Jul. 20, 1861	Muh	CEM2
Mathis	G.	A.	Mar. 15, 1835	Aug. 16, 1872	Muh	CEM2
Mathis	Joseph	B.	Dec. 28, 1872	Jul. 18, 1889	Hdn	CEM1
Mathis	Mrs. Fannie			Dec. 13, 1887	Muh	Ch1
Mathis	Berry		Aug. 8, 1832	Feb. 1, 1903	Muh	CEM2
Mathis, Jr.	J.	W.	No Date	No Date	Muh	CEM2
Matilda (Black)				Jun. 9, 1856	Bre	C1
Matilda (Slave)			1858ca	Jun. 14, 1861	Brk	C1
Matthews	Elizabeth			Jun. 7, 1855	Brk	C1
Matthews	Fanny		Dec. 5, 1836	Feb. 21, 1870	Har	CEM2
Matthews	J.	C.	1824ca	Jun. 19, 1904	Brk	C1
Matthews	James	L.	1919	Jul. 20, 1950	KY	KMIL

Last Name	First Name	I	Birth	Death	Co	Source
Matthews	Mary		1800ca	Dec. 22, 1852	Grn	C1
Matthews	Vincent	H.	1817ca	Jun. 22, 1855	Brk	C1
Matthews	Willie	S.	May 4, 1865	Sep. 29, 1895	Har	CEM2
Mattingly	David		1872ca	Aug. ??, 1878	Brk	C1
Mattingly	Elizabeth	J.	1848ca	Dec. 12, 1878	Brk	C1
Mattingly	Elizabeth		1853ca	Aug. 7, 1854	Brk	C1
Mattingly	Gerald	J.	1929	Oct. 17, 1951	KY	KMIL
Mattingly	H.	J.	Oct. 26, 1836		Gray	C2
Mattingly	H.		1860ca	Mar. 16, 1875	Brk	C1
Mattingly	Hardin	T.	1857ca	Dec. 9, 1878	Brk	C1
Mattingly	John		1838ca	Jul. 24, 1856	Dav	C1
Mattingly	M.	A.	1859ca	Feb. 16, 1878	Brk	C1
Mattingly	Mary	C.	1836ca	Sep. ??, 1857	Dav	C1
Mattingly	Mary	E.	1841ca	Nov. 16, 1858	Brk	C1
Mattingly	Mary	J.	1862ca	Dec. 17, 1878	Brk	C1
Mattingly	Robert	L.	1877	1959	Hdn	CEM2
Mattingly	S.		Mar. 21, 1834		Gray	C2
Mattingly	Susan	M.	1839ca	Aug. 13, 1857	Dav	C1
Mattingly	Terry		1842ca	Aug. 7, 1852	Brk	C1
Maxwell	Thomas			1844	NWS1	8/3/1844
May	Charley		1873ca	Jan. 25, 1875	Brk	C1
May	Joseph		1816ca	Nov. 8, 1856	Dav	C1
May	Mary	A.	1834ca	Nov. 29, 1856	Dav	C1
May	Rob.	T.	1871ca	Oct. 3, 1878	Brk	C1
May	Samuel		1799ca	Aug. 10, 1875	Brk	C1
May	Thomas	P.	1833ca	Aug. 20, 1852	Dav	MCDR
May (Lewis)	Lucretia		1828ca	Oct. 18, 1877	Brk	C1
May, Jr.	Samuel		1832ca	Dec. 25, 1874	Brk	C1
Mayes	Nancy		Sep. 13, 1799	Jun. 5, 1852	Ful	CEM9
Mayes	T. David		Dec. 22, 1799	Feb. ??, 1852	Ful	CEM9
Mayhon	Martha		1883ca		Grn	Marr1
Maynard	Donald	R.	1932	Jan. 12, 1952	KY	KMIL
Mays	Thomas		1800ca	Jul. 2, 1859	Bre	C1
Mays	Unknown Female			Feb. 15, 1859	Bre	C1
Maysey	Little	B.	1856ca	Feb. 25, 1874	Brk	C1
McAdams	Ann A.	J.	1790ca	Oct. 18, 1855	Brk	C1
McAdams	E.	P.	Jul. 23, 1847		Han	Bk1
McAtee	Charles	H.	1929	Dec. 1, 1950	KY	KMIL
McAtee	Madison	B.	1933	Feb. 3, 1951	KY	KMIL
McBrayer	Lena		1890ca		Grn	Marr1
McCague	Weltha		Jan. 29, 1798	Nov. 13, 1887	Hdn	CEM2
Mccall	Julia	A.	1849ca	Oct. 14, 1853	Grn	C1
McClanahan	Ellen		Aug. 9, 1833	Dec. 1, 1908	Ful	CEM7
McClanahan	Joseph		Nov. 4, 1832	Apr. 21, 1900	Ful	CEM7
McClean	America		Sep. 19, 1840	Aug. 23, 1884	Har	CEM1
McClean	Cynthia		Sep. 20, 1828	Mar. 13, 1860	Har	CEM1
McClean	Cynthia		1797	1888	Har	CEM1

Last Name	First Name	I	Birth	Death	Co	Source
McClean	Elbert		Mar. 30, 1877	Oct. 22, 1878	Har	CEM1
McClean	Mary	E.	Jan. 23, 1857	Apr. 26, 1863	Har	CEM1
McClean	Samuel	G.	Jan. 5, 1822	Oct. 26, 1880	Har	CEM1
McClean	William	H.	1823	1907	Har	CEM1
McCleod	Helen		Aug. 17, 1850	May 5, 1933	Har	CEM1
McCleod	John		May 31, 1849	Jun. 11, 1907	Har	CEM1
McConnell	Ollie		1892ca		Grn	Marr1
McCormick	Howard		Jul. 6, 1930	Sep. 13, 1951	KY	KMIL
McCormick	Hynix		1889ca		Grn	Marr1
McCormick	Whitney	N.		May 21, 1985	Boy	MCDR
McCowan	Richard	C.	1932	Feb. 12, 1951	KY	KMIL
McCoy	Conly		1922	Apr. 12, 1951	KY	KMIL
McCoy	Jennie		1888ca		Grn	Marr1
McCoy	John	R.	1931	Jul. 21, 1950	KY	KMIL
McCoy	John		1817ca	Jan. 9, 1852	Brk	C1
McCoy	Mary	F.	1850ca	Jul. 27, 1852	Brk	C1
McCoy	Sarah	E.	1849ca	Jul. 19, 1852	Brk	C1
McCoy (Brown)	Mary		1850ca	Oct. 12, 1878	Brk	C1
McCubbin	Sophia		1850ca	1852	Brk	C1
McCullough	Elizabeth			1852	Brk	C1
McCumpsey	James		Oct. 8, 1858		Dav	CEM2
McCumpsey	Sabina		Jan. 16, 1856	May 8, 1923	Dav	CEM2
McDaniel	Allen		Jun. 16, 1820		Gray	C2
McDaniel	Billy	J.	May 11, 1925	Jun. 24, 1952	KY	KMIL
McDaniel	Eliza	V.	1868ca	Oct. 19, 1874	Brk	C1
McDaniel	Elizabeth		1784ca	May 25, 1874	Bre	C1
McDaniel	Homer		1931	Nov. 28, 1950	KY	KMIL
McDaniel	J.	B.	Mar. 31, 1826		Gray	C2
McDaniel	John	A.	1809ca		Gray	C1
McDaniel	Judith			Aug. 22, 1835	NWS4	9/18/1835
McDaniel	July		1857ca	Mar. 19, 1859	Bre	C1
McDaniel	Thomas			1852	Bre	C1
McDaniel	James	F.	1834ca	Apr. 16, 1861	Dav	C1
McDaniel (Payne)	Ann		1826ca	Oct. 19, 1857	Dav	C1
McDavid	Beatris		Apr. 15, 1907		Car	C1
McDavid	Lora		Jan. 20, 1907		Car	C1
McDowel	Junior	R.	1925	Jul. 25, 1950	KY	KMIL
McDowell	Abram Irvine		Apr. 24, 1793		KY	BK2(P76)
McDowell	Caleb Wallace		Apr. 17, 1774		KY	BK2(P98)
McDowell	Charles		1743	1815	KY	Bk2(P18)
McDowell	Dr. Ephraim		Nov. 11, 1771		KY	BK2(P95)
McDowell	Dr. Ephraim			1830	KY	BK2(P97)
McDowell	Dr. James		1804	1837	KY	BK2(P60)
McDowell	James			Dec. 25, 1742	KY	BK2(P14)
McDowell	James		1739	1771	KY	BK2(P27)
McDowell	Joe		1756		KY	BK2(P18)
McDowell	John Hall			1865	KY	BK2(P98)

Last Name	First Name	I	Birth	Death	Co	Source
McDowell	John Lyle			Dec. ??, 1878	KY	BK2(P64)
McDowell	Joseph		Sep. 13, 1768		KY	BK2(P93)
McDowell	Joseph			Jun. 27, 1856	KY	BK2(P94)
McDowell	Judge Wm.		Mar. 9, 1762		KY	BK2(P66)
McDowell	Magdelen		Oct. 9, 1775		KY	BK2(P99)
McDowell	Martha		Jun. 20, 1766		KY	BK2(P100)
McDowell	Mary		Jun. 12, 1787		KY	BK2(P82)
McDowell	Sallie		1801		KY	BK2(P82)
McDowell	Samuel		1735		KY	BK2(P3)
McDowell	Samuel			Sep. 25, 1817	KY	BK2(P38)
McDowell	Sarah		Oct. 9, 1775		KY	BK2(P99)
McDowell	Wm. Adair		Mar. 21, 1795		KY	BK2(P77)
McDowell (Cloyd)	Elizabeth			1810	KY	BK2(P28)
McDowell, Sr.	Joseph		1715		KY	BK2(P17)
McDowll	Anne		1810		KY	BK2(P76)
McElfresh	M.		1886ca		Grn	Marr1
McElroy	James		1761		All	RP1
McFarland	Belle		Jan. 26, 1861	Aug. 4, 1945	Dav	CEM3
McFarland	Edna	H.	Nov. 12, 1885	Feb. 20, 1886	Dav	CEM3
McFarland	Hallie		Feb. 2, 1887	Jan. 12, 1893	Dav	CEM3
McFarland	James		Sep. 20, 1858	Jun. 3, 1920	Dav	CEM3
McFarland	John	J.	1831ca	Jul. 31, 1852	Dav	MCDR
McFarland	Laura	N.	Jul. 6, 1856	Feb. 8, 1895	Dav	CEM3
McFarland	Mary	E.	Mar. 11, 1886		Dav	CEM3
McFarland	Roy		Feb. 24, 1884		Dav	CEM3
McFarland	Samuel		Jan. 16, 1853	Jan. 15, 1934	Dav	CEM3
McFarland	William Owen		1912	1947	Dav	CEM3
McGarey	Adeline		1894ca		Grn	Marr1
McGaw	John	P.	1860		Cam	MCDR
McGee	Marshall	H.	1927	Mar. 30, 1953	KY	KMIL
McGehee	Gewen Erroll		1888	1942	Ful	CEM7
McGehee	Unknown Male			Aug. 26, 1911	Ful	CEM7
McGehee (Milner)	Vivian		Oct. 4, 1889	Aug. 1, 1912	Ful	CEM7
McGiffin	Samuel		1845ca	Aug. 10, 1854	Brk	C1
McGiffin (Slave)	Samuel		1842ca	Oct. 12, 1854	Brk	C1
McGiffin (Slave)	Susan		1850ca	Aug. 15, 1854	Brk	C1
McGill	Emily	R.	Nov. 27, 1806	May 6, 1888	Hdn	CEM2
McGill	G.	A.	Mar. 10, 1839		Han	Bk1
McGill	Martha		1793ca	Oct. 24, 1855	Dav	C1
McGinnis	Nance	F.	1877ca	May 19, 1935	Jef	MCDR
McGlone	James		Sep. 15, 1904		Car	C1
McGlone	Ruthie		Apr. 23, 1904		Car	C1
McGowan	William	G.	1928	Aug. 31, 1950	KY	KMIL
McGrue	Miles		1830ca		Gray	C1
McGuffin	C.	R.	1863	1936	Hdn	CEM3
McGuffin	Galan		Jul. 12, 1904		Hdn	CEM3
McGuffin	Josephine		1870	1921	Hdn	CEM3

Last Name	First Name	I	Birth	Death	Co	Source
McGuffin	Lonnie		1889	1919	Hdn	CEM3
McGuffin	Magnolia		Apr. 12, 1878	Dec. 6, 1957	Hdn	CEM3
McGuffin	Ruthie		Nov. 7, 1894	Sep. 10, 1960	Hdn	CEM3
McGuffon	Chas.	R.	1870ca	Sep. 20, 1878	Brk	C1
McGuire	Emily		1824ca	Jul. 22, 1910	Sim	CEM1
McGuire	Sidney		Aug. 1, 1846	Jun. 10, 1875	Sim	CEM1
McGuire	William	M.	Jul. 8, 1822	Aug. 28, 1884	Sim	CEM1
McGuire (Coffer)	Gildy Ann			Apr. 28, 1858	Bre	C1
McGuire (Coffer)	Nancy		1826ca	Apr. 27, 1858	Bre	C1
McIntoash	Unknown Male			Feb. 15, 1875	Bre	C1
McIntosh	Absalom			Aug. 20, 1876	Bre	C1
McIntosh	Alfred			Jun. 16, 1878	Bre	C1
McIntosh	Edward		1852ca	Feb. ??, 1853	Bre	C1
McIntosh	Goldan		1851ca	Mar. 7, 1876	Bre	C1
McIntosh	John			Apr. 13, 1858	Bre	C1
McIntosh	Lucey Ann			Jun. 12, 1876	Bre	C1
McIntosh	Susan		1828ca	Oct. 25, 1875	Bre	C1
McIntosh	Unknown Female			Dec. 27, 1875	Bre	C1
McIntosh	Unknown Male			Dec. 1, 1874	Bre	C1
McIntosh	Unknown Male			Sep. 10, 1877	Bre	C1
McIntosh	William		1872ca	Dec. 16, 1875	Bre	C1
McIntosh (Harvey)	Catharine			Mar. 11, 1855	Bre	C1
McKaughan (West)	Elizabeth		1789ca	Aug. 17, 1852	Brk	C1
McKee	Catherine		Apr. 10, 1835		KY	RP1
McKenney	James		1773ca	Aug. 24, 1853	Dav	C1
McKennon	Mahala		1836ca	Jan. 28, 1853	Dav	C1
McKensey	Dora		1884ca		Grn	Marr1
McKenzie	Hattie		1891ca		Grn	Marr1
McKenzie	Neil	S.	1913	Jul. 20, 1950	KY	KMIL
McKie	Robert	J.	1930	Oct. 2, 1950	KY	KMIL
McKinley	Dr. Andrew			1786	KY	BK2(P226)
McKinney	Elizabeth	A.	1826ca	Feb. 17, 1857	Dav	C1
McKinney	John	M.	1845		But	Bk1
McKnight	Andrew		1773		KY	BK2(P159)
McKnight	Virgil		1798		KY	BK2(P161)
M'Clanahan	John		1772ca		NWS5	1/12/1793
McLean	Chapman	S	Jan. 11, 1870	Mar. 26, 1893	Dav	CEM1
McMullen	Jno.	A.		Aug. 13, 1901	Brk	C1
McMullin	Eliza	B.	Oct. 10, 1835	Oct. 26, 1892	Hen	CEM1
McMullin	Eliza		Mar. 17, 1841	Mar. 29, 1864	Hen	CEM1
McMullin	Elnora	H.	Sep. 23, 1837	Aug. 3, 1904	Hen	CEM1
McMullin	Frances	R.	1853	1903	Hen	CEM1
McMullin	Harriett		Mar. 23, 1837	Mar. 7, 1861	Hen	CEM1
McMullin	J.	H.	1836	1919	Hen	CEM1
McMullin	Jane		Jul. 29, 1799	Apr. 10, 1875	Hen	CEM1
McMullin	John	S.	Sep. 5, 1836	Jun. 20, 1914	Hen	CEM1
McMullin	John		Feb. 13, 1830	Mar. 21, 1916	Hen	CEM1

Last Name	First Name	I	Birth	Death	Co	Source
McMullin	Joseph		Feb. 3, 1822	Mar. 18, 1853	Hen	CEM1
McMullin	Nan	L.	Feb. 14, 1842	Feb. 25, 1927	Hen	CEM1
McMullin	S.	H.	Jan. 15, 1832	May 3, 1909	Hen	CEM1
McMullin	Samuel		Oct. 4, 1797	Dec. 17, 1862	Hen	CEM1
McMullin	Stacy		Aug. 16, 1834	Mar. 9, 1897	Hen	CEM1
McMullin	William	C.	Jun. 19, 1836	Jun. 15, 1924	Hen	CEM1
McMurray	Sadie	H.	1880ca		Grn	Marr1
Mcntosh	Margaret		1825ca	Oct. 19, 1857	Bre	C1
McPherson	Hardin			Oct. 2, 1877	Bre	C1
McQuin	Charles		1785ca	Nov. 1, 1874	Bre	C1
McQuin	Nancy		1855ca	Feb. 8, 1875	Bre	C1
McQuinn	Francis Jane		1831ca	Jul. 2, 1855	Bre	C1
McQuinn	July Ann		1843ca	Jun. 1, 1858	Bre	C1
McReynolds	Joseph	M.	1854		But	Bk1
McRoberts	Anna		1881ca	Nov. 2, 1931	Fay	
McRoberts	Anna		1872ca	Oct. 5, 1918	Jef	
McRoberts	William	B.	1848ca	Nov. 23, 1924	Jef	
M'Donald	Barnabas		1770ca		NWS5	7/2/1791
Meade	Creed		Aug. 8, 1821	Jan. 4, 1903	Dav	CEM3
Meade	David		1852	1904	Dav	CEM3
Meade	John		Nov. 20, 1870	Oct. 5, 19??	Dav	CEM3
Meade	Mary	J.	Jun. 25, 1836	Jan. 31, 1896	Dav	CEM3
Meade	Merida		Jun. 25, 1872	Apr. 11, 1892	Dav	CEM3
Meade	Samuel		1899		Dav	CEM3
Meade	Susannah		1859	1944	Dav	CEM3
Meador	C.		1862ca	Apr. 30, 1904	Brk	C1
Meador	Frank		1865ca	Dec. 18, 1878	Brk	C1
Meador	Iva			Nov. 1, 1878	Brk	C1
Meador	Jolly		1865ca	Jun. 29, 1894	Brk	C1
Meador	Lou Ella		Jan. 19, 1907	Mar. 26, 1921	Sim	CEM1
Meadors	Whitney	A.		Feb. 28, 1986	Fay	MCDR
Meadow	W.	H.	1892ca	Jul. 3, 1894	Brk	C1
Meadows	Annie	L.	1895ca		Grn	Marr1
Meadows	Effie		1891ca		Grn	Marr1
Meadows	Jordan			Aug. 22, 1863	KY	Cem2
Medcalf	Mary	E.	May 8, 1841	May 17, 1879	Oh	CMIL2
Medcalf	Rebecca Ellen		1837ca	Aug. 2, 1854	Dav	C1
Medding	Pearlie	M.	1880ca		Grn	Marr1
Mehling	William	U.	1848ca	Nov. 8, 1912	Cam	MCDR
Melton	J.	P.	1928	Jun. 6, 1951	KY	KMIL
Melton	James		Jan. 10, 1849		Cam	MCDR
Melton	James	L.	Mar. 19, 1823		Cam	MCDR
Mendel	Leopold		1848		But	Bk1
Menken	Donald	L.	1932	Jun. 10, 1953	KY	KMIL
Mercer	Ann Elizabeth		1852ca	Mar. 21, 1854	Brk	C1
Mercer	Ed	F.	1920	Sep. 4, 1950	KY	KMIL
Mercer	Ellen			Aug. 20, 1883	Muh	Ch1

Last Name	First Name	I	Birth	Death	Co	Source
Mercer	Emeline		1871ca	Apr. 18, 1876	Brk	C1
Mercer	John	C.	Jun. 16, 1827		Han	Bk1
Mercer	Moses	R.	1833ca		Gray	C1
Mercer	William		1844ca	Sep. 29, 1852	Brk	C1
Mercer (Marlowe)	Emily		Jun. 10, 1851		Han	Bk1
Meredith	Bet		Sep. 10, 1840		Gray	C2
Meredith	J.	J.	Feb. 9, 1834		Gray	C2
Merrit	Stephen		1757		All	RP1
Merriweather	Mildred		1739		KY	BK2(P156)
Messer	Gertrude		1885ca		Grn	Marr1
Messer	Helen		1887ca		Grn	Marr1
Messer	John	W.		Nov. 5, 1877	Grn	C2
Metzker	William			Jan. 14, 1886	Muh	Ch1
Meyer	Joseph John		Nov. 19, 1928	Mar. 4, 1952	KY	KMIL
Midkiff	David	D.	Jul. 29, 1870	May 4, 1943	Oh	Cem2
Midkiff	Dempsey	B.	Jan. 9, 1876		Oh	Cem2
Midkiff	Elizabeth	A.	Jun. 12, 1840	Jan. 8, 1909	Oh	Cem2
Midkiff	J.	P.	Aug. 19, 1829		Oh	Cem2
Midkiff	James		1806ca	Jul. 14, 1855	Oh	Cem2
Midkiff	Joseph	B.	Nov. 16, 1839	Dec. 23, 1871	Oh	Cem2
Midkiff	Thomas	F.	Dec. 18, 1866	Mar. 12, 1931	Oh	Cem2
Midlock	James		1827ca	Feb. 1, 1859	Bre	C1
Milam	R.	J.	1860ca	Oct. 6, 1861	Brk	C1
Milam (Roberts)	Catherine		1848ca	May 8, 1894	Brk	C1
Milburn	Wm.		1824ca	Sep. 24, 1878	Brk	C1
Miles	Sarah		1872ca	Oct. 17, 1874	Bre	C1
Miller	Amanda	T.	1885ca		Grn	Marr1
Miller	Benjamin		1803ca	Sep. 15, 1859	Bre	C1
Miller	Chas.	L.	1816ca	Oct. 15, 1854	Brk	C1
Miller	Chester		1924	Jul. 14, 1950	KY	KMIL
Miller	Daniel			Dec. 14, 1857	Bre	C1
Miller	General Sherman		1873ca	Oct. 20, 1875	Bre	C1
Miller	George	W.	1803ca	May 4, 1875	Bre	C1
Miller	George		1756ca		NWS5	7/2/1791
Miller	Hant		1891ca		Grn	Marr1
Miller	Hiram		1852ca	Aug. 8, 1859	Bre	C1
Miller	Huram		1862ca	Jan. 4, 1875	Bre	C1
Miller	Isabell			Jan. 6, 1861	Brk	C1
Miller	Janice	T.	1832ca	1857	Dav	C1
Miller	Jerrilda			Apr. 7, 1878	Bre	C1
Miller	John	R.	1928	Jul. 20, 1950	KY	KMIL
Miller	Julia	A.	1816ca	Aug. 5, 1855	Dav	C1
Miller	Leonard		1815ca	Jul. 6, 1852	Brk	C1
Miller	Lloyd	K.	1930	May 26, 1953	KY	KMIL
Miller	Luther		1828ca	Aug. 1, 1854	Brk	C1
Miller	Martin		1798ca	Nov. 13, 1858	Bre	C1
Miller	Mary	G.		Mar. 19, 1852	Brk	C1

Last Name	First Name	I	Birth	Death	Co	Source
Miller	Nancy Belle			Sep. 18, 1878	Bre	C1
Miller	Peter		1825ca	Feb. 8, 1875	Dav	MCDR
Miller	Rebecca		Dec. 14, 1799	Sep. 27, 1875	Hdn	CEM3
Miller	Rhoda	A.	1838ca	Dec. 14, 1854	Brk	C1
Miller	Sally		1858ca	Nov. 29, 1861	Brk	C1
Miller	Samuel		1833ca	Dec. 14, 1854	Brk	C1
Miller	Samuel		1833ca	Nov. 15, 1854	Brk	C1
Miller	Susannah			Sep. 9, 1857	Bre	C1
Miller	Unknown Male			Mar. 5, 1861	Brk	C1
Miller	Von	L.		Aug. 27, 1967	Fay	MCDR
Miller	George	M.	May 11, 1866	Apr. 16, 1900	Har	Cem1
Miller	Samuel	R	1788ca	Sep. 23, 1843	NWS1	9/30/1843
Miller (Smith)	Rhoda		1833ca	Nov. 8, 1854	Brk	C1
Miller, Jr.	Anderson			1835	NWS4	7/17/1835
Milley	Thomas		1822ca	Dec. 22, 1854	Dav	C1
Milligan	Dr. Geo. Hen.		1846		But	Bk1
Milliron	Drusila		1895ca		Grn	Marr1
Millner	Charles			Nov. 25, 1854	Brk	C1
Mills	Crawford		1932	May 26, 1953	KY	KMIL
Mills	Mary		1765ca	Nov. 18, 1861	Brk	C1
Millsyaubh (sic)	Male		1842ca	Mar. 18, 1845	NWS1	4/5/1845
Milly (Slave)			1839ca	Nov. 18, 1854	Brk	C1
Milly (Slave)			1837ca	Nov. 14, 1854	Brk	C1
Milner	Ida May		1872	1932	Ful	CEM7
Milner	Narc		1838ca	1856	Brk	C1
Milner	Unkn			Dec. 12, 1893	Ful	CEM7
Milner	Yancy		1862	1943	Ful	CEM7
Milner (Tucker)	Dedida		1832ca	Oct. 25, 1854	Brk	C1
Milner (Tucker)	Richd.		1798ca	Jul. ??, 1854	Brk	C1
Milnor	James		1834ca		Gray	C1
Milnor	John	G	1828ca		Gray	C1
Milton	Sally	E.	1809ca	Mar. ??, 1853	Dav	C1
Mingus	Unknown Female			Oct. 25, 1855	Brk	C1
Minnick	Adam	P.	1903ca	Sep. 29, 1974	Cam	MCDR
Minor	Charles	W.	1927	Oct. 21, 1951	KY	KMIL
M'Intire	James		1765ca		NWS5	9/12/1798
Minton	Emma			Sep. ??, 1900	McL	CH1
Minton	Rachel			Apr. 20, 1876	McL	CH1
Minton	Thomas			May 23, 1871	McL	CH1
Minton	William	N.	Mar. 3, 1827		Gray	C2
Minyard	Harold	C.	1931	Jan. 20, 1951	KY	KMIL
Mires	Soloman			1835	NWS4	8/14/1835
Mitchell	Goldia		1881ca		Grn	Marr1
Mitchell	Joseph		Jan. 17, 1818		Cam	MCDR
Mitchell	Mrs. James	G.	1820ca	Jul. 3, 1853	Dav	MCDR
Mitchell	Nelle		1888ca		Grn	Marr1
Mitchell	Richard	M.		Jul. ??, 1855	Dav	C1

Last Name	First Name	I	Birth	Death	Co	Source
Mitton (Slave)				Feb. 10, 1854	Brk	C1
M'Math	Lieut.			1791ca	NWS5	11/12/1791
M'Nickle	Lieut.			1791ca	NWS5	11/12/1791
Mobley	Lula		Apr. 14, 1907		Car	C1
Mobley	Martha		Dec. 16, 1906		Car	C1
Mobley	Rowentuce		1869ca	Sep. 4, 1878	Brk	C1
Mogg	Lanily		1859ca	Mar. 15, 1861	Brk	C1
Molton	Annie		Feb. 23, 1871	Jun. 16, 1895	Row	CEM1
Molton	David		Mar. 29, 1838	May 20, 1916	Row	CEM1
Molton	George	W.	Oct. 27, 1868	Dec. 8, 1952	Row	CEM1
Molton	Nancy	J.	May 22, 1842	Feb. 15, 1916	Row	CEM1
Molton	Nannie	J.	May 11, 1868	May 17, 1959	Row	CEM1
Molton	Robert Allen		Apr. 22, 1969	Jun. 19, 1969	Row	CEM1
Molton	Susie		May 23, 1877	Jul. 15, 1889	Row	CEM1
Molton	Susie		May 23, 1877	Jul. 15, 1889	Row	CEM1
Monahan	Julia		1803ca	Sep. 29, 1853	Dav	C1
Monarch	Henty	F.	1834ca	Jul. 28, 1857	Dav	C1
Monroe	Henry		1813ca	May 8, 1853	Dav	C1
Montgomery	R.	L.	Oct. ??, 1840		Gray	C2
Montgomery	Ann	C.	1835ca	May ??, 1856	Dav	C1
Montgomery, Jr.	John		1828		Cam	MCDR
Montgomery, Jr.	Thomas	G.	1831		Cam	MCDR
Moore	Bernie Lee		Nov. 10, 1906		Car	C1
Moore	Bessie	L.	1894ca		Grn	Marr1
Moore	Charles			May 1, 1874	Bre	C1
Moore	Dr. W.	L.	1844		Cam	MCDR
Moore	Effy		1765ca	Oct. 19, 1855	Bre	C1
Moore	Elizabeth	F.	Jan. 25, 1858	Oct. 1, 1858	Log	CEM1
Moore	Ernest		1877ca	Jul. 16, 1878	Brk	C1
Moore	Goldie		1889ca		Grn	Marr1
Moore	John	W.	1930	Dec. 31, 1950	KY	KMIL
Moore	Mary Jane			Dec. 14, 1854	Dav	C1
Moore	Michael		1770ca		NWS5	9/20/1794
Moore	Sidney Carter		1826		Cam	MCDR
Moore	William	A.	Feb. 7, 1826	Oct. 18, 1868	Log	CEM1
Moore	William	H.	Feb. 13, 1832	Nov. 1, 1861	Muh	CEM3
Moore	William		1757		All	RP1
Moore	Winnie		1890ca		Grn	Marr1
Moores	Sinai		1767ca	Mar. 8, 1832	Lew	CEM1
Moorman	Henry	C.		Sep. 19, 1903	Brk	C1
Moorman	James		1773ca	Aug. 9, 1852	Brk	C1
Moorman	James		1856ca	Mar. 15, 1877	Brk	C1
Moorman	Unknown Female			Oct. 2, 1855	Brk	C1
Moorman (Owen)	Elizabeth	H.	1807ca	Jul. 24, 1854	Brk	C1
Moorman (Robertson)	M.	L.	1852ca	Dec. ??, 1894	Brk	C1
Moran	Charles Barthell		Apr. 17, 1924	Apr. 21, 1952	KY	KMIL
Moran	R.	M.	1888	1944	Ful	CEM4

Last Name	First Name	I	Birth	Death	Co	Source
Morehead	Dr. David		1821		Cam	MCDR
Morehead	Dr. Rbt. Burns		1827		But	Bk1
Morehead	James	T	1843/44ca	Jan. 23, 1845	NWS1	1/25/1845
Morgan	Joseph		No Date	No Date	Muh	CEM3
Morgan	William		1784ca	Oct. 4, 1854	Dav	C1
Morrill	Corp. Benoni		1771ca		NWS5	6/9/1792
Morris	Charles	E.	1842ca	Sep. ??, 1857	Dav	C1
Morris	Cora		1894ca		Grn	Marr1
Morris	Gertie		Aug. 6, 1891	Sep. 7, 1891	Ful	CEM7
Morris	Guy		Jun. 18, 1890	Oct. 22, 1890	Ful	CEM7
Morris	John		1848ca	Apr. ??, 1853	Bre	C1
Morris	John	J.	Nov. 19, 1852	Sep. 2, 1926	Ful	CEM7
Morris	Joseph Edward		Nov. 30, 1864	Oct. 3, 1908	Ful	CEM7
Morris	Martha		Jan. 21, 1834	Feb. 27, 1900	Ful	CEM7
Morris	Unknown Female			Sep. 15, 1858	Bre	C1
Morris	Unknown Female			Jun. 12, 1877	Bre	C1
Morris	Wesley		1833ca	Oct. 5, 1858	Bre	C1
Morris	Buck		1845ca	Aug. 13, 1875	Brk	C1
Morris (Skillman)	Sallie		1793ca	Jan. 8, 1874	Brk	C1
Morrison	C.	L.	1862	1951	Hdn	CEM1
Morrison	Eliza		Aug. 31, 1831	Aug. 15, 1902	Hdn	CEM1
Morrison	Florence Webb		1872	1911	Hdn	CEM1
Morrison	Hugh		1751	Dec. 23, 1823	All	RP1
Morrison	Maurice		Feb. 11, 1922	Nov. 15, 1953	Hdn	CEM1
Morrison	Millard		1857	1942	Hdn	CEM1
Morrison	Nancy Emma		1857	1934	Hdn	CEM1
Morrison	Nita Trigg		Jan. 25, 1925	Feb. 25, 1928	Hdn	CEM1
Morrison	William	C.	Jul. 29, 1825	Jul. 4, 1887	Hdn	CEM1
Morrow	Alfred	A.	Jan. 26, 1870	Dec. 31, 1911	Ful	CEM7
Morrow	Bobby Joe		Aug. 5, 1937		Ful	CEM7
Morrow	John Lee		Feb. 17, 1937	Feb. 18, 1939	Ful	CEM7
Morrow	John Watkins		Feb. 27, 1893	Dec. 4, 1918	Ful	CEM7
Morrow	M.	S.	Sep. 26, 1823	Oct. 12, 1886	Ful	CEM7
Morrow	Mary			Sep. 5, 1811	Cal	CEM1
Morrow	Sallie	E.	Feb. 17, 1838	Oct. 6, 1880	Ful	CEM7
Morrow	Tina		Sep. 29, 1894	Oct. 20, 1894	Ful	CEM7
Morrow	Will	A.	1825		Cam	MCDR
Morton	Ester	M.	1884ca		Grn	Marr1
Morton	Juliet	M.	1888ca		Grn	Marr1
Morton	Nancy		1852ca	Sep. 25, 1857	Brk	C1
Morton	Nellie		1888ca		Grn	Marr1
Morton	Joseph	W.		1835	NWS4	8/14/1835
Morton, Jr.	William			1835	NWS4	8/14/1835
Mosher	Absalom		1771ca		NWS5	9/20/1794
Mount	Everette		Feb. 3, 1914	Dec. 16, 1944	Hdn	CEM2
Mount	Hattie Given		Oct. 26, 1888	Feb. 21, 1972	Hdn	CEM2
Mounts	Campbell	T.	1846		Cam	MCDR

Last Name	First Name	I	Birth	Death	Co	Source
Mourning	Adroin	E.	1933ca	Nov. 25, 1934	Dav	KMIL
Mourning	Eddie		1890ca	Jan. 8, 1958	Dav	KMIL
Mourning	Elizabeth	J.	1944ca	Jul. 3, 1984	Jef	MCDR
Mourning	Garland	H.	1884ca	Feb. 25, 1943	Jef	MCDR
Mourning	Garland	H.	1838ca	Jul. 12, 1924	Jef	MCDR
Mourning	Ina	M.	1930ca	Mar. 4, 1945	Dav	MCDR
Mourning	Margaret	D.	1912ca	Jun. 16, 1960	Boy	MCDR
Mourning	Mary			Nov. 3, 1919	Dav	MCDR
Mourning	Matalea	W.	1880ca	May 27, 1931	Jef	MCDR
Mourning	Nancy	A.	1840ca	Sep. 10, 1924	Jef	MCDR
Mowery	Iva		1890ca		Grn	Marr1
Mudd	E.	E.	1875	1913	Hdn	CEM2
Mudd	Jas.		Mar. 5, 1836		Gray	C2
Mudd	Lee		1844	1927	Hdn	CEM2
Mudd	Margaret	B.	1878	1958	Hdn	CEM2
Mudd	Robert	L.	1880	1930	Hdn	CEM2
Mudd	Rosa	M.	1876	1959	Hdn	CEM2
Mullen	Amanda Elizabeth		Jul. 12, 1867	Sep. 6, 1922	Har	CEM1
Mullen	Ella		1862	1947	Har	CEM1
Mullen	Ellen	E.	Mar. 19, 1838	May 17, 1903	Har	CEM1
Mullen	George	D.	1864	1935	Har	CEM1
Mullen	George	M.	May 11, 1866	Apr. 16, 1900	Har	CEM1
Mullen	J.	N.	Sep. 1, 1830	May 11, 1884	Har	CEM1
Mullen	James	M.	Jul. ??, 1858	Nov. 27. 1874	Har	CEM1
Mullen	John	M.	Nov. 10, 1858	Oct. 29, 1861	Har	CEM1
Mullen	Joseph	S.	1879	1940	Har	CEM1
Mullen	Martha	A.	Oct. 30, 1886		Har	CEM1
Mullen	Mary	J.	Jul. 27, 1835	Jan. 30, 1863	Har	CEM1
Mullen	Sarah	A.	Oct. 23, 1843	Dec. 18, 1866	Har	CEM1
Mullen	Thomas	J.	Nov. 25, 1834	Aug. 5, 1871	Har	CEM1
Mullen	Thomas		Mar. 29, 1865	Feb. 9, 1905	Har	CEM1
Mullen	Thomas Everett		May 25, 1861	Apr. 11, 1863	Har	CEM1
Mullen	William	T.	Mar. 18, 1834	Nov. 12, 1906	Har	CEM1
Mullens	Alice	B.	1886ca		Grn	Marr1
Mullens	Eliza		1887ca		Grn	Marr1
Mullens	John Leonard		Mar. 15, 1907		Car	C1
Mullin	Nelly		1850ca	Aug. 27, 1852	Bre	C1
Mullins	Carlo Vertice		1892ca		Grn	Marr1
Mullins	Elmer		1928	Dec. 1, 1950	KY	KMIL
Mullins	James	C.	1930	Jul. 22, 1950	KY	KMIL
Mullins	John			Dec. 25, 1877	Bre	C1
Mullins	Lottie		1889ca		Grn	Marr1
Mundy	Mike	H.	1895	Jun. 16, 1951	KY	KMIL
Mungus	Nancy	A.	1846ca	Jul. 27, 1852	Brk	C1
Muntz	Joseph	R.	Feb. 28, 1901	Dec. 8, 1903	Har	CEM1
Muntz	Joseph Haron		1868	1929	Har	CEM1
Muntz	Mollie Kate		1869		Har	CEM1

Last Name	First Name	I	Birth	Death	Co	Source
Murphy	R.	H.	Aug. 2, 1880		McL	Sch1
Murphy	Robert Elbridge		Jul. 30, 1929	Aug. 7, 1950	KY	KMIL
Murray	Bessie		1891ca		Grn	Marr1
Murray	David	R.	1793		KY	BK2(P249)
Murray	Eli	H.	Feb. 10, 1843		KY	BK2(P250)
Murray	Gracie		1893ca		Grn	Marr1
Murray (Allen)	Anna Maria			1877	KY	BK2(P251)
Murry	John		1760ca		NWS5	12/27/1788
Musick	Charles		1829ca	1852	Grn	C1
Musick	Laura Belle		1890ca		Grn	Marr1
Myers	Emma Helsley		Apr. 5, 1860		Muh	CEM3
Myers	John		1812ca	Sep. 6, 1857	Dav	C1
Nall	Emma	J.	1868	1928	Hdn	CEM2
Nall	Gerorge	W.	1834		Cam	MCDR
Nall	Rebecca		Apr. 20, 1842	Jun. 17, 1923	Hdn	CEM2
Nall	T.	C.	Sep. 6, 1836	Jan. 28, 1903	Hdn	CEM2
Nalley	Ruth			Nov. 23, 1875	McL	CH1
Nance	Alfred		1876ca	Apr. 27, 1916	Oh	MCDR
Nancy (Slave)				Feb. 5, 1861	Brk	C1
Napier	Peggy			Mar. 22, 1877	Bre	C1
Napier	Zachariah			Mar. 6, 1855	Bre	C1
Napier (McIntosh)	Cynthia		1831ca	May 28, 1855	Bre	C1
Nathen	Riley		1828ca	Sep. 15, 1878	Brk	C1
Nave	Beulah		1896ca	Jun. 30, 1928	Cam	MCDR
Nave	Catherine	R.	1888ca	Feb. 22, 1959	Fay	MCDR
Nave	Clarence		1887ca	Dec. 15, 1944	Fay	MCDR
Nave	N.	J.	1843ca	Jan. 18, 1861	Dav	C1
Nay	William			May 29, 1844	NWS1	7/6/1844
Neace	Daniel		1854ca	Feb. 15, 1856	Bre	C1
Neace	Hinly		1854ca	Apr. 12, 1856	Bre	C1
Neace	Malinda		1775ca	Feb. 20, 1875	Bre	C1
Neal	Adeline		No Date	No Date	Oh	Cem3
Neal	Daniel	B.	1873ca	Aug. 25, 1874	Bre	C1
Neal	Mattilbelle			Apr. 3, 1877	Bre	C1
Neal	Nannie	K.	1837		Other	Bk1(P307)T
Neal	Rebecca	J.	1867ca	Feb. 14, 1874	Bre	C1
Neel	C.	W.	1852		But	Bk1
Neighbors	Charlie	H.	Aug. 26, 1876	Dec. 11, 1897	Hdn	CEM2
Neighbors	J. Fred		1883	1929	Hdn	CEM2
Neighbors	Jesse	T.	Feb. 19, 1881	Aug. 4, 1941	Hdn	CEM2
Neighbors	Joseph Earl		1888	1960	Hdn	CEM2
Neighbors	W.	C.	Mar. 2, 1848	Nov. 30, 1888	Hdn	CEM2
Neighbors	Wm. Robert		1878	1925	Hdn	CEM2
Neighbors (Downey)	Rena		Jun. 18, 1856	Aug. 4, 1930	Hdn	CEM2
Neighbors (Hicks)	Ina		1898	1965	Hdn	CEM2
Neighbors (Morehead)	Maude		1880	1965	Hdn	CEM2
Neighbors, Jr.	Earl		Apr. 27, 1917	Oct. 28, 1918	Hdn	CEM2

Last Name	First Name	I	Birth	Death	Co	Source
Neill	Josephine		1881ca		Grn	Marr1
Nelson	Addie		1893ca		Grn	Marr1
Nelson	Eddie		Feb. 17, 1880	Apr. 14, 1880	Hdn	CEM1
Nelson	Edwin	J.	Mar. 2, 1866	Jul. 31, 1890	Hdn	CEM1
Nelson	Fred		Feb. 2, 1827		Gray	C2
Nelson	Gabriel	K.	Jan. 28, 1878	Apr. 29, 1892	Hdn	CEM1
Nelson	Joshua		1818ca	Jul. 1, 1853	Dav	C1
Nelson	Lucie		Oct. 18, 1867	Oct. 28, 1867	Hdn	CEM1
Nelson	M.	J.	Aug. 15, 1838		Gray	C2
Nelson	Mary Scott		Nov. 26, 1839	Aug. 21, 1872	Hdn	CEM1
Nequirt	Unknown Male			Apr. 18, 1876	Bre	C1
Netherly	Clela Pearl		Jun. 21, 1926		Row	CEM1
Netherly	Roy		Oct. 5, 1904	Jul. 2, 1976	Row	CEM1
Newgent	John		1769ca		NWS5	4/18/1799
Newman	Harrison	D.		Aug. 20, 1904	Brk	C1
Newman (Moxley)	Adaline		1799ca	May 24, 1878	Brk	C1
Newton	Ancil	S.	1834ca	Sep. 8, 1858	Bre	C1
Newton	Ann		1787ca	Mar. 16, 1857	Dav	C1
Newton	Bertha Ellen		1860ca	Apr. 17, 1861	Brk	C1
Newton	Madison		1827ca	Jul. 20, 1854	Brk	C1
Newton	Mary	J.	1848ca	May 15, 1878	Bre	C1
Newton	Ransom		1836ca	Sep. 4, 1858	Bre	C1
Newton	Thomas	V.	1836ca	Aug. 4, 1854	Brk	C1
Newton	W.	A.	1857		But	Bk1
Nichol	Orman	G.	1850ca	Sep. 20, 1927	Grn	MCDR
Nichols	Annie		1889ca		Grn	Marr1
Nichols	Aura		1882ca		Grn	Marr1
Nichols	Birdetta		1888ca		Grn	Marr1
Nichols	Dan		1849	1927	Har	CEM1
Nichols	Emma	J.	1836ca	Apr. 14, 1854	Dav	C1
Nichols	Nellie Mae		1891ca		Grn	Marr1
Nichols	Sallie	E.	1853	1922	Har	CEM1
Nicholus	Thomas	N.	1853ca	Jan. 24, 1855	Brk	C1
Nickel	Lucy		188ca		Grn	Marr1
Niece	Anderson		1856ca	Mar. 6, 1859	Bre	C1
Niece	Rachel			Aug. ??, 1853	Bre	C1
Nielsen	John	E.	1935	Mar. 17, 1953	KY	KMIL
Nisbett	William		1782ca	Nov. 7, 1854	Brk	C1
Niswonger	Alexander		1860		Cam	MCDR
Nix	Leory			Jun. 3, 1864	KY	C1
Nix	Nancy		1839ca	Jan. 15, 1858	Bre	CMIL2
Nixon	Clavin	K.	1927	Jul. 16, 1950	KY	KMIL
Noakes	Jno.	B.		Jan. 22, 1861	Brk	C1
Noble	Abner		1852ca	Dec. 1, 1854	Bre	C1
Noble	July Ann		1853ca	Sep. ??, 1854	Bre	C1
Noble	Nathan		1761ca	Mar. 23, 1858	Bre	C1
Noble	Nathan		1841ca	Apr. 8, 1859	Bre	C1

Last Name	First Name	I	Birth	Death	Co	Source
Noble	Rada Jane		1854ca	Oct. 11, 1856	Bre	C1
Noble	Tarine		1858ca	Dec. 29, 1859	Bre	C1
Noble	Unknown Female			Nov. 20, 1876	Bre	C1
Noble	Unknown Male			Nov. 10, 1876	Bre	C1
Noble	Washington		1845ca	Feb. 1, 1853	Bre	C1
Noble (Saliers)	Sarah		1810ca	Nov. 16, 1856	Bre	C1
Noe	Joshua		1854ca	Sep. 15, 1858	Bre	C1
Norris	John	L.	1840		But	Bk1
Norris	Ryan		1792ca	Aug. 17, 1856	Brk	C1
Northen	Wm.	S.	1852		Cam	MCDR
Norton	Clinton			Aug. 28, 1859	Brk	C1
Norton	David		1854ca	Sep. 15, 1857	Brk	C1
Norton	John	S.	1877ca	Oct. 18, 1878	Brk	C1
Norton	Mary	A.	1860ca	Mar. 7, 1861	Brk	C1
Norton	Letie		1884ca	Oct. 12, 1903	Brk	C1
Norton (McCoy)	M.	J.	1840ca	May 30, 1894	Brk	C1
Nourse	Hershel Enrie		May 6, 1889	Oct. 26, 1904	Muh	CEM3
Nourse	Michael		Aug. 20, 1813	Sep. 21, 1886	Muh	CEM3
Nourse	Sarah H.	C.	Aug. 13, 1809	Aug. 12, 1891	Muh	CEM3
Nuel	James		1779ca		NWS5	11/12/1796
Nugent	Edward Dewitt		1886	1962	Ful	CEM7
Nugent	Oscar		1884	1950	Ful	CEM7
Nunes	Thomas	F.	1924	Nov. 30, 1950	KY	KMIL
Nutty	Pitt	M.	1893ca	Dec. 25, 1935	Dav	MCDR
Oaks	James		1856ca	Dec. 15, 1874	Bre	C1
Oaks	Maranda		1875ca	Feb. 15, 1876	Bre	C1
Oaks (Napier)	Mary		1804ca	Nov. 24, 1878	Bre	C1
O'Bannon	Elizabeth			1835	NWS4	8/14/1835
Obenshain	Unknown		1797ca	Dec. 6, 1853	Dav	C1
O'Bryan	Geo.	T.	1877ca	May 24, 1878	Brk	C1
O'Calleghan(Shehan)	Mary		1787ca	Dec. 24, 1861	Dav	C1
O'Connell	M.	R.	1873ca	Apr. ??, 1894	Brk	C1
O'Connell	Thomas	E.		May 17, 1855	Brk	C1
Oldfield	Eliza Ellen		Mar. 2, 1855	Feb. 14, 1921	Sim	CEM1
Oldfield	James		Nov. 18, 1816	Nov. 3, 1881	Sim	CEM1
Oldham	Col.			1791ca	NWS5	11/12/1791
Oldham	G.	S.	1841ca	May 4, 1861	Dav	C1
Oldham	J.	T.		Feb. 13, 1893	McL	CH1
Oldham	Jane	B.		Aug. ??, 1898	McL	CH1
Oldham	Thomas		1831ca	Mar. 20, 1853	Dav	MCDR
Oldham	William		1843ca		Web	C1-Pg.3
Oliver	Harold	E.	1931	Aug. 8, 1950	KY	KMIL
Oliver	James	C.	1931	Oct. 6, 1951	KY	KMIL
Oliver	John Davis		1808ca	Nov. 13, 1854	Dav	C1
Oliver	Joshua		1789ca	Jul. 11, 1853	Bre	C1
Oliver (Mays)	Ora		Mar. 24, 1869	Apr. 12, 1963	Ful	CEM6
Oller	William		Apr. 2, 1828		Gray	C2

Last Name	First Name	I	Birth	Death	Co	Source
Olliver (Duff)	Rachel		1793ca	Jul. 14, 1856	Bre	C1
O'Neal	Olie	T.	1872ca	Feb. 2, 1878	Brk	C1
Oney	Nora		1886ca		Grn	Marr1
Orman	Elizabeth		1837ca	Nov. 20, 1920	Byl	MCDR
Orman	Henry		1870ca	Jan. 27, 1917	Byl	MCDR
Orman	Leroy		1933ca	Mar. 12, 1934	Ken	MCDR
Orman	Orris	C.	1881ca	Aug. 27, 1957	Ken	MCDR
Orr	Mrs.			1835	NWS4	8/14/1835
Osborn	Emma		1890ca		Grn	Marr1
Osborn	J.	F.	Jul. 11, 1861	Feb. 3, 1877	Ful	CEM4
Osborn	M.	M.	Feb. 11, 1833	Apr. 27, 1887	Ful	CEM4
Osborn	Martha		1850ca	Aug. ??, 1852	Grn	C1
Osborn	Mary	B.	Sep. 10, 1820	Jun. 9, 1909	Men	CEM1
Osborn	Mattie		Aug. 23, 1875	Aug. 26, 1878	Ful	CEM4
Osborne	J.	T.	Jul. 9, 1874	Feb. 19, 1899	Dav	CEM3
Osborne	John R.	M.	Mar. 25, 1857	Jan. 19, 1860	Hdn	CEM3
Osburn	Isaac		1820		Cam	MCDR
Osburn	R.	M.	1841		Cam	MCDR
Otey	Edw. Lee		Oct. 6, 1863	Jan. 23, 1948	Hen	CEM1
Otey	Mary	E.	1865	1916	Hen	CEM1
Ott	Kenneth	J.	1928	Sep. 19, 1951	KY	KMIL
Overbee	Clayton		1932	Nov. 27, 1950	KY	KMIL
Overbee	Elizabeth	S.		Feb. 17, 1853	Bre	C1
Overby	Y.		1800ca	Apr. 28, 1853	Dav	C1
Overfield	T.	C.	1862	1927	Hen	CEM1
Overfield	Virginia		1868	1934	Hen	CEM1
Overlay	Alice		Mar. 13, 1871	Aug. 1, 1943	Hdn	CEM2
Overton	Daniel	B.	1856ca	Sep. 15, 1861	Brk	C1
Overton	James	T.		1852	Brk	C1
Owen	Frank	A.	1845		Cam	MCDR
Owsley	Clinton Roy		Feb. 1, 1911	Feb. 20, 1911	Hdn	CEM1
Owsley	J.	H.	1841	1916	Hdn	CEM1
Owsley	Mary		1850	1933	Hdn	CEM1
Owsley	Nathan	S.	1893	1911	Hdn	CEM1
Owsley	Roy	S.	Oct. 12, 1873	Aug. 24, 1902	Hdn	CEM1
Pack	Ransom		3-May-32	Jul. 19, 1954	KY	KMIL
Pack	UnKnown Female			Sep. 21, 1861	Brk	C1
Packo	Irvin	H.	1916	Mar. 8, 1951	KY	KMIL
Pagget	Henry		1766ca		NWS5	12/27/1794
Pagget	Peter		1771ca		NWS5	12/27/1794
Paine	Elizabeth		1882ca	Dec. 20, 1973	Cam	MCDR
Paine	Samanthy		1771ca	May 10, 1853	Dav	C1
Palmer	Forest McLee		Aug. 23, 1930	Apr. 25, 1951	Ful	CEM4
Palmer	James	D.	1832		Cam	MCDR
Palmer	Rueben		1851ca	Nov. 22, 1855	Bre	C1
Palmer	Thomas	F.	1931	Nov. 29, 1950	KY	KMIL
Palmer	Tillman	J.	1879	Jul. ??, 1924	Ful	CEM4

Last Name	First Name	I	Birth	Death	Co	Source
Palmer	William	J.	1896	1919	Ful	CEM4
Pantress	Lawson	A.		Apr. 1, 1861	Brk	C1
Parker	Edith Rees		1886		Har	CEM1
Parker	Geo.	W.	Apr. 15, 1827	Feb. 3, 1854	Har	CEM1
Parker	George		1825		Cam	MCDR
Parker	James			Mar. 6, 1797	NWS	3/2/1797
Parker	Jesse	H.	1889	1965	Har	CEM1
Parker	John	C.	1845		Cam	MCDR
Parker	John	H.	1835		Cam	MCDR
Parker	Wm. Randolph		1849		Cam	MCDR
Parks	L.	N.		Aug. 1, 1865	KY	C1
Parks(Sandefur)	Elizabeth	J.	1834ca	Mar. 30, 1857	Dav	CMIL2
Parr	J.	B.	1836ca	Jun. 20, 1904	Brk	C1
Parr	Jasper		Feb. 13, 1886	May 19, 1956	Hdn	CEM2
Parr	Paul Edward		Jun. 26, 1932	Jun. 27, 1932	Hdn	CEM2
Parr	Susan	G.	Oct. 2, 1891	Jul. 1, 1973	Hdn	CEM2
Parrish	Peyton	L.		1835	NWS4	8/14/1835
Parson	Mary	E.	Jun. 14, 1810	Nov. 10, 1899	Hen	CEM1
Parsons	Christopher		Mar. 30, 1821	Aug. 9, 1884	Dav	CEM1
Parsons	E. Warren		Feb. 17, 1861	Oct. 29, 1882	Dav	CEM1
Paschall	Richard	B.	1928	May 20,1951	KY	KMIL
Pate	Elizabeth		1829ca	Jun. 12, 1861	Brk	C1
Pate	Jane		1858ca	Jun. 18, 1861	Brk	C1
Pate	Rebecca		1806ca	Jul. 14, 1855	Oh	Cem2
Pate (Brickey)	Winina		1867ca	Dec. 29, 1893	Brk	C1
Paten, Jr.	Chas. Carroll		Apr. 14, 1929	Sep. 19, 1950	KY	KMIL
Patre	Mary Marcella			Feb. 22, 1904	Brk	C1
Patten	Mrs.			1835	NWS4	8/14/1835
Patterson	Female			Oct. 31, 1875	Dav	MCDR
Patterson	Garvie	F.	Jan. 23, 1889	Jun. 28, 1972	Hdn	CEM2
Patterson	Harold	F.	1932	Apr. 17, 1953	KY	KMIL
Patterson	John	W.	1849		Cam	MCDR
Patterson	Mary		1827ca	Nov. 11, 1861	Brk	C1
Patterson	Mary Ann		Mar. 24, 1868	Aug. 9, 1949	Hdn	CEM2
Patterson	Maude	A.	Dec. 19, 1988	Jul. 15, 1955	Hdn	CEM2
Patterson	Thomas	B.		Nov. 27, 1861	Brk	C1
Patterson	William	B.	Nov. 7, 1868	Jun. 7, 1946	Hdn	CEM2
Patterson (Pierson)	Theoclia		Feb. 24, 1891	Nov. 4, 1967	Hdn	CEM2
Patton	Benjamin	T.	1816ca	Aug. 27, 1835	NWS4	9/4/1835
Patton	Hattie		1889ca		Grn	Marr1
Patton	Lizzie	M.	1889ca		Grn	Marr1
Patton	Margaret		1856ca	Dec. 9, 1859	Bre	C1
Patton	Martha		1890ca		Grn	Marr1
Patton	Sarah	B.	1873ca		Grn	Marr1
Paul	Amanda	J.	Apr. 18, 1865	Jul. 13, 1949	Hdn	CEM3
Paul	E.			Sep. 7, 1856	Hdn	CEM3
Paul	Gay	E.		Nov. 5, 1877	Brk	C1

Last Name	First Name	I	Birth	Death	Co	Source
Paul	Sarah Ellen		May 14, 1856	Jan. 18, 1929	Hdn	CEM3
Paul	Thos.		1806ca	Feb. 11, 1858	Brk	C1
Pauley	Sadie		1894ca		Grn	Marr1
Paulley	Robert	L.	1932	Noc. 2, 1950	KY	KMIL
Paxton	Baby of Tom			May 7, 1883	Muh	Ch1
Paxton	Joseph		Apr. 20, 1799	Aug. 15, 1884	Muh	Ch1
Payne	Clara		Jan. 5, 1852	Dec. 31, 1922	Hdn	CEM1
Payne	Elizabeth		Feb. 19, 1852	Jan. 19, 1919	Hdn	CEM1
Payne	Female		Oct. 8, 1889	Nov. 26, 1889	Hdn	CEM1
Payne	Frank Burr		Apr. 3, 1892	Jul. 29, 1925	Hdn	CEM1
Payne	Henry		Nov. 13, 1811	Oct. 3, 1893	Hdn	CEM1
Payne	J.	B.	Dec. 16, 1850		Hdn	CEM1
Payne	John		1926	Jan. 1, 1951	KY	KMIL
Payne	Logo	W.	1843ca	Feb. 29, 1861	Brk	C1
Payne	M.	D.	1837		But	Bk1
Payne	Mahala	J.	Mar. 10, 1817	Feb. 21, 1885	Hdn	CEM1
Payne	Mary	E.	1837ca	Aug. 3, 1855	Dav	C1
Payne	Mary	M.	Aug. 11, 1882	Nov. 3, 1902	Hdn	CEM1
Payne	Mary Ona		Jul. 27, 1886	Nov. 16, 1915	Hdn	CEM1
Payne	Miss			1835	NWS4	8/14/1835
Payne	Richard		Oct. 21, 1846	Jul. 9, 1922	Hdn	CEM1
Payne	Thomas	B.	1843		Cam	MCDR
Payne	Widow Susie		1890ca		Grn	Marr1
Payne	William			Aug. 31, 1835	NWS4	9/4/1835
Payne	Alice		1865ca	Sep. 4, 1878	Brk	C1
Payne (Scott)	Elizabeth		1825ca	Apr. 22, 1878	Brk	C1
Payton	Catherine		Jun. 28, 1839		Gray	C2
Payton	Female		Jun. 27, 1884	Jun. 27, 1884	Hdn	CEM2
Payton	J.	N.	Sep. 20, 1839		Gray	C2
Payton	Josephine		May 26, 1862	Jan. 6, 1948	Hdn	CEM2
Payton	Louisa		1885ca		Grn	Marr1
Payton	Male		Mar. 8, 1905	Mar. 8, 1905	Hdn	CEM2
Payton	Nancy	L.	May 31, 1862	Feb. 20, 1947	Hdn	CEM2
Payton	Theodore		Nov. 4, 1891	May 1, 1952	Hdn	CEM2
Payton	W.	R.	Apr. 17, 1857	Mar. 10, 1927	Hdn	CEM2
Peace	J.	D.	1831ca	Dec. 22, 1876	Brk	C1
Pearce	G.	C.	1827ca	Mar. ??, 1861	Dav	C1
Pearl	Dorah		1852ca	Jul. 30, 1876	Brk	C1
Pearl	Unknown		1830ca	Sep. 6, 1853	Dav	C1
Peay	Perry	M.	1852		But	Bk1
Pegram	Virgenious		1828ca	Jan. 12, 1852	Dav	MCDR
Pence	Amanda		1892ca		Grn	Marr1
Pence	Betty	J.	1936	1937	Row	CEM1
Pence	Easter		1869ca	May 13, 1877	Bre	C1
Pence	Emily		1872ca	Nov. 15, 1875	Bre	C1
Pence	George Allen		Nov. 13, 1922	Dec. 7, 1950	KY	KMIL
Pence	Matilda			Nov. 22, 1854	Bre	C1

Last Name	First Name	I	Birth	Death	Co	Source
Pence	Maude	M.	Sep. 28, 1884	May 20, 1959	Hdn	CEM2
Pence	Sarah Jane		1851ca	Dec. 10, 1854	Bre	C1
Pence	Shelton			Apr. 19, 1858	Bre	C1
Pence	Stella May		1890ca		Grn	Marr1
Pence	Unknown Female			Mar. 22, 1875	Bre	C1
Pence	Unknown Male			Dec. 3, 1877	Bre	C1
Pendleton	Davis			1797	NWS5	10/4/1797
Pendleton	William A.		1802ca	Aug. 18, 1845	NWS1	8/23/1845
Pendley	David Hall		1836		But	Bk1
Penington	Randolph Miller		Jan. 8, 1907		Car	C1
Penix	Ida		1891ca		Grn	Marr1
Pennington	Ellen			Nov. 11, 1861	Brk	C1
Pennington	Len Emma		1857ca	Oct. 25, 1861	Brk	C1
Pennington	Lona		1889ca		Grn	Marr1
Perenll	Bettie		1890ca		Grn	Marr1
Perrin	William Clapton		1773ca		NWS5	9/19/1795
Perry	Roderick		1803ca	Aug. 17, 1845	NWS1	8/23/1845
Peters	Evaline		1842ca	Sep. 1, 1856	Brk	C1
Peters	Martin		1814ca	Jun. 9, 1894	Brk	C1
Peters	Nancy		1839ca	Oct. 18, 1856	Brk	C1
Petit	Nancy			Jan. 28, 1904	Brk	C1
Petry	Prof. Henry		1859		Web	Bk1
Pettit, Jr.	Thomas		Aug. 17, 1930	Feb. 28, 1954	KY	KMIL
Peveler	Oscar	P.	1931	Jul. 5, 1952	KY	KMIL
Peyton	Francis		1820ca	Oct. 10, 1852	Brk	C1
Peyton	Frankrun		1842ca	Dec. 25, 1861	Brk	C1
Pharris	Frances		1828	Mar. 26, 1895	But	CEM1
Pharris	J.	W.	Mar. 11, 1868	Jan. 28, 1948	But	CEM1
Pharris	Laura	I.	Feb. 8, 1869	Aug. 28, 1922	But	CEM1
Pharris	Rheubin		Nov. 21, 1848	Mar. 17, 1927	But	CEM1
Pharris	Tavender		1823	Apr. 1, 1895	But	CEM1
Phelps	Alma	B.	1895ca		Grn	Marr1
Phelps	James	M.	1827		But	Bk1
Phelps	John		1858		But	Bk1
Phelps	John	M.	1934	Dec. 2, 1952	KY	KMIL
Phelps	John			Nov. 11, 1843	NWS1	11/18/1843
Phelps	Julian	N.	1809		But	Bk1
Phelps	Lucy Jane		1833ca	Aug. 14, 1835	NWS4	8/21/1835
Phelps	Richard		1931	Apr. 12, 1951	KY	KMIL
Phelps	William	U.	1864ca	Aug. 9, 1948	Fay	MCDR
Phelps	H.		Feb. 12, 1834		Gray	C2
Phelps (Gholson)	G.		Dec. 29, 1836		Gray	C2
Phillips	Dr. Granville		Nov. 10, 1832		Other	Bk1(P307)T
Phillips	James	F.	1843		But	Bk1
Phillips	James	W.	1932	Jun. 28, 1952	KY	KMIL
Phillips	Unknown Female			Aug. 30, 1878	Brk	C1
Philon	Capt.			1791ca	NWS5	11/12/1791

Last Name	First Name	I	Birth	Death	Co	Source
Philpot	Ann		1791ca	Jan. 11, 1861	Dav	C1
Philpott	Barbara Kay		Jan. 21, 1951	May 1, 1951	Hdn	CEM2
Philpott	Paul		1914	1972	Hdn	CEM2
Pickel	Jennie		1886ca		Grn	Marr1
Pickeral	William	A.	1832ca		Gray	C1
Pickerill	Clinton Daniel		Feb. 17, 1880	Jul. 18, 1969	Hdn	CEM2
Pickerill	Henry Smith		May 24, 1918		Hdn	CEM2
Pickerill	John	D.	Aug. 20, 1882	Feb. 6, 1944	Hdn	CEM2
Pickerill	Linia		Aug. 6, 1857	Jan. 8, 1930	Hdn	CEM2
Pickerill	Orleans	F.	1864	1934	Hdn	CEM2
Pickerill	Wm. Henry		Feb. 2, 1854	24-May-00	Hdn	CEM2
Pickerill (Brown)	Martha		Feb. 21, 1922		Hdn	CEM2
Pickerill (Smith)	Carrie		Mar. 29, 1888	Apr. 8, 1974	Hdn	CEM2
Pickford	Daniel		1760		All	RP1
Pierce	Dickson			Aug. ??, 1877	Grn	C2
Pierce	Sarah	W.	1835ca	Aug. 28, 1855	Brk	C1
Pierce(Sims)	T.	A.	1891ca	May 1, 1855	Dav	C1
Pierson	Charles	T.	Apr. 8, 1858	Apr. 21, 1945	Hdn	CEM2
Pierson	Lula	R.	Mar. 6, 1867	Mar. 24, 1956	Hdn	CEM2
Pike	D.	S.		Jul. 9, 1904	Brk	C1
Pinkerman	Maggie		1882ca		Grn	Marr1
Pinkston	Jackson		1811ca	Oct. 14, 1853	Dav	C1
Pinkston	Henson		1849ca	Feb. 11, 1861	Brk	C1
Pinkston (Kaydly)	Anna		1809ca	Feb. 19, 1861	Brk	C1
Pirtle	Bittie		Oct. 23, 1862	Jan. 18. 1938	Ful	CEM7
Pirtle	Commodore		Oct. 29, 1855	Jan. 2, 1923	Ful	CEM7
Pitman	Annie		Apr. 3, 1858	Mar. 20, 1899	Muh	CEM2
Pitman	B.	E.	Jul. 12, 1806	Dec. 30, 1879	Muh	CEM2
Pitman	Burris	E.	Jul. 12, 1806	Dec. 30, 1879	Muh	CEM2
Pitman	M.	J.	Jan. 22, 1827	Oct. 13, 1903	Muh	CEM2
Pitman	Mary	E.	Feb. ??, 1849	Nov. ??, 1915	Muh	CEM2
Pitt	Daviess		1754ca	Apr. 16, 1854	Dav	C1
Plank (McMullin)	Ella		1862ca	Dec. 22, 1903	Brk	C1
Poe	Benjamin		1748		All	RP1
Poland	Calvin	T.	1893ca	Dec. 1, 1975	All	MCDR
Poland	Charles	E.	1887ca	Jan. 6, 1963	Ken	MCDR
Poland	Don	W.		Aug. 5, 1945	Fay	MCDR
Poland	Electa	M.	1875ca	Oct. 26, 1944	Ken	MCDR
Poland	Elmer	E.	1904ca	Feb. 18, 1983	Ken	MCDR
Poland	Frieda		1883ca	Sep. 8, 1959	Cam	MCDR
Poland	Voss	T.	1885ca	Mar. 16, 1953	Cam	MCDR
Polk, Jr.	Robert		1894ca	Mar. 10, 1904	Brk	C1
Pollard	Thomas	J.	Oct. 27, 1805		KY	Bk1(P158)A
Pollett	Wid. Effie		1887ca		Grn	Marr1
Polly	Elizabeth		1822ca	Feb. 24, 1858	Lew	CEM1
Polly	Sally	A.	1836ca	Apr. 15, 1855	Dav	C1
Pool	Martha J.	D.	1841ca	Aug. 9, 1857	Dav	C1

Last Name	First Name	I	Birth	Death	Co	Source
Pool	Mary		1867ca	Aug. ??, 1878	Brk	C1
Pool	Sarah	A.	1858ca	Mar. 30, 1876	Brk	C1
Pool (Horsley)	Percy		1831ca	Aug. 11, 1878	Brk	C1
Poole	Annah		Jan. 7, 1859	Jun. 13, 1894	Hen	CEM1
Poole	Henry	J.	May 13, 1850	Dec. 4, 1907	Hen	CEM1
Poole	Mary	E.	Feb. 2, 1828	Oct. 13, 1885	Hen	CEM1
Poole	Pinkney		1824		But	Bk1
Poole	Queen Tina		Jan. 9, 1853	Jul. 3, 1916	Hen	CEM1
Poole	William	W.	1822		Web	Bk1
Pope	Bettie Ann		Jun. 29, 1843	Jan. 21, 1872	Sim	CEM1
Pope	Ray		Apr. 24, 1923	Dec. 6, 1950	KY	KMIL
Porter	Andrew		Sep. 24, 1793		KY	BK2(P271)
Porter	Clark	T.	1822		But	Bk1
Porter	J.	M.	May 25, 1837		Gray	C2
Porter	Sindie		1891ca		Grn	Marr1
Porter	Thomas	T.	1840		But	Bk1
Porter	Virgil	W.	1845		But	Bk1
Porter (Robinson)	Elizabeth		Mar. 30, 1834		Gray	C2
Potter	George			1852	Brk	C1
Potter	John			Jun. 9, 1852	Brk	C1
Potter	Lewis		1849ca	Jun. 30, 1852	Brk	C1
Potter	Lizzie		1881ca		Grn	Marr1
Potter	Unknown Female		Jan. 28, 1945	Feb. 1, 1945	Row	CEM1
Potter	Virgie		1882ca		Grn	Marr1
Powell	J.	A.	1835		Web	Bk1
Powell	Joseph	C.	1920	Jun. 3, 1951	KY	KMIL
Powell	Roy	L.	1929	Dec. 2, 1950	KY	KMIL
Powers	Betsey		1842ca	Sep. 20, 1855	Brk	C1
Powers	Edward		1791ca	Jul. 29, 1856	Brk	C1
Powers	Mary Ann			Jan. 2, 1861	Brk	C1
Powers	Ottis		Nov. 15, 1887	Mar. 7, 1959	Row	CEM1
Prater	James		Apr. 23, 1904		Car	C1
Prather	Robert	L.	1931	Feb. 13, 1951	KY	KMIL
Pratt	Capt.			1791ca	NWS5	11/12/1791
Prechtel	Anthony	J.	1926ca	Mar. 16, 1983	Dav	MCDR
Presson	James	H.	1907ca	May 6, 1977	Dav	MCDR
Pretlow	Edward Lynch		1839ca	May 17, 1845	NWS1	5/24/1845
Price	Amealia	B.	Aug. 21, 1873	Aug. 25, 1953	Hdn	CEM2
Price	Andrew		1839ca	Nov. 6, 1845	NWS1	11/8/1845
Price	Ann		1785ca	Oct. 8, 1844	NWS1	10/12/1844
Price	Capt.			1791ca	NWS5	11/12/1791
Price	Capt. Samuel			1799	NWS5	10/3/1799
Price	Charles	H.	1839		Web	Bk1
Price	Dr. B.	H.	1853		Web	Bk1
Price	J.	D.	1836		Web	Bk1
Price	John	H.	1820ca	Aug. 29, 1852	Grn	C1
Price	Nannie		Oct. 24, 1887	May 4, 1955	Hdn	CEM1

Last Name	First Name	I	Birth	Death	Co	Source
Price	S. Benton		Jul. 19. 1871	Dec. 11, 1942	Hdn	CEM2
Price	Sarah		1850ca	Oct. 25, 1852	Grn	C1
Price	Thomas	E.	1838		Web	Bk1
Price	William	E	1844ca	June 1, 1845	NWS1	6/15/1845
Price	William	H.	Jul. 25, 1873	Nov. 18, 1953	Hdn	CEM1
Priest	Fleming		1811ca	Feb. 17, 1852	Brk	C1
Prince	Hannah Eliz.		1888ca		Grn	Marr1
Prince	Pearl	M.	1890ca		Grn	Marr1
Proctor	Ann		May 12, 1798		KY	RP1
Proctor	Betsey		Feb. 22, 1801		KY	RP1
Proctor	Catherine		May 18, 1787		KY	RP1
Proctor	Eber		Feb. 29, 1832		KY	RP1
Proctor	Elizabeth		Dec. 15, 1759		KY	RP1
Proctor	Elizabeth		Dec. 7, 1835		KY	RP1
Proctor	Frances		Mar. 10, 1834		KY	RP1
Proctor	Jeremiah		Jun. 27, 1807		KY	RP1
Proctor	John		Mar. 23, 1791		KY	RP1
Proctor	Margit		Oct. 5, 1803		KY	RP1
Proctor	Mary		Jan. 18, 1810		KY	RP1
Proctor	Polly		Oct. 2, 1793		KY	RP1
Proctor	Sally		Feb. 9, 1789		KY	RP1
Proctor	Sally		Apr. 18, 1830		KY	RP1
Proctor	Sinthey		Jul. 4, 1810		KY	RP1
Proctor	William		Feb. 7, 1760		KY	RP
Proctor	William		Mar. 30, 1796		KY	RP1
Prosser	Alice	B.	1904ca	Apr. 22, 1971	Fay	MCDR
Prosser	Thomas	W.	1889ca	Oct. 13, 1951	Cam	MCDR
Prost	Wilbert	F.	1906ca	Feb. 4, 1969	Cam	MCDR
Pruitt	John	F.	1854ca	Jan. 25, 1931	All	MCDR
Pruitt	John	K.	1967ca	Oct. 29, 1969	All	MCDR
Pruitt (Corum)	Birdie		Jul. 23, 1881	Aug. 27, 1936	Ful	CEM7
Puckett	Anna		1887	1961	Hdn	CEM2
Puckett	Calvin		Sep. 2, 1878	Nov. 7, 1955	Hdn	CEM2
Puckett	Edwin	L.	Nov. 18, 1918	Dec. 7, 1941	Hdn	CEM2
Puckett	Elva	E.	Nov. 11, 1900		Hdn	CEM2
Puckett	Harry Hindman		Mar. 8, 1895	Apr. 3, 1978	Hdn	CEM2
Puckett	J.	F.	Dec. 7, 1863	Aug. 19, 1954	Hdn	CEM2
Puckett	Jennie Ann		Mar. 3, 1876	Feb. 10, 1956	Hdn	CEM2
Puckett	Mamie		Jan. 28, 1894	Sep. 9, 1901	Dav	CEM2
Puckett	Mandy		1891ca		Grn	Marr1
Puckett	Martha		Feb. 8, 1846	Sep. 12, 1876	Sim	CEM1
Pullen	Isiah		1851ca	Sep. 6, 1876	Brk	C1
Pullen	Willard Cecil		Oct. 12, 1929	Sep. 23, 1951	Hdn	CEM2
Pullen	William		1871ca	Jan. 23, 1876	Brk	C1
Pullum	Rev. Benj.	B.	1828		Web	Bk1
Pumphrey	Gilb.	D.	1768ca	Jul. 16, 1854	Brk	C1
Pumphrey	James	I	1812ca	Jul. 15, 1854	Brk	C1

Last Name	First Name	I	Birth	Death	Co	Source
Pumphrey	Nancy		1778ca	Jul. 21, 1854	Brk	C1
Purcell	James	R.	Sep. 7, 1822		Gray	C2
Purcell	John		1834ca	Sep. 13, 1853	Dav	C1
Purcell (Bennett)	Susan		1780ca	Apr. 3, 1853	Dav	C1
Purdie	Capt.			1791ca	NWS5	11/12/1791
Purdie	Ensign			1791ca	NWS5	11/12/1791
Pursley	Benjamin		1780ca		NWS5	2/14/1799
Purvis	Elizabeth		Oct. 2, 1841		KY	RP1
Purvis	Jane		Dec. 12, 1838		KY	RP1
Purvis	William		May 19, 1836		KY	RP1
Push	G.	W.		May ??, 1852	Grn	C1
Qesnell	Mary		1795ca	Jul. 27, 1875	Dav	MCDR
Qualls	Curtis	W.	1928	May 18, 1951	KY	KMIL
Qualls	Squire Jas. Henry		1836		Web	Bk1
Quillen	E. Belle		1894ca		Grn	Marr1
Quilluen	Alice		1895ca		Grn	Marr1
Quinn	Charles	D.	1925	Mar. 27, 1951	KY	KMIL
Quissenberry	J.	H.	1825ca	1894	Brk	C1
Rafferty	B.	B.	1816ca	May 7, 1857	Dav	C1
Rafferty	Sarah	J.	1819ca	Apr. 8, 1853	Dav	C1
Raike	Carrie		1887ca		Grn	Marr1
Railey	William	W.	1816ca	Aug. 10, 1854	Dav	C1
Ralph (Kelley)	Lucinda		1818ca	Nov. 29, 1854	Dav	C1
Ramer	John	H.	Oct. 15, 1837	Sep. 11, 1914	Ful	CEM7
Ramer (Dancy)	Elizabeth	A.	Mar. 16, 1840	Nov. 19, 1900	Ful	CEM7
Rames	Henry	S.	1853ca		Web	C1(P75)
Rames	Robert		1851ca		Web	C1(P63)
Ramey	J.	T.	Dec. 19, 1891		Row	CEM1
Ramey	Lucinda		1858ca		Grn	Marr1
Ramey	Mary	A.	Sep. 27, 1866	Jun. 29, 1888	Row	CEM1
Ramey	Walter		Oct. 27, 1886	1889	Row	CEM1
Ramsey	John		1756ca		Hen	RC1840
Randolph	John			Jul. 27, 1852	Brk	C1
Rankin	Jackson	B.	Dec. 25, 1872	Nov. 29, 1891	Ful	CEM7
Rankin	John	M.	1878	1943	Ful	CEM7
Rankin	Joseph William		Apr. 5, 1831	Jul. 31, 1905	Ful	CEM7
Rankin (Bynum)	Kittie		Oct. 16, 1844	Dec. 10, 1904	Ful	CEM7
Rankin (Carr)	Ora		1883	1944	Ful	CEM7
Ransom, Jr.	Henry		1922	Feb. 12, 1951	KY	KMIL
Rardin	Willie	A.	1886ca		Grn	Marr1
Ratcliff	Rebecca		1884ca		Grn	Marr1
Ratcliff	William		1825ca	Aug. 15, 1852	Grn	C1
Ratecliff	Maud		1886ca		Grn	Marr1
Rather	Boen			Aug. 30, 1852	Brk	C1
Rauten	Chesley	C.	Aug. 16, 1885	Sep. 17, 1885	Ful	CEM7
Rauten	James	H.	Nov. 3, 1877	Sep. 14, 1878	Ful	CEM7
Rauten	Lillie	L.	Jan. 23, 1888	Jul. 5, 1894	Ful	CEM7

Last Name	First Name	I	Birth	Death	Co	Source
Rawland (Gilbert)	Nancy		1822ca	Aug. 30, 1857	Dav	C1
Rawly	Meranda		1854ca	Feb. 15, 1855	Bre	C1
Ray	Durward Allen		Dec. 19, 1932	Dec. 28, 1953	KY	KMIL
Ray	Elizabeth		1790ca	Mar. 1, 1861	Brk	C1
Ray	Walter	R.	1853ca	Apr. 26, 1923	But	MCDR
Ray	Wm. Damon		Jul. 7, 1922		Hdn	CEM2
Ray (Conatser)	Charlene		Jun. 4, 1924	Feb. 14, 1973	Hdn	CEM2
Rayburn	Annie		1883ca		Grn	Marr1
Read	Wm. Wash.		1819		But	Bk1
Reardon	L.	U.		Jun. 21, 1894	Brk	C1
Redman	Addie	M.	1865	1929	Hdn	CEM2
Redman	Albin	H.	1838	1908	Hdn	CEM2
Redman	Betty	M.	Oct. 6, 1887	May 14, 1964	Hdn	CEM2
Redman	Clarence		Sep. 19, 1875	Jan. 17, 1897	Hdn	CEM2
Redman	James	F.	1864	1948	Hdn	CEM2
Redman	John	A.	Mar. 16, 1869	Jul. 27, 1955	Hdn	CEM2
Redman	Nellie		Dec. 4, 1878	Mar. 30, 1896	Hdn	CEM2
Redman	Robert	I.	Jan. 15, 1888	Nov. 2, 1951	Hdn	CEM2
Redman	Robert	L.	Feb. 27, 1911	Feb. 12, 1962	Hdn	CEM2
Redman	Thomas		Nov. 16, 1791	Dec. 16, 1877	Hdn	CEM1
Redman (Friend)	Harriet	M.	1839	1908	Hdn	CEM2
Redmon	Hugh Irwin		Sep. 27, 1928	Nov. 2, 1950	KY	KMIL
Reed	Lieut.			1791ca	NWS5	11/12/1791
Reed	Thomas		1765ca		NWS5	12/27/1788
Reeder	Male		Apr. 13, 1880	Jul. 11, 1882	Sim	CEM1
Rees	Amanda		Jan. 19, 1856	May 12, 1860	Har	CEM1
Rees	Amelia	G.	Sep. 29, 1892	Feb. 2, 1898	Har	CEM1
Rees	Amelia		May 15, 1841	Feb. 15, 1903	Har	CEM1
Rees	Carrie	M.	Nov. 21, 1877	Jan. 28, 1886	Har	CEM1
Rees	Eliza		Mar. 15, 1812	Jun. 30, 1890	Har	CEM1
Rees	Ethel		1880	1967	Har	CEM1
Rees	Hyson	T.	Jun. 8, 1842	Sep. 23, 1924	Har	CEM1
Rees	Hyson		Apr. 4, 1864	Jan. 14, 1895	Har	CEM1
Rees	I.	N.	Dec. 26, 1828	Nov. 11, 1891	Har	CEM1
Rees	Louise		1887	1919	Har	CEM1
Rees	Mary		Apr. 22, 1863	Nov. 23, 1954	Har	CEM1
Rees	Mary	J.	Jan. 10, 1847	Apr. 16, 1886	Har	CEM1
Rees	Rhodes		1885	19??	Har	CEM1
Rees	Willie		Aug. 29, 1870	Jun.25, 1875	Har	CEM1
Reesor	Jack	B.	Aug. 28, 1931	May 25, 1953	KY	KMIL
Reeves	A.	W.	Sep. 3, 1860	Jul. 6, 1919	Ful	CEM4
Reeves	Baby of Jas.			Sep. 9, 1887	Muh	Ch1
Reeves	Ethel		May 22, 1907		Car	C1
Reeves	Huron			Feb. 22, 1889	Muh	Ch1
Reeves	Orman	G.	1901ca	Sep. 9, 1979	Jef	MCDR
Reid	Lloyd	W.	1931	Sep. 7, 1951	KY	KMIL
Reidel	Walter		1874ca	Aug. 8, 1904	Brk	C1

Last Name	First Name	I	Birth	Death	Co	Source
Remine	Samuel		1765ca		NWS5	1/12/1793
Render	John Wilson		1837		But	Bk1
Renfro	Edward		1822		But	Bk1
Reynolds	D.		Nov. 30, 1839		Gray	C2
Reynolds	John Wesley		1835		Web	Bk1
Reynolds	Quarter Master			1791ca	NWS5	11/12/1791
Rhoades	America	W.	Sep. 7, 1854	Oct. 8, 1883	Muh	CEM3
Rhoades	D.	W.	Jul. 20, 1847	Aug. 9, 1924	Muh	CEM3
Rhoades (Tompkins)	Maria	D.	1819ca	Jul. 7, 1878	Brk	C1
Rhoden	Troy	V.	Apr. 25, 1904		Car	C1
Rhodes	B.	W.	Jun. 11, 1805	Jul. 31, 1887	Muh	CEM3
Rhodes	Barney	A.	1880	1940	Muh	CEM3
Rhodes	Mary		Aug. 29, 1808	Aug. 12, 1855	Muh	CEM3
Rice	Chester		1930	Dec. 12, 1950	KY	KMIL
Rice	Humphrey		1821ca	Nov. 24, 1854	Brk	C1
Rice	J.	L.	1835		Web	Bk1
Rice	John	H.	1808ca	Sep. 14, 1845	NWS4	9/18/1835
Rice	Julia			1835	NWS4	8/14/1835
Rice	Lizzie	E.	1890ca		Grn	Marr1
Rice	Miss Lura			Sep. 27, 1887	Muh	Ch1
Rich	Alfred		1811ca	Jul. 11, 1843	NWS1	6/24/1843
Richards	Ben	H.	Jan. 8, 1871	Mar. 28, 1901	Hdn	CEM2
Richards	Charles Hugh		1885	1963	Hdn	CEM2
Richards	D.	H.	1844	1930	Hdn	CEM2
Richards	David	H.	Nov. 19, 1898	Jun. 17, 1902	Hdn	CEM2
Richards	Davie		Aug. 31, 1882	Jul. 30, 1883	Hdn	CEM2
Richards	Docata		1850ca	Jul. 23, 1852	Grn	C1
Richards	Elizabeth		1824ca	May 3, 1884	Har	Cem1
Richards	Estella	M.	1887ca		Grn	Marr1
Richards	Grace	E.	1889ca		Grn	Marr1
Richards	J.	H.	1872	1924	Hdn	CEM2
Richards	James	D.	1857	1938	Hdn	CEM2
Richards	James	M.	Apr. 22, 1851	Feb. 23, 1914	Hdn	CEM2
Richards	John	R.	Feb. 21, 1817	Dec. 10, 1909	Hdn	CEM2
Richards	Josephine White		Dec. 24, 1843		Sim	CEM1
Richards	Louisa		Apr. 9, 1824	Sep. 17, 1901	Hdn	CEM2
Richards	Margaret		1839ca	Nov. 9, 1877	Grn	C2
Richards	R.	P.	Jun. 7, 1837	Mar. 4, 1864	Sim	CEM1
Richards	Sophia	M.	1848	1931	Hdn	CEM2
Richards	William	W.	1805ca	Dec. 23, 1854	Dav	C1
Richardson	A.	F.	1864	1934	Hdn	CEM2
Richardson	Clarence		Mar. 23, 1867	Dec. 24, 1948	Hdn	CEM2
Richardson	Daisy		Mar. 29, 1879	Oct. 11, 1907	Muh	CEM3
Richardson	Ella		Jun. 16, 1858	Oct. 15, 1935	Hdn	CEM1
Richardson	Fowler		1894	1975	Hdn	CEM2
Richardson	Hattie	L.	1869	1950	Hdn	CEM2
Richardson	Henry	M.	May 19, 1847	Nov. 25, 1916	Hdn	CEM2

Last Name	First Name	I	Birth	Death	Co	Source
Richardson	J. Burch		Mar. 23, 1881	Sep. 3, 1948	Hdn	CEM2
Richardson	James	D.	1857	1938	Hdn	CEM2
Richardson	Jane	W.	1840	1911	Hdn	CEM1
Richardson	Jerry		1849ca	Dec. 10, 1874	Brk	C1
Richardson	John		Aug. 27, 1904	Jan. 25, 1926	Hdn	CEM2
Richardson	Joseph Duncan		1833	1922	Hdn	CEM1
Richardson	Katie		Feb. 1, 1876	Oct. 15, 1888	Dav	CEM2
Richardson	Landie		1778ca		NWS5	10/31/1795
Richardson	Lucretia		Oct. 7, 1862	Dec. 31, 1927	Hdn	CEM1
Richardson	Maria		1846ca	Oct. 23, 1874	Brk	C1
Richardson	Mary	S.	Jan. 4, 1871	Jan. 30, 1939	Hdn	CEM2
Richardson	S. Birtie		Dec. 13, 1880	Mar. 7, 1900	Dav	CEM2
Richardson	Tom			Jun. 3, 1949	Hdn	CEM3
Richardson	Vira		Jan. 23, 1861	Jul. 23, 1943	Hdn	CEM2
Richardson	Virginia		1897		Hdn	CEM2
Richardson	Wm. Edward		Oct. 13, 1905	Aug. 18, 1905	Muh	CEM3
Richardson	Myrtle Lyddan		Nov. 19, 1890	Jul. 18, 1973	Hdn	CEM2
Richey	John		1746		All	RP1
Richmond	James	C.	1795ca	Oct. ??, 1856	Dav	C1
Riddle	James	W.	1928	Apr. 22, 1951	KY	KMIL
Rider	Dollie	D.	1868	1915	Hdn	CEM2
Rider	George	M.	1870	1933	Hdn	CEM2
Rider	Nora	V.	Sep. 7, 1872	Oct. 28, 1953	Hdn	CEM2
Rider	R.	L.	1867	1922	Hdn	CEM2
Rider	Robert Lamar		1920	1920	Hdn	CEM2
Riffe	Addie		1883ca		Grn	Marr1
Riffe	William	N.		Oct. ??, 1877	Grn	C2
Riffle	Alice		1880ca		Grn	Marr1
Riggle	Ralph	T.	Mar. 18, 1901	Oct. 23, 1901	Har	Cem1
Riggle	William	T.	Oct. 17, 1918	Nov. 9, 1918	Har	Cem1
Riggs	Charles			Aug. 23, 1845	NWS1	9/6/1845
Rile	Mrs. Maranda			Aug. 11, 1886	Muh	Ch1
Riley	Elizabeth			Nov. ??, 1854	Bre	C1
Riley	George		1928	Dec. 10, 1953	KY	KMIL
Riley	Jane		1803ca	Dec. 15, 1858	Bre	C1
Riley	John	D.	1866ca	Nov. 16, 1878	Brk	C1
Riley	Martha		1864ca	Nov. 20, 1878	Brk	C1
Riley	Mary		1868ca	Dec. 15, 1874	Brk	C1
Riley	William		1851ca	Oct. 3, 1852	Bre	C1
Rinehart	William Edgar		Jul. 12, 1929	Jun. 3, 1951	KY	KMIL
Ring	Murrell	B.	Oct. 28, 1810	Mar. 7, 1858	Ful	CEM3
Rivers	Edwin Eugene		Jul. 20, 1919	Sep. 29, 1950	KY	KMIL
Rives	James	T.	1840		But	Bk1
Roach	Margaret		May 2, 1827	Nov. 30, 1923	Dav	CEM2
Roach	Ruth		1769ca	Mar. 27, 1852	Grn	C1
Roach	William		Sep. 4, 1818	Jul. 6, 1900	Dav	CEM2
Roark	Alice	R.		Jul. 17, 1911	Fay	MCDR

Last Name	First Name	I	Birth	Death	Co	Source
Roark	Alvis	K.	1874ca	Mar. 27, 1946	Fay	MCDR
Roark	Amanda	J.	1889ca	Mar. 5, 1928	All	MCDR
Roark	Amelia		1863ca	Nov. 24, 1925	Muh	MCDR
Roark	Anga		1901ca	Jan. 28, 1964	Sim	MCDR
Robards	katie		1878ca	Jan. 20, 1904	Brk	C1
Robbins	Sarah			1878	Brk	C1
Roberson	Unknown Male			Mar. 7, 1875	Bre	C1
Robert	Henry		1829ca	Jan. 7, 1853	Dav	C1
Robert (Slave)			1835ca	Jun. 2, 1855	Brk	C1
Roberts	Alice			Mar. 3, 1852	Grn	C1
Roberts	Charles	E.	Nov. 10, 1904	Oct. 11, 1970	Hdn	CEM2
Roberts	Cyria		1789ca	Apr. 15, 1852	Brk	C1
Roberts	Ella	M.	1883ca		Grn	Marr1
Roberts	Henry	N.	1800ca	Sep. 17, 1857	Dav	C1
Roberts	James			Feb. 24, 1853	Brk	C1
Roberts	John	J.	1822ca	Jun. 23, 1853	Brk	C1
Roberts	Lizzie		Jun. 8, 1868	Sep. 27, 1907	Sim	CEM1
Roberts	Margaret		1788ca	Dec. 9, 1855	Dav	C1
Roberts	Mary Ann		1811ca	Feb. 27, 1853	Dav	C1
Roberts	Mrs. John			1835	NWS4	8/14/1835
Roberts	Thomas	J.	Aug. 10, 1885	Jan. 27, 1918	Ful	CEM7
Roberts	Unknown Male			Nov. 28, 1875	Bre	C1
Roberts	Wade	H.	Jun. 25, 1877	Jun. 21, 1962	Hdn	CEM2
Roberts	Wesley		1811ca	Jul. 25, 1853	Dav	C1
Roberts (Monin)	Anna		Aug. 14, 1903		Hdn	CEM2
Roberts (Neighbors)	Bertha		Sep. 26, 1886	Jul. 1, 1944	Hdn	CEM2
Roberts (Ray)	Marinda		1823ca	Sep. 12, 1852	Brk	C1
Robertson	Jane		1841ca	Sep. 15, 1852	Brk	C1
Robertson	Jerome	B.	Mar. 14, 1815		KY	Bk1(P548)T
Robertson	R.		1864ca	Apr. ??, 1894	Brk	C1
Robertson	Sherril			Aug. 23, 1949	Fay	MCDR
Robertson	Susan		1851ca	Aug. 5, 1852	Brk	C1
Robertson	Thomas	R.	1929	Dec. 2, 1950	KY	KMIL
Robertson (Hayden)	Mary Ann		1830ca	Apr. 2, 1852	Brk	C1
Robinson	Avian		1874ca	Aug. 18, 1878	Brk	C1
Robinson	Horace		Jan. 2, 1871	Jan. 24, 1931	Hdn	CEM2
Robinson	Jennie		Dec. 28, 1870	Nov. 12, 1958	Hdn	CEM2
Robinson	Joe		1930	Aug. 18, 1950	KY	KMIL
Robinson	John	H.	1862	1945	Hdn	CEM2
Robinson	Lawrence		Sep. 17, 1902	Mar. 20, 1920	Hdn	CEM2
Robinson	Mary	E.	Sep. ??, 1839	May 28, 1898	Hdn	CEM2
Robinson	Minnie		1895ca		Grn	Marr1
Robinson	Mrs. Mildred	E.	Jun. 29, 1797	Dec. 24, 1883	NWS2	12/26/1883
Robinson	Nannie	E.	May 25, 1860	Sep. 8, 1910	Hdn	CEM2
Robinson	Samuel	F.	1921	Sep. 18, 1952	KY	KMIL
Robinson	Stanley	E.	1929	Aug. 11,, 1952	KY	KMIL
Robinson	Thomas Griffin			Oct. 31, ??01	Cal	CEM1

Last Name	First Name	I	Birth	Death	Co	Source
Robinson	Victoria		1877	1938	Hdn	CEM2
Robits	Alex			Jul. 22, 1852	Brk	C1
Robrie	Godfrey W.	B.	1851ca	Aug. 22, 1858	Brk	C1
Robson	Charlotte		Aug. 5, 1824	Sep. 14, 1904	Har	Cem1
Roburson (Jarred)	Bettie	A.	1834ca	Aug. 7, 1878	Brk	C1
Roby (Hibbs)	Joan		Jan. 24, 1863	Jan. 24, 1939	Hdn	CEM2
Rockwell	Helena		1888ca		Grn	Marr1
Rockwell	Jessie		1882ca		Grn	Marr1
Rodgers	James	S.	Feb. 1, 1867	Jan. 7, 1913	Ful	CEM7
Rodgers	Mary	L.	Nov. 7, 1847	Jan. 3, 1912	Ful	CEM7
Rodgers	Rev. J.	A.	Oct. 18, 1838	Jul. 10, 1903	Ful	CEM7
Rodgers	Will	C.	1882	1924	Ful	CEM7
Roe	Eva		1892ca		Grn	Marr1
Roe	Mary	N.	1897ca		Grn	Marr1
Rogers	Carrie	B	Aug. 19, 1873	Oct. 27, 1963	Dav	CEM1
Rogers	Joseph Lee		14-May-32	Jun. 16, 1951	KY	KMIL
Rogers	Roy	M	Nov. 24, 1871	Feb. 07, 1948	Dav	CEM1
Rogers (McGuffin)	Lillie		1904	1934	Hdn	CEM3
Rogers, Sr.	H.	C.	Apr. 22, 1826		Gray	C2
Roll	Abraham		May 27, 1798	Jan. 30,1838	Muh	CEM3
Roll	D.	B.	Sep. 16, 1827	Apr. 8, 1898	Muh	CEM3
Roll	D.	F.	May 8, 1864	Aug. 14, 1904	Muh	CEM3
Roll	E.	A.	Nov. 11, 1833	Sep. 5, 18??	Muh	CEM3
Roll	Edward		Mar. 20, 1883	Aug. 28, 1883	Muh	CEM3
Roll	Essie D. Moore		Jan. 29, 1853	May 20, 18??	Muh	CEM3
Roll	Fannie Duncan		Apr. 14, 1825	Sep. 8, 1876	Muh	CEM3
Roll	J.	W.	1860	1940	Muh	CEM3
Roll	M.	F.	1871	1935	Muh	CEM3
Roll	Martha	T.	1837	18?2	Muh	CEM3
Roll	Melissa		Dec. 2, 1852	Mar. 16, 1864	Muh	CEM3
Roll	Michael		1820ca	1838	Muh	CEM3
Roll	Michael		Jun. 30, 1829	Feb. 25, 1890	Muh	CEM3
Roll	Minnie		Sep. 9, 1871	Jul. 20, 1908	Muh	CEM3
Roll	Nancy		Feb. 14, 1828	Jul. 13, 1855	Muh	CEM3
Roll	Nannie	A.	Jun. 17, 1855	Jul. 16, 1902	Muh	CEM3
Roll	Rachel	D.	Apr. 26, 1853	Apr. 6, 1883	Muh	CEM3
Roll	Rachel	V.	Aug. 28, 1807	Jan. 23, 1881	Muh	CEM3
Roll	Rachel		1857		Muh	CEM3
Roll	Ranney	H.	Jul. 3, 1850	Dec. 17, 1920	Muh	CEM3
Roll	Rosa		1866	1940	Muh	CEM3
Roll	Thomas	F.	1835	1859	Muh	CEM3
Roll	Thomas	J.	Jan. 8, 1852	Apr. 9, 1896	Muh	CEM3
Roll	V. ،	R.	No Date	No Date	Muh	CEM3
Roll	W. H. Morton		1855	1917	Muh	CEM3
Roll	William	P.	Mar. 1, 1858	Dec. 11, 1887	Muh	CEM3
Rollins	Jonathan		1815ca	Mar. 1, 1877	Grn	C2
Rollins	Lewis		1848ca	Oct. 9, 1894	Brk	C1

Last Name	First Name	I	Birth	Death	Co	Source
Rolly	Jinnie		1857ca	Sep. 3, 1877	Bre	C1
Rone	Adam		1847		But	Bk1
Roper	Aubrey		1882	1954	Ful	CEM7
Roper	Eugenia		1889	19??	Ful	CEM7
Rorer	Clarence		1890	1892	Har	CEM1
Rorer	Clinton		May 4, 1866	Aug. 13, 1867	Har	CEM1
Rorer	Cynthia		Feb. 9, 1859	Oct. 26, 1860	Har	CEM1
Rorer	F.	A.	Mar. 11, 1825	Mar. 12, 1882	Har	CEM1
Rorer	Thomas	R.	Jan. 16, 1824	Oct. 29, 1878	Har	CEM1
Rork	William	G.	1859		Web	Bk1
Rose	Alice Jane		Aug. 5, 1855	Oct. 9, 1924	Har	Cem1
Rose	Damon	L.	1930	Dec. 12, 1950	KY	KMIL
Rose	Sarah	E.	Jun. 13, 1842	Feb. 10, 1907	Har	Cem1
Rose	William	B.	1846ca	Oct. 30, 1858	Bre	C1
Roseberry	John		Oct. 7, 1798	Mar. 17, 1880	Hen	CEM1
Roses	Anderson		1824ca	Sep. 1, 1878	Bre	C1
Ross	Charlotte		1883ca		Grn	Marr1
Ross	Clara		Oct. 17, 1893	Jan. 2, 1929	Ful	CEM7
Ross	Estella		1871	1934	Muh	CEM3
Ross	J. Wing		1867	1931	Muh	CEM3
Ross	James		1765ca		NWS5	1/12/1793
Ross	Ollie		Nov. 9, 1891		Ful	CEM7
Ross	Shapley	P.	Jan. 18, 1811		KY	Bk1(P524)T
Ross	Unknown			Jul. 7, 1918	Ful	CEM7
Ross, Jr.	Frank	J.	Feb. 3, 1926		Har	Cem1
Roth	Xavier		1826ca	Apr. 23, 1915	Cam	MCDR
Rouse	Hannah		1878ca		Grn	Marr1
Rowan	Mary	E.	1870ca		Grn	Marr1
Rowe	Edward Earl		Jun. 23, 1930	Sep. 7, 1952	KY	KMIL
Rowland	Bertha		1881ca		Grn	Marr1
Rowland (Pruett)	Martha		1799ca	Jul. 23, 1853	Dav	C1
Roy	Charles	A.	1909	Nov. 5, 1950	KY	KMIL
Royalty	Thuday			Dec. 13, 1878	Brk	C1
Royster	Elvira		1856	1940	Hen	CEM1
Royster	Lucy Ann		1849	1927	Hen	CEM1
Royster	Nancy		1886ca		Grn	Marr1
Royster	Theodore		1850	1927	Hen	CEM1
Royster	Thomas		1848	1887	Hen	CEM1
Rual	Mary	B.	1809ca	May 30, 1855	Brk	C1
Ruark	Mary	J	Aug. 11, 1829	May 3, 1911	Lew	CEM1
Rucker	Boyd		Jan. 1, 1907		Car	C1
Rud	John	G.	1847ca	Nov. 10, 1854	Brk	C1
Rudder	David Newton		1850	1935	Har	CEM1
Rudder	Ella	E.	1883	1969	Har	CEM1
Rudder	George	K.	1883	1963	Har	CEM1
Rudder	Ida	E.	1878	1972	Har	CEM1
Rudder	Marguerite	L.	1898	19??	Har	CEM1

Last Name	First Name	I	Birth	Death	Co	Source
Rudder	Sandie	T.	1880	1954	Har	CEM1
Rudder	Virginia McCue		1855	1937	Har	CEM1
Rudy	Pof. Jacob	A.	1851		Web	Bk1
Ruiz	Eugen Louis		Jun. 28, 1923	Jun. 27, 1923	KY	KMIL
Rundy	Pearl		1882ca		Grn	Marr1
Runner	Alex.	C.	1825		But	Bk1
Rush	Eliza Jane		Jun. 27, 1852	Aug. 1, 1872	Sim	CEM1
Rush	F.	M.	Jul. 23, 1843	Nov. 26, 1923	Sim	CEM1
Rush	Female		Aug. 9, 1903	Sep. 9, 1903	Sim	CEM1
Rush	G.	W.	Sep. 28, 1871	Jul. 9, 1939	Sim	CEM1
Rush	Guy Earl		1900ca	Aug. 27, 1946	Sim	CEM1
Rush	Maud		Nov. 28, 1878	Jun. 26, 1901	Sim	CEM1
Rush	Samuel	H.	1839		But	Bk1
Rush	W.	W.	Jul. 9, 1869	Oct. 18, 1872	Sim	CEM1
Russ	Orman			Sep. 16, 1950	Jef	MCDR
Russ	Orman	K.	1895ca	Mar. 6, 1971	Jef	MCDR
Russel	Unknown Male			Mar. 22, 1876	Bre	C1
Russell	B.	C.	1835ca	Sep. 11, 1857	Dav	C1
Russell	F.	M.	1846		Web	Bk1
Russell	Nancy		1874ca	Jun. 13, 1877	Bre	C1
Russell	W. J.	F.	1842		Web	Bk1
Russell (King)	Eliza	A.	1804ca	Oct. 13, 1855	Dav	C1
Ruth	Thomas		Dec. 12, 1907		Car	C1
Rutherford	Johnnie	B.	1928	Aug. 4, 1950	KY	KMIL
Ruthford	Bertha		1885ca		Grn	Marr1
Rutledge	Baby of Rosie			Aug. 30, 1884	Muh	Ch1
Rutledge	Jefferson		1831ca	Sep. ??, 1857	Dav	C1
Ryals	Emanuel		1865ca	Mar. 5, 1912	Ken	MCDR
Ryan	Saml.	M.	1877ca	Nov. 23, 1878	Brk	C1
Ryley	John		1766ca		NWS5	5/19/1792
Saitzer	Cora		1877	Feb. 13, 1878	Brk	C1
Saitzer	Mollie		1855ca	Apr. 30, 1878	Brk	C1
Sallee	Raymod		1906	Jul. 16, 1950	KY	KMIL
Salmons	Nora	W.	1894ca		Grn	Marr1
Saltonstall	G.	F.	1760ca	Jan. 30, 1836	NWS4	2/13/1836
Saltsman (Chance)	Mary	A.	1854ca	Dec. 2, 1878	Brk	C1
Salyer	Nancie		1882ca		Grn	Marr1
Salyer	Virgie		1886ca		Grn	Marr1
Salzer	Adam			Jul. 1, 1876	Bre	C1
Sammons	Randall	G.	1921	May 24, 1951	KY	KMIL
Sammons	Vernal		Jun. 1, 1907		Car	C1
Samms	Jack	C.	1928	Jul. 20, 1950	KY	KMIL
Samples	Quarter Master			1791ca	NWS5	11/12/1791
Sampson	George	L.	1922	Feb. 13, 1951	KY	KMIL
Sampson	James	W.	1931	Feb. 12, 1951	KY	KMIL
Sams	M.	J.	Jan. 21, 1846	Aug. 29, 1902	Ful	CEM7
Sams	T.	G.	May 10, 1828	Dec. 7, 1915	Ful	CEM7

Last Name	First Name	I	Birth	Death	Co	Source
Sandefur	James	B.	1932	Jul. 25, 1950	KY	KMIL
Sanders	Jennings Bryan		Oct. 6, 1898	Nov. 10, 1898	Hdn	CEM2
Sanders	Madison		1850ca	Sep. 28, 1878	Brk	C1
Sandlin	John		1826ca	Dec 13, 1858	Bre	C1
Sandlin	Theopholis			Jan. 15, 1858	Bre	C1
Sands	Col. William	L.		1835	NWS4	8/14/1835
Sands	R.	V.	Oct. 22, 1835		Gray	C2
Sands	Sarah			1835	NWS4	8/14/1835
Sapington	Thomas			1845	NWS1	5/24/1845
Sarah (Slave)			1842ca	Aug. 18, 1854	Brk	C1
Sarah Ellen (Slave)				Jun. 27, 1861	Brk	C1
Satterfield	Allen		1866ca	Dec. 29, 1903	Brk	C1
Satterfield	James	H.	1839		But	Bk1
Saunders	John	S.	Sep. 22, 1826		Other	Bk1(P409)T
Savage	Mary Elizabeth		1821ca	May 27, 1845	NWS1	6/7/1845
Savill	Daniel		1828ca	Nov. 23, 1843	NWS1	11/25/1843
Scharedein	William		1932	Jun. 24, 1953	KY	KMIL
Schildmeyer	Albert	F.	Jun. 16, 1932	Jul. 15, 1953	KY	KMIL
Schmidt	Charles		Mar. 5, 1867	May 16, 1940	Hdn	CEM2
Schmidt (Bush)	Nannie		Jan. 5, 1879	Apr. 12, 1962	Hdn	CEM2
Schmitt	Francis	G.	1929	Sep. 2, 1951	KY	KMIL
Schweingruber	Bobby		1931	Jul. 16, 1950	KY	KMIL
Scott	Annie	E.	Feb. 16, 1865	Dec. 9, 1941	Ful	CEM4
Scott	Charlie	B.	Sep. 13, 1901	Jul. 9, 1902	Hdn	CEM2
Scott	Cyrne		1846ca	Aug. 6, 1852	Brk	C1
Scott	Elisha	G.	Dec. 5, 1853	Nov. 5, 1930	Hdn	CEM2
Scott	Elisha Boyd		Jul. 14, 1914	Apr. 8, 1916	Hdn	CEM2
Scott	Elizabeth Ann		Apr. 28, 1861	Feb. 26, 1936	Hdn	CEM2
Scott	Female		Feb. 17, 1917	Fewb. 17, 1917	Hdn	CEM2
Scott	Frances		Oct. 14, 1843	May 29, 1892	Hdn	CEM1
Scott	Francis Jane		1843ca	Apr. 9, 1852	Brk	C1
Scott	Isham	C.	1887	1953	Ful	CEM4
Scott	James	L.	Jul. 10, 1868	Apr. 18, 1885	Hdn	CEM1
Scott	John	F.	Dec. 8, 1859	Aug. 24, 1942	Ful	CEM4
Scott	Joseph Clara		Dec. 17, 1863	Aug. 17, 1877	Hdn	CEM1
Scott	Laura	A.	1856ca	Apr. 30, 1858	Brk	C1
Scott	Leo Virgil		Nov. 18, 1885	Nov. 2, 1938	Hdn	CEM2
Scott	Maggie Lee		1893	1917	Ful	CEM4
Scott	Rachel		1813ca	Jun. 24, 1861	Brk	C1
Scott	Robert	F.	1931	Aug. 23, 1950	KY	KMIL
Scott	Samuel		Feb. 23, 1798	Mar. 16, 1873	Hdn	CEM1
Scott	Sasepto		1819ca	Sep. 18, 1854	Brk	C1
Scott	Lucretia Ellen	D.	May 27, 1838	Dec. 2, 1876	Hdn	CEM1
Scott (Boyd)	Blanche		Nov. 2, 1885	Dec. 17, 1931	Hdn	CEM2
Scott (Woods)	Addie	H.	1853ca	Feb. 26, 1875	Brk	C1
Sears	George		May 12, 1889	Jun. 5, 1920	Muh	CEM3
Sears	John	F.	May 16, 1877	Apr. 21, 1900	Muh	CEM3

Last Name	First Name	I	Birth	Death	Co	Source
Sears	Joseph			Feb. 23, 1835	All	RP1
Sears	Norma		Aug. 4, 1850	Jun. 7, 1933	Muh	CEM3
Sears	Sally	F.	Aug. 19, 1849	Jan. 21, 1937	Muh	CEM3
Sears	Thomas	E.	Oct. 7, 1939	Nov. 30, 1939	Muh	CEM3
Seat	Ada Lee		Feb. 20, 1873	Dec. 24, 1942	Ful	CEM7
Seat	John L.	D.	Dec. 3, 1870	Mar. 20, 1915	Ful	CEM7
Seaton	Auston			Nov. 6, 1876	Brk	C1
Sebashan	Benjamin		1836ca	Sep. 28, 1857	Bre	C1
Sebastian	Ed			Mar. 2, 1877	Bre	C1
Sebastian	Sally		1804ca	Aug. 28, 1874	Bre	C1
Sebastian (Johnson)	Polly		1836ca	Aug. 5, 1874	Bre	C1
Sebastin	Lewis			Apr. 2, 1853	Bre	C1
Secrest	Emma	L.	1885ca		Grn	Marr1
Self	Frank		Jul. ??, 1896	Nov. ??, 1960	Hdn	CEM2
Self	Jennie		Apr. ??, 1901	Nov. ??, 1977	Hdn	CEM2
Self	Robert		1921	1936	Hdn	CEM2
Sevier	Reuben Jackmon			1835	NWS4	8/14/1835
Sewell	Benjamin			Sep. 1, 1859	Bre	C1
Sewell	M.	E.	1833ca	Aug. 24, 1861	Dav	C1
Sewell	Unknown Female			Jun. 16, 1854	Bre	C1
Sewell	Unknown Male			Oct. 2, 1855	Bre	C1
Sewell	William		1828ca	Dec. 27, 1855	Bre	C1
Sexton	Chas.		Mar. 20, 1907		Car	C1
Shackelford	A.	F.	1795ca	Feb. 23, 1857	Bre	C1
Shackelford	Cegilda			Jan. 26, 1854	Bre	C1
Shackelford	Mary	J.	1854ca	Mar. 26, 1855	Bre	C1
Shackleford (Hufake)	Mariam		1827ca	Nov. 1, 1852	Bre	C1
Shacky	Millie		1863ca	Aug. 9, 1877	Bre	C1
Shadwick	Amos	R.	1838ca	Jan. 22, 1853	Dav	C1
Shain	Edward	E.	Mar. 21, 1839		Gray	C2
Sharer	James Edw.		1846		But	Bk1
Sharp	Absolem	M.		Sep. 10, 1835	NWS4	9/18/1835
Sharp	Felix	G.	1930	Sep. 4, 1951	KY	KMIL
Sharp	Hiram		1855ca	Dec. 12, 1858	Brk	C1
Sharp	Isono		1797ca	Aug. 31, 1854	Brk	C1
Shaw	Billy	D.	1929	Oct. 18, 1951	KY	KMIL
Shaw	Elizabeth		1837ca	Aug. 10, 1854	Brk	C1
Shaw	Kenneth	R.	1929	Sep. 0\6, 1950	KY	KMIL
Shaw	Thomas	W.	Sep. 10, 1851	Feb. 12, 1881	Hdn	CEM2
Sheets	Elbert	H.	1897	1957	Hdn	CEM2
Sheets	Stella	M.	1896		Hdn	CEM2
Sheffield (Tob)	Mary		1783ca	Sep. 7, 1854	Bre	C1
Shelby	H.	W.	May 16, 1802	Nov. 19, 1880	Ful	CEM7
Shelman	Letitia		1850ca	Jul. 5, 1852	Brk	C1
Shelton	Baby of Bill			Jun. 27, 1887	Muh	Ch1
Shelton	R.	R.	Oct. 23, 1858	Feb. 20, 1910	Ful	CEM7
Sheraer	Velmer		1929	Oct. 25, 1951	KY	KMIL

Kentucky Birth and Death Records, Vol. One

Last Name	First Name	I	Birth	Death	Co	Source
Sherill	Henrietta		1907ca	Oct. 22, 1974	Fay	MCDR
Sherill	Nannie		1868ca	Aug. 28, 1936	Ada	MCDR
Sherm	Harriett		1831ca	May 11, 1856	Brk	C1
Sherry	William		1744		All	RP1
Shewmaker	John William		Jun. 21, 1925	Dec. 31, 1953	KY	KMIL
Shivell	Charley	W.	Sep. 13, 1859	Dec. 11, 1887	Hdn	CEM2
Shivell	E. Miles		May 28, 1857	Jul. 24, 1884	Hdn	CEM2
Shivell	Thomas	F.	Feb. 12, 1828	Jun. 24, 1900	Hdn	CEM2
Shivell (Miles)	Miranda		Jun. 27, 1833	Feb. 25, 1902	Hdn	CEM2
Shively	Charles		Mar. 15, 1883	Dec. 19, 1883	Hdn	CEM1
Shively	R.	L.	Aug. 16, 1877	Dec. 22, 1877	Hdn	CEM1
Shoemaker	Cynthia		1794ca	Jul. 16, 1857	Dav	C1
Shope	Marinda		1892ca		Grn	Marr1
Shope	Emma		1882ca		Grn	Marr1
Short	Sally			Mar. 15, 1875	Bre	C1
Shrewsberry	Elizabeth		1810ca	Jan. 19, 1878	Brk	C1
Shrewsberry	J.	B.		1894	Brk	C1
Shrewsberry	Unknown Male			1894	Brk	C1
Shuck	Capt. W.	A.	Apr. 16, 1839	Aug. 7, 1926	Ful	CEM1
Shuck	Jannie Louise		Jul. 5, 1886	Jan. 26, 1902	Ful	CEM1
Shuck	Mary Louise		Apr. 21, 1878	Sep. 24, 1938	Ful	CEM1
Shulty	William			1852	Brk	C1
Shultz	Cyrus	C.	1854		But	Bk1
Shursher	Unknown Female			Feb. 15, 1858	Bre	C1
Sigler	Jennie		Jul. 26, 1853	Aug. 26, 1912	Hen	CEM1
Simions	George	F.		1852	Brk	C1
Simions	Marcus	F.		1852	Brk	C1
Simmons	Alva			Nov. 26, 1878	Brk	C1
Simpson	Charles	L.	1929	Dec. 12, 1950	KY	KMIL
Simpson	Elizabeth		1887ca		Grn	Marr1
Simpson	Isaac	P.	Apr. 24, 1832		KY	Bk1(P374)T
Simpson	Samuel	R.	1906	Nov. 30, 1950	KY	KMIL
Sisco	Bill		1894ca	Mar. 2, 1956	All	MCDR
Sisco	Clarie	N.	1860ca	Sep. 3, 1944	All	MCDR
Sizemore	Clifford		1929	Mar. 8, 1953	KY	KMIL
Sizemore	Felix		1831ca	Aug. 10, 1858	Bre	C1
Sizemore	Isabell		1855ca	Apr. 16, 1875	Bre	C1
Sizemore	John			Jul. 10, 1874	Bre	C1
Sizemore	Lizzie		1886ca		Grn	Marr1
Sizemore	Melda		1861ca		Grn	Marr1
Sizemore (Groce)	Susannah		1832ca	May 12, 1853	Bre	C1
Skaggs	Alice	B.	Aug. 18, 1869	Dec. 30, 1921	Hdn	CEM2
Skaggs	Charlotte	E.	Mar. 30, 1845	Jul. 29, 1919	Hdn	CEM2
Skaggs	Emerson		Nov. 12, 1866	Mar. 10, 1953	Hdn	CEM2
Skaggs	Lottie		Aug. 8, 1877	Jul. 26, 1878	Hdn	CEM2
Skaggs	Mary	E.	Apr. 15, 1879	Feb. 10, 1966	Hdn	CEM2
Skaggs	Robert Taylor		Aug. 27, 1884	Feb. 29, 1888	Hdn	CEM2

116

Last Name	First Name	I	Birth	Death	Co	Source
Skillman	Abraham		1796ca	Dec. 5, 1878	Brk	C1
Skillman	Lucy Lellen	E.	1841ca	Feb. 21, 1852	Brk	C1
Skillman (Moorman)	Fannie	F.	1816ca	Sep. 10, 1876	Brk	C1
Skillman (Slave)	Katey		1788ca	Oct. ??, 1858	Brk	C1
Skrobanek	Charles		1929	Oct. 3, 1951	KY	KMIL
Slaton	Bettie			May 6, 1904	Brk	C1
Slaughter	Catherine	L.	1913	1913	Hdn	CEM3
Slaughter	James	C.		1835	NWS4	8/14/1835
Slaughter	Robert	E.		Mar. 29, 1937	Hdn	CEM3
Slone	Kate		1885ca		Grn	Marr1
Slone	Mahala		1861ca	Oct. ??, 1877	Grn	C2
Slusher	Ashley Lee		Oct. 27, 18982		Row	CEM1
Slyvester (Slave)			1797ca	1857	Brk	C1
Smalley	Happy	J.	Dec. 11, 1847	May 9. 1922	Har	CEM1
Smalley	Susie Arnold		Sep. 28, 1887	Apr. 9, 1905	Har	CEM1
Smallwood	Howard	I.	1930	Aug. 2, 1950	KY	KMIL
Smawly	Evan		1764ca		NWS5	8/22/1789
Smiley	Laura		1872ca	Nov. 4, 1878	Brk	C1
Smiser	Arthur	D.	Jun. 15, 1872	Sep. 21, 1873	Dav	CEM2
Smiser	William	L.	Nov. 28, 1874	May 6,1875	Dav	CEM2
Smith	????	H.		Aug. 25, 1852	Brk	C1
Smith	Anna		1890ca		Grn	Marr1
Smith	B.	A.	Jul. 20, 1889	Nov. 20, 1903	Ful	CEM4
Smith	B.	A.	1829ca	Sep. 7, 1875	Bre	C1
Smith	Bennie Wade		Mar. 15, 1888	Sep. 15, 1935	Hdn	CEM2
Smith	C.	D.	Mar. 6, 1887	Jun. 9, 1888	Ful	CEM4
Smith	Capt.			1791ca	NWS5	11/12/1791
Smith	Carroll			Nov. 26, 1859	Brk	C1
Smith	Cecil	E.	1929	Jul. 20, 1950	KY	KMIL
Smith	Cerrelda	A.	1862	1946	Har	Cem1
Smith	Charles	E.	1918	Feb. 14, 1951	KY	KMIL
Smith	Daniel	M.	1811		But	Bk1
Smith	David	M.	1926	Sep. 1, 1950	KY	KMIL
Smith	Donald		1933	Nov. 28, 1950	KY	KMIL
Smith	Dr. R.	M.	1837ca	Jun. 9, 1904	Brk	C1
Smith	Dudley		1828ca	Dec. 1, 1857	Brk	C1
Smith	E.	F.	Nov. ??, 1823		Muh	CEM8
Smith	E.	G.	Mar. ??, 1839		Muh	CEM4
Smith	Elizabeth		Aug. 12, 1791	Jun. 17, 1879	Ful	CEM7
Smith	Elizabeth		Jan. 22, 1836	Feb. 20, 1878	Ful	CEM4
Smith	Elvira		1848ca	Sep. 2, 1852	Grn	C1
Smith	F.	S.	Feb. ??, 1832		Muh	CEM5
Smith	Gypsie		1887ca		Grn	Marr1
Smith	H.		Jun. ??, 1842		Muh	CEM6
Smith	Infant			1835	NWS4	8/14/1835
Smith	Isaac		1794ca	Jun. 17, 1854	Brk	C1
Smith	Isom	G.	Nov. 13, 1857	Nov. 28, 1912	Ful	CEM4

Last Name	First Name	I	Birth	Death	Co	Source
Smith	J.	W.	1834		Muh	CEM7
Smith	J.	W.	May 6, 1833		Gray	C2
Smith	Jacob		1812ca	Jun. 27, 1857	Dav	C1
Smith	Jessie Alvin		1930	Oct. 26, 1952	KY	KMIL
Smith	Jo Allen		1859ca	Jan. 13, 1876	Brk	C1
Smith	Joanna		Sep. 2, 1874	Mar. 18, 1937	Ful	CEM4
Smith	Jodias		1852ca	Jan. 2, 1854	Brk	C1
Smith	John		May 3, 1840		Gray	C2
Smith	John	T.		Feb. 11, 1852	Grn	C1
Smith	John	W.	1847		Web	Bk1
Smith	John	W.	Mar. 17, 1868	1946	Ful	CEM4
Smith	John		1766ca		NWS5	6/9/1792
Smith	John		1863ca	Apr. 28, 1878	Brk	C1
Smith	John		1857ca	Jul. 15, 1858	Bre	C1
Smith	Joseph	A.		1835	NWS4	8/14/1835
Smith	Julia	E.	Jun. 10, 1856	Jul. 9, 1892	Ful	CEM4
Smith	Katy		Aug. 31, 1888	Aug. 31, 1906	Ful	CEM4
Smith	Lewis	H.	1847ca	Jan. 17, 1858	Bre	C1
Smith	Lillie	E.	Jun. 13, 1880	Mar. 7, 1892	Ful	CEM4
Smith	Linford		1832ca	Oct. 8, 1855	Brk	C1
Smith	Louis	K.	1929	Jul. 20, 1950	KY	KMIL
Smith	Luella		Sep.30, 1878	Nov. 1, 1918	Ful	CEM4
Smith	M.	F.	Feb. 15, 1867	Dec. 9, 1898	Ful	CEM4
SMith	Manvel		1849ca	Jul. 17, 1852	Brk	C1
Smith	Margaret	E.	1831ca	Aug. 13, 1853	Dav	MCDR
Smith	Margaret		May 30, 1809	Jan. 11, 1855	Muh	CEM3
Smith	Margaret		1891ca		Grn	Marr1
Smith	Marvin	W.	1924	Jun. 6, 1951	KY	KMIL
Smith	Mary	E.	1889ca		Grn	Marr1
Smith	Mrs.			1835	NWS4	8/14/1835
Smith	Myrtle		1875ca	Jan. 4, 1877	Grn	C2
Smith	Owen			Aug. 20, 1835	NWS4	9/4/1835
Smith	Persilia		1832ca	Oct. 18, 1877	Bre	C1
Smith	Rachel	A.	1876ca	Oct. 28, 1878	Brk	C1
Smith	Richard	G.	Aug. 29, 1790	Oct. 29, 1871	Ful	CEM7
Smith	Robert	D.	1856	1925	Har	Cem1
Smith	Robert	E.	1831ca	Aug. 13, 1853	Dav	C1
Smith	Roy	L.	1929	Mar. 21, 1953	KY	KMIL
Smith	Roy	L.	1929	Mar. 21, 1953	KY	KMIL
Smith	Sadie		1890ca		Grn	Marr1
Smith	Samuel		1761		All	RP1
Smith	Samuel		1868ca	May 26, 1878	Bre	C1
Smith	Sarah	S.	Nov. 17, 1830	Dec. 12, 1892	Ful	CEM7
Smith	Stout		1843ca	Apr. 9, 1928	Muh	MCDR
Smith	Susan	M.	1891ca		Grn	Marr1
Smith	Unknown Male			Dec. 11, 1855	Bre	C1
Smith	Virgil	J.	1932	Sep. 1, 1951	KY	KMIL

Last Name	First Name	I	Birth	Death	Co	Source
Smith	Wiley		Aug. 8, 1830	Jun. 23, 1900	Ful	CEM4
Smith	Wilford	L.	Jun. 18, 1869	Apr. 20, 1912	Ful	CEM4
Smith	William	H.	1929	Jul. 22. 1950	KY	KMIL
Smith	William Dotson		Jul. 20, 1830	Nov. 24, 1898	Ful	CEM7
Smith	Willie	M.	1922	Aug. 1, 1952	KY	KMIL
Smith	Sanford		1824ca	Jan. 1, 1879	Brk	C1
Smith (Dyer)	Rachel	C.	1841ca	Aug. 23, 1878	Brk	C1
Smoot	Billie	K.	Dec. 22, 1932	Nov. 11, 1933	Row	CEM1
Sneed	Eother	L.	1926	Oct. 7, 1951	KY	KMIL
Snider	J.	M.	Nov. 29, 1828		Gray	C2
Snoddy	Harriett			Aug. 17, 1852	Grn	C1
Snoddy	James			Jul. ??, 1852	Grn	C1
Snodgrass	Christopher		Dec. 24, 1801	Jun. 31, ????	But	CEM2
Snodgrass	Hannah		May 10, 1815	Sep. 11, 1877	But	CEM2
Snodgrass	Thomas	R.	Jun. 27, 1857	Feb. 5, 1880	But	CEM2
Snow	Mrs. Phebe		1816ca	Aug. 22, 1844	NWS1	9/7/1844
Snyder	Elizabeth	M.	1855ca	Jun. 17, 1878	Brk	C1
Sokolski	H.		1834		Web	Bk1
Sottell	George		1838ca	Mar. 20, 1856	Brk	C1
South	Thos.	C.	1802ca	Oct. 18, 1878	Brk	C1
South	Lewis			Mar. 10, 1855	Bre	C1
Southwood	Isaac		1806ca	Sep. 27, 1853	Bre	C1
Southwood	Sarah		1837ca	Sep. 8, 1837	Bre	C1
Soward	Mrs. Mary	P.		Jul. 11, 1845	NWS1	7/19/1845
Soyars	Dr. James	T.	1838		Web	Bk1
Spann	Mrs. Elizabeth			Mar. ??, 1844	NWS1	3/9/1844
Sparks	A.	V.	1874ca	Oct. 15, 1927	Dav	MCDR
Sparks	Agnes	A.	1890ca	Mar. 2, 1974	Cam	MCDR
Sparks	Agnes		1913ca	Mar. 30, 1921	Fay	MCDR
Sparks	Albert		1874ca	Jun. 20, 1944	Dav	MCDR
Sparks	James	E.	1928	Aug. 2, 1950	KY	KMIL
Sparks	Lizzie		1894ca		Grn	Marr1
Sparks	Lucy	L.	1890ca		Grn	Marr1
Sparks	Thomas	J.	1913ca	Dec. 11, 1952	Fay	MCDR
Sparks	Thomas	J.	1913ca	Sep. 28, 1918	Dav	MCDR
Sparks	Thomas	W.	1908ca	Oct. 25, 1966	Fay	MCDR
Sparks	Thomas	W.	1937ca	Oct. 11, 1951	Bur	MCDR
Sparks	Thomas		1861ca	Jan. 26, 1941	Fay	MCDR
Spears	Dottie		1883ca		Grn	Marr1
Speer	Geneva		1888ca		Grn	Marr1
Speer	Lieut.			1791ca	NWS5	11/12/1791
Spencer	Albert		Nov. 1, 1885	Apr. 27, 1961	Hdn	CEM2
Spencer	Allen		1822ca	Dec. 18, 1878	Bre	C1
Spencer	Chas.	W.	1850		Web	Bk1
Spencer	Delila		1856ca	Jun. 20, 1858	Bre	C1
Spencer	Elizabeth			Sep. 17, 1852	Brk	C1
Spencer	Ida		Dec. 25, 1889	Apr. 11, 1976	Hdn	CEM2

Last Name	First Name	I	Birth	Death	Co	Source
Spencer	Lavina		1804ca	Nov. 27, 1854	Dav	C1
Spencer	Margaret Ann		Aug. 24, 1881	Dec. 31, 1915	Row	CEM1
Spener	Evaline			Jan. 14, 1856	Bre	C1
Spicer	Benjamin		1797ca	Sep. 12, 1877	Bre	C1
Spicer	Elizabeth		1829ca	Oct. 15, 1859	Bre	C1
Spicer	Elizabeth		1874ca	Sep. 31, 1875	Bre	C1
Spicer	James		1852ca	May 15, 1856	Bre	C1
Spicer	Nancy		1846ca	Feb. 12, 1853	Bre	C1
Spicer	Nancy Jane			Aug. 9, 1856	Bre	C1
Spicer	Scytha			Nov. 15, 1859	Bre	C1
Spicer	Tabitha		1857ca	Oct. 15, 1858	Bre	C1
Spiers	Bettie		Apr. 5, 1863	Jun. 2, 1865	Hdn	CEM3
Spiers	John	M.	Apr. 18, 1870	Sep. 5, 1871	Hdn	CEM3
Spiers	Richard		Aug. 12, 1812	Aug. 25, 1851	Hdn	CEM3
Spiller	Adline		1852ca	Sep. 22, 1917	Fay	MCDR
Spiller	Alice	M.	1878ca	4-May-45	Cam	MCDR
Spiller	Anna	M.		Feb. 7, 1948	Cam	MCDR
Spiller	Catheim		1876ca	Mar. 25, 1914	Cam	MCDR
Spiller	Elmer		1870ca	Mar. 8, 1946	Cam	MCDR
Spiller	Ernest		1923ca	Oct. 22, 1980	Fay	MCDR
Spiller	James	H.		Apr. 13, 1955	Fay	MCDR
Spiller	Lawless	T.	1909ca	Nov. 15, 1986	Fay	MCDR
Spiller	Lucy	O.	1868ca	Apr. 8, 1943	Fay	MCDR
Spiller	Margret	M.	1888ca	Oct. 30, 1965	Cam	MCDR
Spiller	Maria		1872ca	Jul. 14, 1926	Fay	MCDR
Spillers	Columbus Levy		Dec. 1, 1865	Oct. 27, 1954	Ful	CEM4
Spillers	Maggie		Mar. 16, 1878	Dec. 25, 1944	Ful	CEM4
Spillman	Thomas			Dec. 28, 1844	NWS1	1/4/1845
Spradlin	Perlina		1886ca		Grn	Marr1
Spriggs	Mary		1889ca		Grn	Marr1
Springer	Alma		1888ca		Grn	Marr1
Spry	Sarah		1889ca		Grn	Marr1
Spurlock	Eveline		1839ca	Mar. 30, 1853	Bre	C1
Spurlock	John	W.	1931	Dec. 1, 1950	KY	KMIL
Spurlock	William		1791ca	Nov. 14, 1854	Bre	C1
Spurrier	Ada	J.	1854	1925	Hdn	CEM1
Spurrier	Edward	B.	Jun. 6, 1873	May 24, 1874	Hdn	CEM1
Spurrier	Walter	C.	Jul. 23, 1882	Nov. 3, 1883	Hdn	CEM1
Spurrier	William	B.	1844	1925	Hdn	CEM1
Stacy	Benjamin		1767ca	Mar. 10, 1856	Bre	C1
Stacy, Jr.	James	I.	1932	Jun. 3, 1951	KY	KMIL
Stacy, Jr.	Lenox		1924	Nov. 1, 1952	KY	KMIL
Stakelin	Katherine		1895		Har	CEM1
Stakelin	Ruby	K.	1925	1927	Har	CEM1
Stakelin	William	B.		1862	Har	CEM1
Stallings	Mary		1838	1915	Ful	CEM7
Stallings	Thomas		1836	1875	Ful	CEM7

Last Name	First Name	I	Birth	Death	Co	Source
Stamper	Anna		1851ca	Mar. 9, 1853	Bre	C1
Stamper	Ellen		1850ca	Dec. 23, 1855	Bre	C1
Stamper	Elvina		1877ca	Jun. 16, 1878	Bre	C1
Stamper	Erasch		1806ca	Feb. 27, 1856	Bre	C1
Stamper	James		1849ca	Dec. 21, 1852	Bre	C1
Stamper	Jonathan		1842ca	Dec. 17, 1852	Bre	C1
Stamper	Nancy		1852ca	Dec. 4, 1855	Bre	C1
Stanfield	Annie Bell		Dec. 26, 1885	1959	Ful	CEM4
Stanfield	Curtis		Jun. 13, 1930	Dec. ??, 1932	Ful	CEM4
Stanfield	Henry		Aug. 11, 1900	Aug. 27, 1960	Ful	CEM4
Stanfield	Jimmie		Aug. 24, 1910	1918	Ful	CEM4
Stanfield	Unknown		Oct. 23, 1917	Nov. ??, 1917	Ful	CEM4
Stanley	John		1928	May 30, 1951	KY	KMIL
Stanly (Slave)				Mar. 5, 1854	Brk	C1
Stanoberry	Mary		1869ca	Mar. 17, 1894	Brk	C1
Staples	Jas.		1876ca	Feb. 25, 1878	Brk	C1
Stapp	Sherill		1878ca	Jun. 18, 1955	Fay	MCDR
Starling	Edmund Alexander		1827		KY	BK2(P91)
Starling	Lyne		1806		KY	BK2(P83)
Starling	William		Sep. 19, 1807		KY	BK2(P83)
Starns	Isaac			Oct. 27, 1800	NWS5	11/3/1800
Statham	D.	M.	May 1, 1873	Dec. 16, 1897	Ful	CEM7
Statham	Gid	B.	1866ca	Jul. 28, 1962	Ful	CEM7
Statham	H.		Apr. 4, 1835	Oct. 29, 1883	Ful	CEM7
Statham	Iner	M.	Jan. 11, 1892	Feb. 9, 1892	Ful	CEM7
Statham	Martha		Jun. 13, 1842	Oct. 10, 1899	Ful	CEM7
Statham	Martha		Aug. 6, 1881	Dec. 17, 1886	Ful	CEM7
Statham	Ronnie		Sep. 28, 1882	Sep. 23, 1895	Ful	CEM7
Statham	Unknown			Sep. 30, 1898	Ful	CEM7
Statham	Unknown Female		Nov. 7, 1903	May 6, 1907	Ful	CEM7
Statham	Unknown Male		Aug. 2, 1902	Jul. 17, 1903	Ful	CEM7
Statham	Wade		Feb. 3, 1895	Apr. 8, 1895	Ful	CEM7
Statham	Woodson	T.	Jul. 25, 1888	Nov. 10, 1903	Ful	CEM7
Steele	Daniel		1788		Car	Bk1
Steele	Dr. John	H.	Sep. 28, 1830		Car	Bk1
Steele	Mary		1845ca	Aug. 25, 1861	Brk	C1
Steele (Stuart)	Eliza	A.		1884		Bk2(P222)
Steen	Dr. Marion	W.	Jan. 25, 1855		Car	Bk1
Steenes	Alice	E.	Apr. 7, 1890	Nov. 21, 1938	Har	Cem1
Stephen (Slave)			1811ca	May 18, 1861	Brk	C1
Stephens	Cora	B.	1888ca		Grn	Marr1
Stephens	G.	W.	Feb. 16, 1832	Mar. 9, 1890	Ful	CEM7
Stephens	J.	S.	Oct. 7, 1845	Mar. 27, 1878	Men	CEM1
Stephens	John Thomas		1873	Jun. 28, 1864	Ful	CEM7
Stephens	Maggie		1883ca		Grn	Marr1
Stephens	Nora	F.	Mar. 1, 1907		Car	C1
Stephens	Raymond	G.	1928	Nov. 28, 1950	KY	KMIL

Last Name	First Name	I	Birth	Death	Co	Source
Stephens	Susan	C.	Feb. 7, 1833	Feb. 19, 1890	Ful	CEM7
Stephens (Wills)	Polly	A.	Jan. 25, 1823	Jan. 2, 1906	Men	CEM1
Stephenson	Delia		1864	1923	Hdn	CEM2
Stephenson (Jones)	K.		1872ca	May 9, 1894	Brk	C1
Stevens	Martha		Oct. 14, 1800	May 20, 1882	Ful	CEM7
Stewart	Alexander		1784ca		NWS5	4/3/1800
Stewart	Eva		1888ca		Grn	Marr1
Stewart	Eva	J.	1888ca		Grn	Marr1
Stewart	James	N.		Sep. 14, 1845	NWS1	10/25/1845
Stewart	Kate	C.	May 25, 1851	Jan. 25, 1881	Hdn	CEM1
Stewart	Lillie		1888ca		Grn	Marr1
Stewart	Von	C.		Oct. 10, 1934	Oh	MCDR
Stice	Reno	D.	1930	Oct. 2, 1952	KY	KMIL
Stidham	Henry		1924	Jul. 16, 1950	KY	KMIL
Stidham	Lloyd	D.	1930	Nov. 27, 1950	KY	KMIL
Stiltner	Sallie		1892ca		Grn	Marr1
Stinson	Ada	B.	1883ca	Jan. 21, 1976	Sim	MCDR
Stinson	Ada		1896ca	Nov. 13, 1914	Muh	MCDR
Stinson	Albert		1911ca	Dec. 4, 1979	Fay	MCDR
Stinson	Albert	B.	1907cca	Mar. 23, 1985	Fay	MCDR
Stinson	Altolene			May 2, 1920	Muh	MCDR
Stinson	Amanda	L.	1857ca	Dec. 25, 1912	All	MCDR
Stinson	C.	W.	Apr. ??, 1833		Gray	C2
Stinson	Squire		Dec. 21, 1837		Gray	C2
Stinson	Susan		Jun. 21, 1836		Gray	C2
Stone	Alexander		1856ca		Web	C1-Pg. 11
Stone	Barton Warren		Nov. 5, 1817		Other	Bk1(P212)T
Stone	Belle	A.	Aug. 23, 1843	Jun. 5, 1925	Dav	CEM2
Stone	Charlie	C.	1921	Sep. 1, 1950	KY	KMIL
Stone	J.	B.	1835ca	Jul. 15, 1861	Dav	C1
Stone	James		1855ca		Web	C1-Pg. 21
Stone	Joshua		Apr. 25, 1907		Car	C1
Stone	Margaret		1823ca	Sep. 10, 1858	Brk	C1
Stone	Martha		1885ca		Grn	Marr1
Stone	Nannie	E.	1856ca	Jun. 28, 1878	Brk	C1
Stone	William	A.	Oct. 14, 1831	Jun. 20, 1899	Dav	CEM2
Stone	William		1790ca	Jan. 16, 1853	Dav	C1
Stone (Alexander)	Julie Ann		Nov. 25, 1821	Mar. 17, 1892	Men	CEM1
Stono	Vina			Oct. 1, 1876	Bre	C1
Story	Mary		1878ca		Grn	Marr1
Stout	Alexander		1859ca	Nov. 24, 1923	Fay	MCDR
Stout	Alfred		1949ca	Nov. 30, 1983	Fay	MCDR
Stout	Allie			Dec. 19, 1912	Fay	MCDR
Stout	Mr.			1787	NWS5	9/15/1787
Stovall	George		1761		All	RP1
Stowers	John			1826	Han	Bk1
Strand	Catherine		1819ca	Feb. 24, 1854	Dav	C1

Last Name	First Name	I	Birth	Death	Co	Source
Strangel	Daniel		1836	Jan. 29, 1865	Ful	CEM7
Strawsburg	J.		Jul. 1, 1836		Gray	C2
Strickland	Sue	A.	Dec. 20, 1842	Sep. 18, 1898	Hdn	CEM2
Strong	Charlotte		1877ca	Nov. 16, 1878	Bre	C1
Strong	John	C.	1873ca	Sep. 5, 1875	Bre	C1
Strong	Unknown Male			Apr. 11, 1857	Bre	C1
Strong	Unknown Male			Nov. 18, 1859	Bre	C1
Strong	Unknown Male			Jun. 14, 1874	Bre	C1
Strother	Henry		1860		Web	Bk1
Strother	Jaems			1761	KY	BK2(P87)
Strother	Jeremiah			1741	KY	BK2(P87)
Stuart	Annie	E.	Jun. 13, 1865	Aug. 12, 1945	Hdn	CEM2
Stuart	David Russell		Nov. 10, 1894	Jun. 20, 1952	Hdn	CEM2
Stuart	James Melvin		Nov. 11, 1920	Jun. 28, 1972	Hdn	CEM2
Stuart	John Todd		Nov. 10, 1807			BK2(P223)
Stuart	Lula	A.	1864	1923	Hdn	CEM2
Stuart	Lula	M.	Dec. 8, 1890	Nov. 7, 1968	Hdn	CEM2
Stuart	Mary	S.	Apr. 1, 1903		Hdn	CEM2
Stuart	Myrtle	N.	Sep. 19, 1895	Aug. 2, 1961	Hdn	CEM2
Stuart	R.	E.	Dec. 8, 1865	Jul. 17, 1908	Hdn	CEM2
Stuart	Robert	V.	Aug. 10, 1900	Jan. 28, 1969	Hdn	CEM2
Stuart	Robert		Aug. 14, 1772			BK2(P222)
Stuart	W.	T.	1863	1943	Hdn	CEM2
Stuart	Wm. Melford		1896	1961	Hdn	CEM2
Stubblefield	R.	G.	Feb. 11, 1838	May 4, 1908	Sim	CEM1
Stucker	Frederick	P.	Dec. 8, 1908	Jul. 25, 1958	Hdn	CEM2
Stucker	James Russell		1906	1924	Hdn	CEM2
Stucker	Joseph	E.	Sep. 26, 1911	Mar. 13, 1976	Hdn	CEM2
Stucker	Pauline	D.	Jun. 14, 1918		Hdn	CEM2
Stucker	Warren	E.	May 19, 1877	Dec. 7, 1968	Hdn	CEM2
Stucker (Averitt)	Bettie		Feb. 3, 1883	Mar. 22, 1961	Hdn	CEM2
Stumbo	Samuel	T.	Dec. 19, 1928	Jul. 11, 1953	KY	KMIL
Stump	Mr.			1799	NWS5	4/18/1799
Sturgel	Wilbur		1836ca	Nov. 29, 1853	Bre	C1
Sturgill	Della		1891ca		Grn	Marr1
Sturgill	Margie		1886ca		Grn	Marr1
Stutson	Luther		1771ca		NWS5	6/9/1792
Sublett	Asher	B.	1932	Nov. 27, 1950	KY	KMIL
Sudduth	W.	A.	1854		KY	BK2(P63)
Sullivan	Ella	R.	1873ca		Grn	Marr1
Sullivan	Florence		1873ca		Grn	Marr1
Sullivan	Martha		1888ca		Grn	Marr1
Sullivan	Ralph	F.	1927	Jun. 15, 1953	KY	KMIL
Summers	Sharilda	M.	1863	1947	Hdn	CEM2
Summers	Sharon Ann		Jan. 21, 1960	Jan. 24, 1960	Hdn	CEM2
Summers	William Perry		1854	1927	Hdn	CEM2
Summers	Alonzo	C.	1899	1954	Hdn	CEM2

Last Name	First Name	I	Birth	Death	Co	Source
Summers (Grizzle)	Aline		1902	1939	Hdn	CEM2
Summers (Monin)	Lucile		Jan. 8, 1896	Jul. 20, 1966	Hdn	CEM2
Summers, Jr.	W.	P.	Jul. 4, 1927	Jul. 4, 1927	Hdn	CEM2
Surrell	Sandy Jane		Dec. 3, 1961	Dec. 3, 1961	Row	CEM1
Survert	John		1832ca	Jun. ??, 1857	Dav	C1
Sutberry	Rebecca	A.	1842ca	May 14, 1865	Ful	CEM7
Sutherland	Adrian		1878ca	Dec. 22, 1956	Dav	MCDR
Sutherland	Adron	C.	1912ca	Nov. 7, 1968	Dav	MCDR
Suttle	J.	H.	Jun. 15, 1855		Sim	C1
Suttle	Mary	E.	Sep. 22, 1852		Sim	C1
Suttle	R.	W.	Apr. 9, 1856		Sim	C1
Suttle	S.	A.	May 4, 1854		Sim	C1
Sutzer	Hugh		May 7, 1891	Nov. 10, 1962	Hdn	CEM2
Sutzer (Craig)	Nancy	L.	Jan. 20, 1893	Apr. 29, 1961	Hdn	CEM2
Swann	Martha		Oct. 17, 1811	Aug. 7, 1861	Hen	CEM1
Swearingen	Capt.			1791ca	NWS5	11/12/1791
Sweatt	James	L.	1834		But	Bk1
Sweatt	John Turner		1832		But	Bk1
Swem	Maud	L.	1886ca		Grn	Marr1
Swift	P.	B.	Nov. 2, 1839		Gray	C2
Swim	Sarah	E.	1879ca		Grn	Marr1
Tabb	Bailey	S.	Oct. 12, 1834	Jan. 3, 1917	Hdn	CEM1
Tabb	Edmund	H.	1905	1962	Hdn	CEM2
Tabb	Ethel Shannon		1909		Hdn	CEM2
Tabb	Lafayette		Jan. 28, 1860	Apr. 11, 1913	Hdn	CEM1
Tabb	Mary	E.	Mar. 18, 1874	Mar. 16, 1948	Hdn	CEM2
Tabb	Susan	D.	Jul. 8, 1821	Nov. 18, 1916	Hdn	CEM1
Tabb	William	W.	Oct. 8, 1869	Apr. 25, 1940	Hdn	CEM2
Taber	Benjamin	M.	Oct. 22, 1850	Jul. 15,1853	Hdn	CEM3
Taber	Eliza			1874	Brk	C1
Taber	Jennie		Mar. 30, 1876		Hdn	CEM3
Taber	Justus			Apr. 21, 1850	Hdn	CEM3
Taber	Mary	E.	May 9, 1834	Jul. 24, 1926	Hdn	CEM3
Taber	Mary	F.	Nov. 14, 1839	Jan. 16, 1843	Hdn	CEM3
Taber	Robert	M.	Aug. 26, 1815	Oct. 19, 1874	Hdn	CEM3
Taber	Samuel	M.	Feb. 19, 1818	Sep. 7, 1875	Hdn	CEM3
Taber	Samuel M.	T.	Jul. 7, 1841	Jan. 8, 1843	Hdn	CEM3
Taber	Robert Lee		1863	1925	Hdn	CEM2
Taber (Hicks)	Edna		1872	1933	Hdn	CEM2
Tabor	Charles	A.	1931	Jul. 16, 1950	KY	KMIL
Tabor (Wills)	Verla		Sep. 2, 1892	Sep. 12, 1922	Men	CEM1
Tackett	Donald	F.	1932	Sep. 20, 1950	KY	KMIL
Tackett	Ollie		1892ca		Grn	Marr1
Talbott	A.	H.	1810ca	1857	Dav	C1
Talbott	Mrs. Sally	B.		Oct. 7, 1835	NWS4	10/9/1835
Tanner	Richard		1834ca	Feb. ??, 1853	Dav	C1
Tanner	Sanuel	H.	1844		But	Bk1

Last Name	First Name	I	Birth	Death	Co	Source
Tanner(Luckee)	L.		1804ca	Apr. ??, 1853	Dav	C1
Tapp	Robert Calvin		1856		Web	Bk1
Tarry	Ebb	L.	1930	May 31, 1951	KY	KMIL
Tate	James			Apr. 12, 1889	Muh	Ch1
Tate	Willis			Oct. 21, 1884	Muh	Ch1
Tate (Matthews)	Crillar		1868ca	May 10, 1904	Brk	C1
Tate (Robinson)	Cindarilla		1812ca	Jan. 25, 1855	Brk	C1
Taulbee	Elizabeth		1843ca	Aug. 22, 1878	Bre	C1
Taulbee	John	F.	1873ca	May 12, 1875	Bre	C1
Taulbee	Mary	E.		Jul. 29, 1859	Bre	C1
Taulbee	William	T.	1875ca	Jul. 27, 1878	Bre	C1
Taulbee (Banks)	Lousana		1853ca	Dec. 28, 1878	Bre	C1
Taulbee (Dunn)	Dannil	J.	1841ca	Feb. 28, 1878	Bre	C1
Taylor	Armstead		Aug. 10, 1810	Nov. 13, 1853	Har	CEM1
Taylor	Ben	H.	Mar. 28, 1890		Hdn	CEM2
Taylor	Charles Augusta		Feb. 18, 1929	Nov. 28, 1950	KY	KMIL
Taylor	Col. William			1846	KY	BK2(P28)
Taylor	Dora		1862	1894	Har	CEM1
Taylor	Dr. Pigman		1825		Web	Bk1
Taylor	Earnest	A.	1931	Nov. 21, 1950	KY	KMIL
Taylor	Estell	J.		Mar. 29, 1867	Dav	CEM2
Taylor	F.	D.	Mar. 12, 1830	Mar. 21, 1891	Har	CEM1
Taylor	Garrard Banks		1813		But	Bk1
Taylor	George		Aug. 26, 1821	Nov. 19, 1883	Ful	CEM7
Taylor	Isaac		1871		Har	CEM1
Taylor	John		1775ca	Jul. ??, 1857	Dav	C1
Taylor	John		1830ca	Aug. 9, 1852	Brk	C1
Taylor	Jos.	M.	May 4, 1823	Nov. 5, 1851	Har	CEM1
Taylor	Joseph	J.	Oct. 7, 1865	Mar. 5, 1887	Ful	CEM7
Taylor	Joseph		1774ca		NWS5	1/12/1793
Taylor	Joseph		1851		But	Bk1
Taylor	Joseph			Mar. 29, 1863	Dav	CEM2
Taylor	Josephine			Sep. 16, 1903	Brk	C1
Taylor	Laura	A.	1859ca	May 1, 1860	Har	CEM1
Taylor	Louisa		Sep. ??, 1848	Feb. 13, 1882	Hdn	CEM1
Taylor	Lydia Ann		Oct. 8, 1820	Mar. 25, 1875	Hdn	CEM1
Taylor	Martha	A.	Jul. 24, 1845	Jan. 19, 1889	Har	CEM1
Taylor	Mary	E.	Jun. 30, 1855	Aug. 18, 1855	Har	CEM1
Taylor	Mary		Aug. 18, 1901	Feb. 6, 1907	Ful	CEM7
Taylor	Mary Ann		Jun. 20, 1822	Jun. 17, 1876	Har	CEM1
Taylor	Millard		1873		Har	CEM1
Taylor	Nancy	P.	Nov. 2, 1810	Aug. 6, 1873	Har	CEM1
Taylor	Nora		Apr. 3. 1859	Mar. 14, 1911	Har	CEM1
Taylor	Ona	M.	Jan. 8, 1892	Aug. 9, 1948	Hdn	CEM2
Taylor	Rebecca Jane		Aug. 25, 1834	Jun. 12, 1906	Har	CEM1
Taylor	Sarah	A.	Jun. 9, 1840	Nov. 30, 1857	Har	CEM1
Taylor	Sarah	L.	1894		Har	CEM1

Last Name	First Name	I	Birth	Death	Co	Source
Taylor	Septimus		1822		But	Bk1
Taylor	W.	S.	1853		But	Bk1
Taylor	Wraymond	V.	Jul. 8, 1900	Sep. 16, 1900	Ful	CEM7
Taylor (Tucker)	Susan	E.	1815ca	Jan. 6, 1861	Dav	C1
Taylor (Williams)	Elizabeth	G.	1821ca	Oct. 8, 1855	Dav	C1
Teager	Adaline		1831ca	Sep. 5, 1832	Lew	CEM1
Teager	Elizabeth	E	1842ca	Apr. 3, 1844	Lew	CEM1
Teager	Herman		1852ca	Dec. 5, 1855	Lew	CEM1
Teager	John		1790ca	Jun. 18, 1833	Lew	CEM1
Teager	Lewis	B	Aug. 11, 1801	Mar. 21, 1870	Lew	CEM1
Teager	Lucretia	D		Apr. 11, 185?	Lew	CEM1
Teager	Mary		1766ca	Sep. 23, 1833	Lew	CEM1
Teager	Mary		1820ca	Jul. 8, 1833	Lew	CEM1
Teager	Moses		1829ca	Apr. 20, 1859	Lew	CEM1
Teager	Nancy	B	Jan. 5, 1807	Aug. 28, 1883	Lew	CEM1
Teager	Napoleon	B	1836ca	Sep. 14, 1856	Lew	CEM1
Teal	Effie	M.	1889ca	Feb. 14, 1916	Dav	MCDR
Teel	Anitra		1934ca	Jun. 29, 1979	Bat	MCDR
Teel	Marcus	A.	1858ca	Mar. 14, 1931	Dav	MCDR
Teel	Margaret	I.	1860ca	Jun. 6, 1940	Dav	MCDR
Temple	Marvin		1929	Mar. 5, 1953	KY	KMIL
Terry	Andrew			Jul. 15, 1853	Bre	C1
Terry	Angeline		1850ca	Apr. 22, 1853	Bre	C1
Terry	Barbara		Nov.19, 1815	Jan. 30, 1869	Hdn	CEM1
Terry	Harriett	S.	Dec. 6, 1828	Sep. 23, 1862	Hdn	CEM1
Terry	Isaac		1849ca	Sep. 15, 1853	Bre	C1
Terry	Joe	A.	Jan. 28, 1871	Jan. 30, 1906	Ful	CEM7
Terry	Laura	O.	May 14, 1847	Sep. 2, 1875	Muh	CEM2
Terry	Mary	E.	Mar. 13, 1856	Feb. 13, 1862	Hdn	CEM1
Terry	Moses		Jan. 26, 1817	Jan. 27, 1879	Hdn	CEM1
Terry	Samuel		Jan. 21, 1865	Mar. 22, 1866	Hdn	CEM1
Terry	Sarah	E.	Feb. 27, 1841	Jan. 1, 1861	Hdn	CEM1
Terry	Simon		1930	Jul. 11, 1950	KY	KMIL
Terry	Stephen		1873ca	Aug. 28, 1875	Bre	C1
Terry	Walter		1874ca	Sep. 21, 1875	Dav	MCDR
Testerman	Wilda	F.	1900ca	Sep. 25, 1981	Fay	MCDR
Tharp	Dodson		1774ca		NWS5	4/18/1799
Tharp	George	W.	1917	Nov. 30, 1950	KY	KMIL
Thibodeaux	Irvin	J.	1930	Jul. 20, 1950	KY	KMIL
Thixton, Sr.	John		1792ca	Apr. 16, 1852	Dav	MCDR
Thom	Mark		1851ca	Sep. 1, 1852	Grn	C1
Thomas	A.		1805ca	Sep. 13, 1853	Dav	C1
Thomas	Eliza		1859ca	Dec. ??, 1875	Dav	MCDR
Thomas	Erastus	O.	1866		But	Bk1
Thomas	F.	M.	1853	1920	Ful	CEM4
Thomas	Isaac	W.	1819ca	Jun. 10, 1852	Brk	C1
Thomas	Isaac		1793ca	Jun. 30, 1858	Bre	C1

Last Name	First Name	I	Birth	Death	Co	Source
Thomas	Isham		1804			Bk1(P279)T
Thomas	Jake	R.	1928	Oct. 21, 1951	KY	KMIL
Thomas	James	M.	1848ca	Jun. ??, 1852	Grn	C1
Thomas	Jane		1865	1938	Ful	CEM4
Thomas	Joseph	H.	Aug. 24, 1862	Apr. 22, 1863	Hdn	CEM1
Thomas	Martha		1815ca	Apr. 20, 1875	Bre	C1
Thomas	Mary Ann			Sep. 11, 1852	Brk	C1
Thomas	Mattie		1887cq		Grn	Marr1
Thomas	Mealie		1883ca		Grn	Marr1
Thomas	Royce	V.	1928	1932	Ful	CEM4
Thomas	Sarah	F.	May 10, 1907		Car	C1
Thomas	Susan	M.	Sep. 5, 1860	Oct. 11, 1884	Hdn	CEM2
Thomas	Unknown Female		May 10, 1907		Car	C1
Thomas	W.	H.	Mar. 11, 1829		KY	Bk1(P279)T
Thomas (Coo)	Mary	A.	1820ca	Sep. ??, 1853	Dav	C1
Thomas (Slave)	Rufus	J.	1853ca	Apr. 14, 1861	Brk	C1
Thomas (Slave)			1860ca	Sep. 10, 1861	Brk	C1
Thomas (Slave)			1860ca	Sep. 10, 1861	Brk	C1
Thompson	Annie	C.	Aug. 4, 1864	Jun. 25, 1894	Hdn	CEM2
Thompson	B.		1802ca	Oct. ??, 1861	Dav	C1
Thompson	Clarence		1928	Sep. 5, 1950	KY	KMIL
Thompson	Cleveland		1933	May 20, 1951	KY	KMIL
Thompson	Cora	L.	1891ca		Grn	Marr1
Thompson	Ely		1827ca	Sep. 15, 1858	Bre	C1
Thompson	Emma		1871ca		Grn	Marr1
Thompson	Eugene	R.	1930	Jul. 25, 1950	KY	KMIL
Thompson	G.	W.	1818ca	Sep. ??, 1861	Dav	C1
Thompson	H.	S.	1823	1883	Hdn	CEM2
Thompson	Infant			1835	NWS4	8/14/1835
Thompson	Iva Dorris		Jan. 30, 1889	Mar. 15, 1889	Hdn	CEM2
Thompson	J.	R.	1853	1902	Hdn	CEM2
Thompson	Matthew		1850ca	Mar. 7, 1853	Grn	C1
Thompson	Mrs.			1835	NWS4	8/14/1835
Thompson	Rebecca	A.	1829	1908	Hdn	CEM2
Thompson	Roland	D.	1933	Oct. 20, 1952	KY	KMIL
Thornton	Bobby	J.	1931	Sep. 1, 1950	KY	KMIL
Thornton	Sivilla		1833ca	Apr. 3, 1855	Dav	C1
Thurman	Christie		1848		Hdn	CEM1
Thurman	D.	R.	1846	1918	Hdn	CEM1
Thurman	Lucretia		1829ca	Jul. 27, 1856	Brk	C1
Tibbaulds	Jle.		1831ca	Feb. 19, 1833	Dav	C1
Tibbs	Jessie	T.	1931	Apr. 24, 1951	KY	KMIL
Tidball	Thomas	A.	Mar. 24, 1838		Other	Bk1(P172)T
Tiffany	Walter		1745	Apr. 1, 1826	All	RP1
Timberlake	Ann	E.	1847ca	Sep. 25, 1877	Grn	C2
Timberlake	Dora		1885ca		Grn	Marr1
Timmons	Harriet		Feb. 16, 1857	May 20, 1861	Web	CEM1

Last Name	First Name	I	Birth	Death	Co	Source
Timmons	J.	E.	1847		Web	Bk1
Timmons	Mary	L.	Apr. 20, 1865	Sep. 23, 1866	Web	CEM1
Tinsley	John	M.	1819		But	Bk1
Tinsley	Mary		1881ca		Grn	Marr1
Tipton	Capt.			1791ca	NWS5	11/12/1791
Titus	Vesta	V.	1893ca		Grn	Marr1
Todd	David		Apr. 8. 1823		KY	BK2(P210)
Todd	David			Feb. 8, 1785	KY	BK2(P210)
Todd	Hannah			1832	KY	BK2(P222)
Todd	Levi		1756		KY	BK2(P212)
Todd	Robt. Smith		Feb. 25, 1791	Jul. 15, 1849	KY	BK2(P215)
Tolbert	Matilda			Oct. 15, 1876	Brk	C1
Toler	Walter		1932	May 28, 1951	KY	KMIL
Toll	Henrietta		1787	1851	Har	CEM1
Toll	William	H.	Nov. 22, 1822	Nov. 23, 1892	Har	CEM1
Tolle	Clarence Lee		1891	1942	Har	CEM1
Tolle	Homer Robert		1893	1940	Har	CEM1
Tolle	James	G.	Aug. 5, 1888	Dec. 17, 1956	Har	CEM1
Tomer (Demeyers)	Elenor		1824ca	Dec. 1, 1852	Brk	C1
Tomos	Jasper Newt.		Oct. 15, 1840		Gray	C2
Toon	Albert	E.	1917	Sep. 26, 1950	KY	KMIL
Torian	Peter		1810ca	Sep. 14, 1835	NWS4	9/18/1835
Torrence	Elizabeth		1815ca	Apr. ??, 1855	Dav	C1
Towry	George	H.	1834		Web	Bk1
Toy	Elizabeth		Feb. 4, 1849	Mar. 6, 1910	Hen	CEM1
Toy	Joseph		Feb. 6, 1785	May 13, 1876	Hen	CEM1
Toy	Sarah		Jun. 22, 1793	Dec. 23, 1862	Hen	CEM1
Trautman	Ruth		1890ca		Grn	Marr1
Trent	Arminda		1846ca	Mar. 4, 1876	Bre	C1
Trent	Franklin		1852ca	Mar. 31, 1856	Bre	C1
Trent	Ira	V.	1931	Nov. 4, 1950	KY	KMIL
Trent	June		1831ca	Jul. 31, 1876	Bre	C1
Trent	Louis			Apr. 1, 1855	Bre	C1
Triplett	Gideon		1864ca	Aug. 20, 1878	Brk	C1
Triplett	Harriet		1830ca	Apr. ??, 1855	Dav	C1
Triplett	Robert	H.	1831ca	Jan. 9, 1852	Dav	MCDR
Triplett	Sallie	K.	1833ca	Jan. 23, 1852	Dav	MCDR
Triplett	William			Aug. 6, 1853	Grn	C1
Trowel	Cornelius		1930	Apr. 25, 1951	KY	KMIL
Truitt	Ida	M.	1878ca		Grn	Marr1
Truitt	Vina	W.	1877ca		Grn	Marr1
Truman	Ellinor		1784ca	May 18, 1852	Grn	C1
Truman	William	T.	1809ca	Mar. ??, 1845	NWS1	3/22/1845
Tuck	Philip Henry		1822		But	Bk1
Tucker	Addie Page		Jul. 17, 1890		McL	Sch1
Tucker	Arra		Feb. 12, 1886		McL	Sch1
Tucker	Catherine	A.	Oct. 15, 1845	Sep. 29, 1872	Oh	Cem2

Last Name	First Name	I	Birth	Death	Co	Source
Tucker	Clarence		Dec. 14, 1890		McL	Sch1
Tucker	Collie		Aug. 5, 1893		McL	Sch1
Tucker	Dannie		Feb. 5, 1890		McL	Sch1
Tucker	David		1833ca	May 7, 1855	Brk	C1
Tucker	Donnie		Aug. 9, 1888		McL	Sch1
Tucker	E.	T.	Feb. 18, 1839	Nov. 13, 1892	Oh	Cem2
Tucker	Elias		1874ca	De. 29, 1878	Brk	C1
Tucker	Elisha		1836ca	Sep. 16, 1852	Brk	C1
Tucker	Emma		Jun. 16, 1881		McL	Sch1
Tucker	Gus		Mar. 11, 1883		McL	Sch1
Tucker	Hammon		May 9, 1882		McL	Sch1
Tucker	John		Jul. 9, 1883		McL	Sch1
Tucker	May		May 12, 1884		McL	Sch1
Tucker	Steve		Sep. 18, 1886		McL	Sch1
Tucker	William	A.		Sep. 11, 1852	Brk	C1
Tucker	William	W.	1796ca	Sep. 8, 1852	Brk	C1
Tucker (Basham)	Lucretia		1816ca	Oct. 3, 1856	Brk	C1
Turmer	Ellis		1850ca	May 1, 1854	Bre	C1
Turnball	Eliza	J.	1815ca	Jun. 30, 1855	Dav	C1
Turner	Alfred		1836ca	Sep. 6, 1852	Bre	C1
Turner	Annie	N.	1854	1934	Hdn	CEM2
Turner	Blanche		Aug. 4, 1906	Aug. 8, 1906	Ful	CEM7
Turner	Dr. Hamilton	B.	1821		But	Bk1
Turner	Elizabeth			Oct. 15, 1875	Bre	C1
Turner	Ensign			1791ca	NWS5	11/12/1791
Turner	Henry		1864ca	Jul. 6, 1874	Bre	C1
Turner	James		1791ca	Sep. 13, 1856	Bre	C1
Turner	James		1805ca	Dec. 20, 1858	Bre	C1
Turner	John	F.	1848	1914	Hdn	CEM2
Turner	John	H.	1876	1946	Ful	CEM7
Turner	Lewis		1838ca	Jan. 1, 1853	Bre	C1
Turner	Mittie	I.	Feb. 9, 1878	May 21, 1938	Ful	CEM7
Turner	Nancy		1847ca	Jul. 21, 1853	Bre	C1
Turner	Oscar	N.	Sep. 26, 1878	Jun. 6, 1931	Ful	CEM7
Turner	Patsy		1833ca	Jan. 24, 1853	Bre	C1
Turner	Permelia		1834ca	Mar. 1, 1856	Dav	C1
Turner	Rozer		1838ca	Dec. 2, 1853	Bre	C1
Turner	Samuel		1850ca	Dec. 20, 1853	Bre	C1
Turner	Unknown Female			Oct. 24, 1857	Bre	C1
Turner	Unknown Male			Dec. 31, 1861	Brk	C1
Turner	Unknown Male			Jul. 30, 1875	Bre	C1
Turner (Johnson)	Mary		1814ca	May 20, 1853	Bre	C1
Turnipseed	Alva	C.	1901ca	Apr. 12, 1955	Cam	MCDR
Turnipseed	Mary	B.	1864ca	Sep. 26, 1953	Jef	MCDR
Turpin (Allen)	Charity		1795ca	Mar. 1, 1878	Brk	C1
Turpin (Sipes)	Eliz.		1812ca	Dec. 8, 1878	Brk	C1
Tusey	Annie		1891ca		Grn	Marr1

Last Name	First Name	I	Birth	Death	Co	Source
Tussey	Mary		1881ca		Grn	Marr1
Tutsae	Harriet		1833ca	Dec. 25, 1878	Brk	C1
Tuttle	George	W.		Aug. 30, 1852	Brk	C1
Tuttle	Mathew		1930	Sep. 4, 1950	KY	KMIL
Twredle	Xavier		1911ca	Apr. 15, 1915	Dav	MCDR
Underwood	Benjamin	F.	1823ca	Dec. 11, 1852	Grn	C1
Underwood	Herbert		1928	Apr. 25, 1951	KY	KMIL
Underwood	Patsy			1835	NWS4	8/14/1835
Underwood	Samuel	A.	1834ca	Jan. 17, 1852	Grn	C1
Underwood	Betty		May 3, 1902	Dec. 20, 1903	Ful	CEM2
Underwood (Asbell)	Elizabeth Jane			Mar. 12, 1842	Ful	CEM2
Unknown Male (Slave)				Jun. 26, 1854	Brk	C1
Usher	David Newton			Sep. 29, 1835	NWS4	10/2/1835
Usher	Frances	J.	Jan. 27, 1832	Dec. 20, 1876	Dav	CEM2
Usher	John		No Date	No Date	Dav	CEM2
Usher	Robert		1743ca	Apr. 23, 1836	NWS4	4/30/1836
Utter	William			Sep. ??, 1797	NWS5	9/23/1797
Uzell	Claire	L.	1880ca	Aug. 12, 1948	Muh	MCDR
Uzell, Jr.	Cecil		1910ca	Jul. 7, 1920	Muh	MCDR
Vahlsies (Cathelow)	Mahala	P.	1843ca	Mar. 31, 1878	Brk	C1
Vallance	Kate		1897ca		Grn	Marr1
Van Meter	Barbara	A.	Dec. 12, 1835	Feb. 22, 1899	Hdn	CEM2
Van Meter	Carrie	P.	Sep. 2, 1876	Nov. 29, 1879	Hdn	CEM1
Van Meter	Chas. Leonard		Apr. 20, 1910	Jul. 25, 1964	Hdn	CEM2
Van Meter	Claude		1885	1958	Hdn	CEM2
Van Meter	Della Pence		Feb. 14, 1882	Aug. 6, 1963	Hdn	CEM2
Van Meter	Edgar	L.	1887		Hdn	CEM2
Van Meter	Edward	R.	May 1, 1803	Jan. 11, 1887	Hdn	CEM2
Van Meter	Emma	I.	1883	1948	Hdn	CEM2
Van Meter	Fannie	A.	Dec. 21, 1892	Jan. 27, 1941	Hdn	CEM2
Van Meter	Hattie		1887	1970	Hdn	CEM2
Van Meter	Jacob		Feb. 8, 1837		Hdn	CEM2
Van Meter	John	H.	Oct. 9, 1828	Mar. 2, 1904	Hdn	CEM2
Van Meter	Malvina	B.	Nov. 4, 1868	Jun. 20, 1948	Hdn	CEM2
Van Meter	Margaret		Jan. 11, 1828		Hdn	CEM2
Van Meter	Robert Russell		Dec. 23, 1926	Dec. 5, 1927	Hdn	CEM2
Van Meter	W. Proctor		Jun. 2, 1881	Aug. 26, 1944	Hdn	CEM2
Van Meter	William	T.	Mar. 1, 1863	Mar. 25, 1940	Hdn	CEM2
Van Metre	Claude Elmo		Nov. 12, 1906	Oct. 27, 1944	Hdn	CEM2
Van Metre	Clyde	H.	1878	1954	Hdn	CEM2
Van Metre	Gladys		1905	1905	Hdn	CEM2
Van Metre	Joseph	C.	Oct. 27, 1839	Aug. 16, 1922	Hdn	CEM2
Van Metre	L.	W.	Aug. 3, 1874	Mar. 2, 1957	Hdn	CEM2
Van Metre	Louisa		Jun. 19, 1852	Apr. 19, 1938	Hdn	CEM2
Van Metre	Male		Feb. 14, 1912	Feb. 14, 1912	Hdn	CEM2
Van Metre	Van		Feb. 5, 1847		Hdn	CEM2
Van Metre (Brown)	Laura		Oct. 24, 1846	Feb. 5, 1926	Hdn	CEM2

Last Name	First Name	I	Birth	Death	Co	Source
Van Metre (Gibson)	Lena		May 8, 1914		Hdn	CEM2
Vance	Dennis	L.	Oct. 11, 1948	Dec. 2, 1969	Hdn	CEM2
Vancleve	Unknown Male			Sep. 19, 1858	Bre	C1
Vanclive	Elizabeth		1792ca	Nov. 15, 1877	Bre	C1
Vanderhoof	Allie		1889ca		Grn	Marr1
Vandgriff	Samuel		1829ca	Dec. 20, 1904	Brk	C1
Vanhoose	Robert	G.	1930	Jul. 20, 1950	KY	KMIL
Vass, Jr.	Thomas		1841		But	Bk1
Vaughn	Mamie		1893ca		Grn	Marr1
Veatch	Martha	E.	Mar. 3, 1871	1910	Ful	CEM7
Veatch	Mrs. Matilda		1820ca	Oct. 23, 1875	Dav	MCDR
Ventress	Elderidge		1834	1904	Hdn	CEM1
Ventress	Sophronia	B.	Jul. 22, 1837	3-May-10	Hdn	CEM1
Ventress	Susan Alice		Feb. 27, 1865	Mar. 7, 1885	Hdn	CEM1
Vessels (Lewis)	Gertrude			May 6, 1874	Brk	C1
Viers	Jackson		1848ca	Oct. 2, 1853	Bre	C1
Vires	Mary Ann		1868ca	Sep. 1, 1877	Bre	C1
Vires	Merrica		1852ca	Oct. 1, 1874	Bre	C1
Vires	Randolph		1812ca	Mar. 23, 1875	Bre	C1
Virgin	Catharine		1888ca		Grn	Marr1
Voss	Agnes		1880ca	Jun. 5, 1942	Ken	MCDR
Voss	Albert		1891ca	Mar. 24, 1955	Cam	MCDR
Voss	August		1857	Jan. 4, 1933	Ken	MCDR
Voss	Caroline		1864ca	Mar. 20, 1953	Cam	MCDR
Voss	Cecil		1905ca	Nov. 27, 1953	Ken	MCDR
Voss	Edward	J.	1893ca	May 3, 1937	Fay	MCDR
Voss	Edwin	H.	1907ca	Feb. 28, 1978	Oh	MCDR
Vuers	Unknown Female			Dec. 25, 1856	Bre	C1
Wade	Eula		1904	1906	Ful	CEM6
Wade	Henry	F.	1854	1933	Ful	CEM6
Wade	James	G.	1875	1944	Ful	CEM6
Wade	Josiah	W.	1845		But	Bk1
Wade	Lena	B.	1877	1946	Ful	CEM6
Wade	Major William	M	1798ca	Sep. 26, 1843	NWS1	9/30/1843
Wade	Rebecca	A.	1848	1900	Ful	CEM6
Wadkins	Elizabeth		1852ca	Nov. 27, 1855	Bre	C1
Wadkins	Jannie		1890ca		Grn	Marr1
Wadkins	Polly			Jun. 7, 1874	Bre	C1
Wadkins	Unknown Female			Feb. 15, 1875	Bre	C1
Wadkins	William		1874ca	Oct. 13, 1875	Bre	C1
Waford	Everett	W.	1932	Dec. 2, 1950	KY	KMIL
Wagers	Daniel	H.	1928	Feb. 4, 1951	KY	KMIL
Waggoner	Clyde		Feb. 10, 1940	Jul. 2, 1941	Row	CEM1
Waggoner	Dudley		1848ca	Aug. 10, 1859	Brk	C1
Waggoner	George	W.		Jul. 15, 1859	Brk	C1
Waggoner	George Earl		Jan. 13, 1930	Jan. 1, 1953	KY	KMIL
Waggoner	Nannie	R.	1859ca	May 26, 1904	Brk	C1

Last Name	First Name	I	Birth	Death	Co	Source
Waggoner	Will		1786ca	Aug. 20, 1859	Brk	C1
Wainscott	Carrie		Dec. 9, 1878	Sep. 23, 1886	Sim	CEM1
Wainscott	Female		Aug. 11, 1897		Sim	CEM1
Wainscott	M.	Z.	Dec. 27, 1840	Dec. 9, 1898	Sim	CEM1
Waite (Fife)	Minnie	E.	Oct. 1, 1874	Jul. 7, 1950	Hdn	CEM2
Walford	Sarah		1892ca		Grn	Marr1
Walgamott	Mary	P.	Sep. 11, 1851	Feb. 18, 1865	Ful	CEM5
Walgamott	Mary	R.	Jun. 16, 1835	Jul. 23, 1882	Ful	CEM5
Walk	Wid. Mary Jane		1861ca		Grn	Marr1
Walker	Ann	E.		Feb. ??, 1899	McL	CH1
Walker	Arthur		1874	1943	Hdn	CEM2
Walker	Claude	D.	Jul. 12, 1898	Nov. 13, 1918	Ful	CEM4
Walker	Donald Morrris		Apr. 16, 1931	Dec. 7, 1950	KY	KMIL
Walker	Earnest		Oct. 9, 1894	Jul. 30, 1895	Hdn	CEM2
Walker	Edgar	T.	Apr. 3, 1876	Jul. 15, 1957	Hdn	CEM2
Walker	Ephraim		Dec. 8, 1904	May 24, 1943	Hdn	CEM2
Walker	Frances Jan		Jul. 14, 1854	Apr. 1, 1904	Ful	CEM7
Walker	Glenn	R.		Feb. 10, 1951	KY	KMIL
Walker	Harry		Jun. 15, 1871	Oct. 22, 1908	Hdn	CEM2
Walker	Hazel Goldie		1888ca		Grn	Marr1
Walker	J.	H.	1866ca	May 5, 1894	Brk	C1
Walker	James	S.	1926	Feb. 9, 1953	KY	KMIL
Walker	James		1856ca	Sep. 18, 1877	Grn	C2
Walker	Lucrestia	R.	1875	1935	Hdn	CEM2
Walker	Mamie Roby		Jun. 21, 1883	Mar. 14, 1970	Hdn	CEM2
Walker	Martha		1876ca		Grn	Marr1
Walker	Mary	W.	1850ca	Sep. 1, 1852	Brk	C1
Walker	Mattie	L.	1893ca	Oct. 9, 1894	Brk	C1
Walker	Mrs. Ailcie		1831ca	Dec. 28, 1875	Dav	MCDR
Walker	Mrs. Thomas		1721		KY	BK2(P156)
Walker	Nellie		Nov. 9, 1841	Sep. 25, 1928	Hdn	CEM2
Walker	Roy Flatt		1920	1938	Ful	CEM7
Walker	Sally	S.	Apr. 15, 1801	Sep. 22, 1878	Hdn	CEM2
Walker	Unknown			Jan. 27, 1853	Grn	C1
Walker	Unknown Male			Mar. 17, 1852	Brk	C1
Walker	Vennie	M.	May 22, 1872	Oct. 18, 1952	Hdn	CEM2
Walker	Widow Lizzie		1870ca		Grn	Marr1
Walker	William		Feb. 6, 1816		Other	Bk1(P175)A
Walker	Wm. Edgar		Feb. 25, 1900	Aug. 2, 1932	Hdn	CEM2
Walker (Lewis)	Cordie		Feb. 5, 1886	Mar. 21, 1911	Hdn	CEM2
Walker (Walters)	Martha		1835ca	Oct. 14, 1903	Brk	C1
Wall	Eliz. Clementina		1844ca	1845	NWS1	6/28/1845
Wall	Finley	W.	1819ca	Feb. 8, 1852	Dav	MCDR
Wallace	Clarence		Jun. 14, 1888	Jun. 14, 1888	Hdn	CEM3
Wallace	David Ann		Jan. 5, 1845	Nov. 4, 1870	Sim	CEM1
Wallace	Essie		May 8, 1889	Sep. 12, 1889	Hdn	CEM3
Wallace	Martha	E.	1891ca		Grn	Marr1

Last Name	First Name	I	Birth	Death	Co	Source
Waller	Samuel		1820ca	Apr. 3, 1961	Brk	C1
Walls	Lewis		1876ca	Dec. 14, 1878	Brk	C1
Walls	Missouri		1838ca	Oct. 31, 1878	Brk	C1
Walls (Beauchamp)	M.		1822ca	Jun. 29, 1894	Brk	C1
Walter	Frederick		1834ca	Aug. 25, 1904	Brk	C1
Walter	Raymond	J.	1899ca	Jan. 13, 1982	Cam	MCDR
Walton	F.	A.	May 25, 1818	Jan. 24, 1878	Sim	CEM1
Walton	James		1810ca	Jun. 8, 1852	Grn	C1
Walton	Mary		Dec. 8, 1829	Sep. 9, 1905	Sim	CEM1
Wand	William		1847		But	Bk1
Ward	Araminta		1873ca	Nov. 15, 1875	Bre	C1
Ward	Bertha		1885ca		Grn	Marr1
Ward	Dovey		1890ca		Grn	Marr1
Ward	Isaac		Jan. 30, 1861	Apr. 9, 1900	Oh	CEM1
Ward	James	R.	Sep. 9, 1834	Nov. ??, 1867	Oh	CEM1
Ward	James		Jan. ??, 1798	May 13, 1885	Oh	CEM1
Ward	Mary Jane		1834ca	Dec. 11, 1854	Bre	C1
Ward	Nancy		1807ca	Nov. 8, 1890	Oh	CEM1
Ward	Otis		Jan. 3, 1886	Jun. 11, 1889	Oh	CEM1
Ward	Quarter Master			1791ca	NWS5	11/12/1791
Warden	Elisha		1761		All	RP1
Wardrip	Catherine			Oct. 4, 1875	Brk	C1
Wardrip	Nat.		1877ca	Jun. 8, 1878	Brk	C1
Wardrip	Yoauger		1819ca	Dec. 17, 1878	Brk	C1
Ware	A.	E.	1899ca	Apr. 14, 1955	Ken	MCDR
Ware	Alene	E.	1899ca	Apr. 24, 1979	Ken	MCDR
Ware	Elias		1848ca	Jun. ??, 1852	Grn	C1
Warman	Candace	M.	1883ca		Grn	Marr1
Warnock	Julia		1875ca	Oct. 25, 1877	Grn	C2
Warnock	Willie		1868ca		Grn	Marr1
Warren	Jno.	H.	1813ca	Jul. 14, 1878	Brk	C1
Warren	Lieut.			1791ca	NWS5	11/12/1791
Warren	Martin	W.	1920	Nov. 28, 1950	KY	KMIL
Warren	Mrs. William	E.		1835	NWS4	8/14/1835
Warrington	Leonvill			May 28, 1878	Brk	C1
Washer	O.		Mar.19, 1837		Gray	C2
Wathen	Unknown Female			Jul. 7, 1861	Brk	C1
Watson	Allen		1832		Web	Bk1
Watson	B.		1840		Web	Bk1
Watson	Daniel	W.	Aug. 6, 1871	Nov. 11, 1953	Hdn	CEM2
Watson	Della	J.	1874	1906	Hdn	CEM2
Watson	Harold	L.	1930	Jul. 4, 1952	KY	KMIL
Watson	Hollis	V.	1904	1942	Ful	CEM4
Watson	Jennie	R.	Jan. 22, 1871	Feb. 6, 1904	Ful	CEM4
Watson	Margaret		Jul. 24, 1841	Nov. 6, 1904	Ful	CEM4
Watson	Richard Prather			Apr. 4, 1938	Ful	CEM4
Watson	Robert	A.	1881	1952	Ful	CEM4

Last Name	First Name	I	Birth	Death	Co	Source
Watson	William		1846ca	Apr. ??, 1861	Dav	C1
Watson	William		Aug. 28, 1904		Car	C1
Watson (Scott)	Mattie		Sep. 6, 1882	Jul. 30, 1971	Hdn	CEM2
Watts	Arnold		1927	Nov. 24, 1951	KY	KMIL
Watts	Bobbie	E.	1932	Aug. 4, 1951	KY	KMIL
Watts	Wright		1874		Brk	C1
Wayman	William			Sep. ??, 1843	NWS1	9/16/1843
Wayse	W.	C.	Nov. 29, 1834		Gray	C2
Weatherford			1793ca	Apr. 10, 1874	Brk	C1
Weatherholt	Gertrude		Feb. 22, 1888	Feb. 22, 1888	Dav	CEM2
Weatherholt	Unknown Female			Nov. 22, 1861	Brk	C1
Weatherholt	Unknown Female			Nov. 22, 1861	Brk	C1
Weaver	Elder Bird		1843		But	Bk1
Weaver	Jennie		1889ca		Grn	Marr1
Weaver	John		1742		All	RP1
Webb	C.	J.	Feb. 4, 1875	Jul. 24, 1902	Hdn	CEM1
Webb	Edna		Dec. 19, 1879	Sep. 29, 1902	Hdn	CEM1
Webb	Ellen		Jun. 19, 1920	Jun. 29, 1920	Ful	CEM4
Webb	James	D.	1928	Oct. 13, 1950	KY	KMIL
Webb	John	S.	1827ca	Jul. 15, 1854	Brk	C1
Webb	Jonas	B.	1930	Apr. 16, 1951	KY	KMIL
Webb	Leya			Jul. 14, 1852	Brk	C1
Webb	Mary Ellen		1889ca		Grn	Marr1
Webb	Mattie		1883ca		Grn	Marr1
Webb (Wright)	Lucy	A.	1857ca	Feb. 13, 1904	Brk	C1
Welch	Gobel	J.	1933	Feb. 14, 1951	KY	KMIL
Welch	James	D.	Jun. 10, 1932	Jul. 17, 1953	KY	KMIL
Welch	Mr.		1769ca		NWS5	12/22/1792
Well	Paschal			Aug. 18, 1852	Brk	C1
Well	Nancy Ann			Aug. 15, 1852	Brk	C1
Well (Wallace)	Martha	J.	1827ca	Aug. 12, 1852	Brk	C1
Wellman	Daisy	L.	May 12, 1871	May 12, 1871	Dav	CEM2
Wellman	Sarah	K.	Dec. 30,1874	Jan. 5, 1877	Dav	CEM2
Wells	J.	A.		Aug. ??, 1894	Brk	C1
Wells	J.	F.	Aug. 30, 1833		Gray	C2
Wells	Jos.	T.		Feb. 16, 1878	Brk	C1
Wells	Malinda Jane		1830ca	Nov. 20, 1854	Dav	C1
Welsh	James Douglas		Aug. 19, 1929	Nov. 7, 1950	KY	KMIL
West	Alexander		1776ca	Apr. 12, 1852	Brk	C1
West	Elizabeth		1841ca	Apr. 11, 1852	Brk	C1
West	James	R.	1833ca	Apr. 3, 1852	Brk	C1
West	Lea	H.	1903ca	Jul. 1, 1904	Brk	C1
West	Lewis	W.		Apr. 17, 1852	Brk	C1
West	Sarah Ann		1831ca	Apr. 12, 1852	Brk	C1
West	William		1801ca	Apr. 6, 1852	Brk	C1
Westefield	Fannie		Apr. 6, 1848	Feb. 7, 1906	Dav	CEM2
Westerfield	Dr. William	P.	1835		But	Bk1

Last Name	First Name	I	Birth	Death	Co	Source
Westerfield	J.	B.	1807ca	May 15, 1861	Dav	C1
Westerfield	W.	H.	Dec. 14, 1842		Dav	CEM2
Whalen	Hannah		Apr. 28, 1858	Jun. 29, 1914	Har	CEM1
Whalen	N.	J.	Jul. 17, 1848	Jun. 22, 1905	Har	CEM1
Whalen	Wesley		1851ca	1894	Brk	C1
Whalen	Wm.		1829ca	May 15, 1894	Brk	C1
Whalin	Granvil Harry		Feb. 14, 1930	Oct. 16, 1952	KY	KMIL
Whalin	James Henry		1835		But	Bk1
Whayne	J.	P.	??? 10, 1850	Sep. 5, 1886	Hdn	CEM1
Wheatley	Ameline		1826ca	Dec. ??, 1856	Brk	C1
Wheatley	Ellen	A.	1834ca	Feb. 9, 1894	Brk	C1
Wheatley	Frances			Aug. 8, 1856	Brk	C1
Wheatley	Jas.	H.		Mar. 16, 1878	Brk	C1
Wheatley	Joseph	C.	1857ca	Sep. 16, 1858	Brk	C1
Wheatley	L.	E.	1825ca	Feb. 18, 1878	Brk	C1
Wheatley	Unknown Male			Mar. 10, 1894	Brk	C1
Wheeler	Cora		1884ca		Grn	Marr1
Wheeler	J.	T.	1833ca	Feb. 8, 1894	Brk	C1
Wheeler	John	W.	1823ca	Mar. 24, 1855	Brk	C1
Wheeler (Huckoby)	Nelly	A.	1832ca	Dec. 17, 1855	Brk	C1
Whitaker	A.	S.	1846	1973	Har	CEM1
Whitaker	Ann		Jan. 17, 1806	Sep. 12, 1886	Har	CEM1
Whitaker	Ann		Jun. 2, 1798	Nov. 12, 1862	Har	CEM1
Whitaker	Arbell Taylor		1842	1929	Har	CEM1
Whitaker	Arch	A.	Jan. 29, 1826	Mar. 22, 1899	Har	CEM1
Whitaker	Asa	F.	Apr. 16, 1824	Nov. 15, 1893	Har	CEM1
Whitaker	Catherine		Sep. 2, 1893		McL	Sch1
Whitaker	Cordelia		Jul. 30, 1866	Oct. 26, 1866	Har	CEM1
Whitaker	Elizabeth	A.	Mar. 31, 1849	Mar. 19, 1869	Har	CEM1
Whitaker	Emma Colvin		1868	1944	Har	CEM1
Whitaker	Eugene		Feb. 4, 1863	Aug. 14, 1911	Har	CEM1
Whitaker	Fannie Duncan		Jan. 9, 1868	May 20, 1899	Har	CEM1
Whitaker	Francis Jane		Jan. 10, 1825	Mar. 7, 1860	Har	CEM1
Whitaker	Golda		Jun. 12, 1888		McL	Sch1
Whitaker	H. Mc.		1817	1906	Har	CEM1
Whitaker	Hannah		1818	1891	Har	CEM1
Whitaker	Harny	T.	1878	1913	Har	CEM1
Whitaker	Hattie		1870	1950	Har	CEM1
Whitaker	J.	T.	Jun. ??, 1834	Nov. 15, 1899	Har	CEM1
Whitaker	Jennie		1868	1940	Har	CEM1
Whitaker	John		1860	1940	Har	CEM1
Whitaker	Josiah Jacob		1842	1923	Har	CEM1
Whitaker	Lucie		Jun. 30, 1887		Har	CEM1
Whitaker	Male		Oct. 23, 1902	Oct. 26, 1902	Har	CEM1
Whitaker	Mary Elizabeth		Apr. 30, 1830	Mar. 14, 1896	Har	CEM1
Whitaker	Nannie	G.	Jul. 22, 1878	Aug. 29, 1962	Har	CEM1
Whitaker	Peter		Nov. 24, 1793	Sep. 22, 1856	Har	CEM1

Last Name	First Name	I	Birth	Death	Co	Source
Whitaker	Presley	G.	1854		But	Bk1
Whitaker	Presley		1826		But	Bk1
Whitaker	Ralph Leslie		Oct. 14, 1889	Mar. 2, 1901	Har	CEM1
Whitaker	Sarah	E.	Jun. 12, 1829	Jul. 21, 1904	Har	CEM1
Whitaker	Sarah	L.	Jun. 6, 1869	Dec. 9, 1898	Har	CEM1
Whitaker	Sarah	S.	Feb. 7, 1862	Oct. 26, 1894	Har	CEM1
Whitaker	Thomas	D.	1866	1948	Har	CEM1
Whitaker	Verna		Feb. 28, 1883		McL	Sch1
Whitaker	W.	P.	Dec. 7, 1864	Oct. 17, 1877	Har	CEM1
Whitaker	Walter	H.	Jan. 28, 1875	Jul. 23, 1939	Har	CEM1
White	Belva		1890ca		Grn	Marr1
White	Elizabeth		Apr. 30, 1835	Dec. 23, 1912	But	CEM2
White	H.	J.	Jan. 6, 1857	Dec. 29, 1922	Hdn	CEM1
White	Hazel Goldie		1893ca		Grn	Marr1
White	Hezekiah		1824		But	Bk1
White	Ida		Apr. 7, 1861	May 28, 1861	Har	CEM1
White	Jane		1846ca	Apr. ??, 1853	Bre	C1
White	John	A.	Jun. 25, 1856	May 12, 1863	Har	CEM1
White	Lafayette		Oct. 9, 1840	Nov. 16, 1862	Sim	CEM1
White	Leslie		Apr. 13, 1884	Sep. 27, 1946	Hdn	CEM1
White	Lora		1889ca		Grn	Marr1
White	Mahalia	J.	Sep. 8, 1860	Jul. 21, 1878	Hdn	CEM1
White	Mary	F.	Apr. 22, 1860	May 23, 1860	Har	CEM1
White	Mary	J.	1892ca		Grn	Marr1
White	Merry	P.	1843	1895	Hdn	CEM1
White	Nancy		Feb. 5, 1799	Jul. 4, 1854	But	CEM2
White	Noah			1835	NWS4	8/14/1835
White	Oliver	C.	1827		But	Bk1
White	Richard		1774ca		NWS5	11/7/1795
White	Robert	S.	Dec. 5, 1887	Oct. 26, 1923	Hdn	CEM1
White	Robert		1852ca	Apr. ??, 1853	Bre	C1
White	Robin			Aug. 2, 1852	Bre	C1
White	Susannah		Dec. 31, 1860	Dec. 24, 1940	Hdn	CEM1
White	T.	J.	Jan. 1, 1862	May 10m 1894	Hdn	CEM1
White	William	E.	1827		But	Bk1
White	William		1815ca	Apr. 6, 1878	Bre	C1
White	Martin	E.	1833	1906	Hdn	CEM1
Whiteaker	Clara		Jan. 5, 1905	Apr. 17, 1906	Har	CEM1
Whiteaker	Laura		1872	1938	Har	CEM1
Whiteaker	Mannie	F.	Jun. 14, 1903	Nov. 5, 1905	Har	CEM1
Whiteaker??	Volney		1867	19??	Har	CEM1
Whiteman	William	S.	1931	Jul. 20, 1950	KY	KMIL
Whiteside	Joseph	E.	1932	Mar. 23, 1951	KY	KMIL
Whiticar	Huran		1847ca	Jan. 3, 1855	Bre	C1
Whitler	Charles	P.	1927	Nov. 2, 1950	KY	KMIL
Whitrock	Nettie	M.	1889ca		Grn	Marr1
Whitson	Dr. Harman	H.	1834		Web	Bk1

Last Name	First Name	I	Birth	Death	Co	Source
Whitt	Mada		1889ca		Grn	Marr1
Whittaker	Melvin	T.	1932	Nov. 17, 1951	KY	KMIL
Whitworth	George	H.	1857ca	Dec. 14, 1861	Brk	C1
Whitworth	George	H.	1858ca	Dec. 14, 1861	Brk	C1
Whright	Rhody		1778ca	Nov. 16, 1856	Brk	C1
Wickliffe	Yost		1852ca	Oct. 11, 1931	Muh	MCDR
Wilborn	Ollie		1882ca		Grn	Marr1
Wilcox	Emma		Mar. 1, 1907		Car	C1
Wilhite	John		1831ca	Apr. ??, 1856	Dav	C1
Wilhite(Taylor)	Eliza	A.	1823ca	Dec. 23, 1857	Dav	C1
Wilhoit	E.	B.	Sep. 19, 1842		Car	Bk1
Wilkerson	Mrs. Robert		1825ca	May 13, 1852	Dav	MCDR
Wilkerson	Orlie	W.	1883	1970	Hdn	CEM2
Wilkerson	Thelma	V.	1901		Hdn	CEM2
Wilkings	Lucy Lellen		Jan. 20, 1858	Aug. 17, 1871	Ful	CEM7
Wilkins	Mary	O.	Feb. 11, 1824	Dec. 26, 1895	Ful	CEM7
Wilkins	N.	E.	May 21, 1867	Nov. 26, 1897	Ful	CEM6
Wilkinson	James		1830ca	Aug. 38, 1845	NWS1	9/6/1845
Wilkinson	Thornton		1795ca	Nov. 13, 1857	Dav	C1
Wilkinson(Bishop)	Eliza		1806ca	Apr. 10, 1857	Dav	C1
Willett	Catherine		1874ca	Dec. 28, 1875	Dav	MCDR
Williams	Alice			Aug. 2, 1853	Grn	C1
Williams	Alvin	C.	1931	Sep. 7, 1950	KY	KMIL
Williams	Annie Ophelia		1884ca	Oct. 1, 1960	Muh	CEM2
Williams	Charles	K.	1929	Aug. 12, 1950	KY	KMIL
Williams	Elizabeth	M.	1851ca	Jun. 17, 1853	Grn	C1
Williams	Henry		1812ca	Dec. 4, 1877	Grn	C2
Williams	J.	H.	Dec. 30, 1830	Sep. 6, 1883	Hdn	CEM2
Williams	James	C.	1824		Web	Bk1
Williams	Joseph	A.	Mar. 2, 1877	May 27, 1937	Muh	CEM2
Williams	Julia	P.	Nov. 27, 1821	Aug. 18, 1904	Hdn	CEM2
Williams	July Ann			Feb. 15, 1859	Bre	C1
Williams	Kenneth	O.	1930	Sep. 8, 1950	KY	KMIL
Williams	L.	P.	May 20, 1872	Sep. 7, 1927	Muh	CEM2
Williams	Marvin		1929	Oct. 14, 1952	KY	KMIL
Williams	Mary	E.		Jan. 21, 1853	Grn	C1
Williams	Ollie		Jul. 28, 1875	Jun. 13, 1952	Muh	CEM2
Williams	Rosa	E.	1890ca		Grn	Marr1
Williams	Rosa		1888ca		Grn	Marr1
Williams	Rosa		1875ca		Grn	Marr1
Williams	Ruby		1888ca		Grn	Marr1
Williams	Sallie		Apr. 5, 1858	Jan. 7, 1900	Ful	CEM4
Williams	Sallie		1857ca	Jul. 11, 1875	Brk	C1
Williams	Stella		1889ca		Grn	Marr1
Williams	Sylvester	H.	1819		Web	Bk1
Williams	Unknown Female			Jun. 16, 1856	Bre	C1
Williams	Unknown Female			Nov. 5, 1857	Bre	C1

Last Name	First Name	I	Birth	Death	Co	Source
Williams	Unknown Female			Mar. 14, 1877	Bre	C1
Williams	Unknown Male			Jun. 20, 1875	Bre	C1
Williams	W.		1856ca	Mar. 15, 1877	Bre	C1
Williams	Wid. Eliza	J.	1872ca		Grn	Marr1
Williams	Bertie		Dec. 6, 1899	Sep. 22, 1901	Har	CEM1
Williams	Dora	L.	Oct. 6, 1908	Nov. 16, 1911	Har	CEM1
Williams	M	T		Jun. 25, 1844	NWS1	6/29/1844
Williams	Mrs. Elijah		1803ca	Jan. 30, 1843	NWS1	2/4/1843
Williams (McDaniel)	Nancy		1813ca	Oct. 13, 1858	Bre	C1
Williams (Richardson)	Frances		Mar. 22, 1921	Aug. 6, 1969	Hdn	CEM3
Williams(Richmond)	Mary	A.	1829ca	Dec. 19, 1857	Dav	C1
Williamson	George	W.	1843ca	Oct. 10, 1852	Brk	C1
Williamson	James		1753		All	RP1
Williamson	Martha	F.	1858ca	Aug. 23, 1861	Brk	C1
Williamson (Barger)	Elfrida		1829ca	Nov. 11, 1852	Brk	C1
Willinghams	J.	A.	1858		Web	Bk1
Willis	Gertrude		1886ca		Grn	Marr1
Willis	Joseph			Apr. 4, 1853	Grn	C1
Willis	Nelson		1890ca		Grn	Marr1
Willis	J.	H.	Aug. 31, 1837		Gray	C2
Willis, Jr.	William		1847		But	Bk1
Wills	Alice		1826		Men	CEM1
Wills	Amanda Jane		Mar. 8, 1849	Sep. 5, 1854	Men	CEM1
Wills	Andrew		Aug. 4, 1829	Apr. 21, 1863	Men	CEM1
Wills	George		1875ca	Aug. 18, 1875	Dav	MCDR
Wills	James		1843ca	Sep. 16, 1852	Grn	C1
Wills	James		Feb. 15, 1801	Feb. 12, 1879	Men	CEM1
Wills	James Thornton		Aug. 28, 1846	May 18, 1863	Men	CEM1
Wills	William		Apr. 16, 1765	Aug. 10, 1834	Men	CEM1
Wills	William		Jul. 8, 1827	Aug. 30, 1829	Men	CEM1
Wills (Anderson)	Aleatha		Apr. 4, 180?	Sep. 28, 1884	Men	CEM1
Wilmington(Bates)	Elizabeth		1786ca	Mar. 30, 1853	Dav	C1
Wilson	J.	R.	1837	1894	Sim	CEM1
Wilson	L.	J.	Nov. 8, 1837		Gray	C2
Wilson	Mahala		1848	1928	Sim	CEM1
Wilson	Mahala		1848	1928	Sim	CEM1
Wilson	Male		Jun. 28, 1906	Jul. 12, 1906	Dav	CEM2
Wilson	Mrs. Harriett		1816ca	Apr. 28, 1844	NWS1	5/4/1844
Wilson	Priscilla		Dec. 5, 1835		Gray	C2
Wilson	Richard	E.	1926	May 10, 1953	KY	KMIL
Wilson	Ruthie		1827	1896	Sim	CEM1
Wilson	Susan		Jan. 18, 1837		Gray	C2
Wilson	William	W.	Sep. 7, 1835	Dec. 6, 1883	Hdn	CEM1
Wilson (Duncan)	R.	A.	1833ca	Oct. 24, 1857	Dav	C1
Wines	William	A.	Aug. 31, 1847	Jul. 13, 1901	Hdn	CEM2
Wingo	Nannie		1885ca		Grn	Marr1
Winkfield	Marshall		1927	Oct. 12, 1951	KY	KMIL

138

Kentucky Birth and Death Records, Vol. One

Last Name	First Name	I	Birth	Death	Co	Source
Winkler	Edward		1834ca	Apr. ??, 1855	Dav	C1
Winn (Winstead)	E.	R.	1833ca	Jun. ??, 1861	Dav	C1
Winstead	Barbour		Mar. 26, 1890	Nov. 18, 1890	Dav	CEM1
Winstead	Caroline		Sep. 19, 1888	Feb. 14, 1889	Dav	CEM1
Winstead	Isaac	C	Apr. 7, 1863	Aug. 19, 1929	Dav	CEM1
Winstead	Ruddle	B	Dec. 12, 1862	Apr. 15, 1945	Dav	CEM1
Winston	James	R.	1931	Jul. 8, 1953	KY	KMIL
Winters	Freda		1893ca		Grn	Marr1
Winters	Mrs. Eliza		1813ca	Nov. 17, 1843	NWS1	11/25/1843
Wireman	Dollie		1886ca		Grn	Marr1
Wirotzious	William		1924	Mar. 8, 1951	KY	KMIL
Wirotzious	William		1924	Mar. 8, 1951	KY	KMIL
Wise	Henry	H.	1832		Web	Bk1
Witten	Addie		Sep. 28, 1887	May 11, 1911	Hdn	CEM2
Witten	Margret Belle		May 11, 1911	May 11, 1911	Hdn	CEM2
Witten	Wm. Lee		Mar. 16, 1877	May 15, 1966	Hdn	CEM2
Womack	Faythe		1887ca		Grn	Marr1
Womack	Oliver	C.	1812		Web	Bk1
Wood	J.	P.	Sep. 20, 1829	Sep. 3, 1884	Har	CEM1
Wood	John		1785ca	Sep. ??, 1855	Dav	C1
Wood	Ottie Logan		Mar. 11, 1932	Oct. 27, 1952	KY	KMIL
Wood	Presley	S.	1861		But	Bk1
Wood	Rachel		Jul. 13, 1834	Jul. 8, 1907	Har	CEM1
Wood	Roy Wilbur		Jun. 25, 1930	Sep. 23, 1950	KY	KMIL
Wood	Tolbert			Dec. 24, 1853	Bre	C1
Wood	Washington		1794ca	Jul. 17, 1855	Bre	C1
Wood (VanClive)	Susannah		1814ca	Nov. 24, 1853	Bre	C1
Woodard	Roger Clinton		Oct. 30, 1919	Dec. 31, 1953	KY	KMIL
Woodring	Ellen		Dec. 17, 1840	Feb. 20, 1918	Hdn	CEM2
Woodring	J.	W.	Jul. 18, 1839	Feb. 4, 1915	Hdn	CEM2
Woodring	Joseph		Nov. 23, 1821	Feb. 11, 1888	Hdn	CEM2
Woodring	Rosie		Sep. 20, 1852	Jul. 17, 1909	Hdn	CEM2
Woodring	Samuel		Feb. 7, 1807	May 15, 1900	Hdn	CEM2
Woodring	Sarah	J.	Mar. 6, 1817	Oct. 4, 1880	Hdn	CEM2
Woodring	Thomas	S.	Feb. 9, 1844	Sep. 7, 1901	Hdn	CEM2
Woodrow	Sarah		1849ca	Jul. 23, 1852	Grn	C1
Woods	Margaret		1777ca	Aug. 15, 1852	Brk	C1
Woods	Maria	J.	1853ca	Sep. 7, 1861	Brk	C1
Woods	William		1852		Brk	C1
Woods	James		1930	Nov. 1, 1952	KY	KMIL
Woodson	John	J.	1839		Web	Bk1
Woodworth	Asa		1764ca		NWS5	1/12/1793
Woodyard	Grace	F.	1861	1942	Hdn	CEM2
Woodyard	J.	W.	1856	1939	Hdn	CEM2
Wooldridge	J.	P.	1831	1909	Hdn	CEM1
Wooldridge	Leria	O.	1872ca	Sep. 29, 1952	Jef	MCDR
Wooldridge	Rhoda	A.	1838		Hdn	CEM1

139

Last Name	First Name	I	Birth	Death	Co	Source
Woosley	Joseph		Jan. 13, 1833		Gray	C2
Woosley	Lewis	F.	1859		But	Bk1
Woosley	M.		Jul. 19, 1838		Gray	C2
Woosley	Mary		Nov. ??, 1839		Gray	C2
Woosley	May		Nov. 30, 1840		Gray	C2
Woosley	Samuel		Dec. 5, 1825		Gray	C2
Worley	Lee		Feb. 24, 1836		Gray	C2
Worth	Allie	R.	Mar. 4, 1864	Apr. 6, 1897	Ful	CEM7
Worth	C.	J.	Sep. 10, 1854	Mar. 20, 1912	Ful	CEM7
Worth	Charles	J.	Oct. 27, 1835	May 20, 1900	Ful	CEM7
Wortham	Christa		1876ca	Jul. 19, 1878	Brk	C1
Wortham	D.	F.	Aug. 20, 1818	Jul. 11, 1898	Hdn	CEM1
Wortham	David	A.	Dec. 21, 1853	May 11, 1865	Hdn	CEM1
Wortham	Jefferies		Apr. 2, 1881	Mar. 12, 1899	Hdn	CEM1
Wortham	John	F.	Dec. 6, 1843	Nov. 8, 1864	Hdn	CEM1
Wortham	Lorabelle		Dec. 4, 1878	Apr. 9, 1895	Hdn	CEM1
Wortham	Martha	B.	1826	1907	Hdn	CEM1
Wortham	Mary	E.	Jan. 29, 1898	Mar. 28, 1859	Hdn	CEM1
Wortham	Mary		1824	1909	Hdn	CEM1
Wortham	Samuel	W.	1834	1919	Hdn	CEM1
Wortham	Susan		Oct. 6, 1823	Apr. 7, 1903	Hdn	CEM1
Worthington	Sally		1890ca		Grn	Marr1
Wright	Anahanan		1877ca		Grn	Marr1
Wright	Jarrett		1757		All	RP1
Wright	Mary	C.	1881ca		Grn	Marr1
Wright	Mrs. Mary		1835ca	Jul. 30, 1844	NWS1	8/3/1844
Wright	Roy Lee		Jun. 9, 1907		Car	C1
Wright	W.			1835	NWS4	8/14/1835
Wright	Willard		1865ca	May 29, 1878	Brk	C1
Wright	William	C.		Mar. ??, 1907	McL	CH1
Wright	William		1799ca	Dec. 26, 1844	NWS1	12/28/1844
Wright (Drane)	Elizabeth		1829ca	Nov. 8, 1856	Brk	C1
Wyatt (Slave)				Aug. 2, 1856	Brk	C1
Wygle	Henry		1764ca		NWS5	1/12/1793
Wynns	John	D.	1848		Web	Bk1
Yandell (Willheite)	Dyca		1793ca	Aug. 20, 1853	Dav	C1
Yates	Leah Martin			Aug. 11, 1952	Sim	CEM1
Yates	Ray	B.	1930	Feb. 12, 1951	KY	KMIL
Yates	Virgil		Feb. 14, 1871	Mar. 27, 1928	Sim	CEM1
Yates	William	A.		Sep. 15, 1852	Grn	C1
Yonts	Robert	B.	1927	Nov. 30, 1950	KY	KMIL
Yopp	Floria		1860ca	Mar. 13, 1911	Fay	MCDR
York	James	D.	1931	Sep. 13, 1952	KY	KMIL
Young	Dellie		1879ca		Grn	Marr1
Young	Elizabeth		Jun. 19, 1888	Jun. 20, 1902	Har	CEM1
Young	Infant		Oct. 5, 1877	Oct. 5, 1877	Har	CEM1
Young	Infant		Nov. 9, 1894	Nov. 9, 1894	Har	CEM1

Last Name	First Name	I	Birth	Death	Co	Source
Young	James	B.	Mar. ??, 1878	Oct. 12, 1886	Har	CEM1
Young	John	B.	Dec. 28, 1890	Aug. 4, 1956	Har	CEM1
Young	Martha		1852	1934	Har	CEM1
Young	Noah		Dec. 20, 1863	Feb. 2, 1952	Hdn	CEM2
Young	W.	H.	1842	1928	Har	CEM1
Young	Willie	D.	Mar. 9, 1881	Oct. 19, 1887	Har	CEM1
Young (Clark)	Temoria		Apr. 1, 1863	Jun. 27, 1936	Hdn	CEM2
Zappa	Anthony		May 14, 1912	Apr. ??, 1981	Cam	MCDR
Zechella	Clara		Jun. 6, 1898	Jan. ??, 1984	Cam	MCDR
Zehusen	Viola		Sep. 15, 1912	Mar. ??, 1987	Ken	MCDR
Zeidler	Norman		Jun. 1, 1894	Aug. ??, 1979	Ken	MCDR
Zeller	Lydia		Mar. 24, 1883	Oct. ??, 1968	Cam	MCDR
Zellers	Elvin		Jan. 25, 1909	Aug. ??, 1979	Ken	MCDR
Zenor	William		1803ca	Sep. 10, 1853	Dav	C1
Ziebold	Dorothy		Aug. 8, 1923	Dec. 28, 1991	Ken	MCDR
Ziegenhardt	Howard		Sep. 16, 1907	Jul. ??, 1972	Ken	MCDR
Zieglar	Carl	R.	1915ca	Jul. 3, 1955	Cam	MCDR
Ziegler	Adam		1875ca	Nov. 9, 1954	Cam	MCDR
Ziegler	Al	J.	1905ca	May 15, 1975	Cam	MCDR
Ziegler	Amelia		1881ca	Aug. 4, 1953	Cam	MCDR
Ziegler	Anthony	T.	1896ca	Sep. 29, 1975	Dav	MCDR
Ziegler	Audrey		1907ca	Feb. 13, 1983	Cam	MCDR
Ziegler	Edward		Sep. 27, 1897	Oct. ??, 1969	Ken	MCDR
Ziegler	Harry		Mar. 18, 1899	Jun. ??, 1972	Cam	MCDR
Ziegler	Nancy		Jul. 11, 1927	Jun. ??, 1993	Ken	MCDR
Zillick	Lawrence		Jul. 16, 1900	Sep. ??, 1978	Ken	MCDR
Zimmer	Edna		Nov. 17, 1895	Jan. ??, 1982	Ken	MCDR
Zimmerman	Clifford		Dec. 17, 1914	Jan. 20, 1990	Cam	MCDR
Zimmerman	Mildred		May 5, 1890	Sep. ??, 1983	Jef	MCDR
Zinck	Charles		May 2, 1902	Jul. ??, 1981	Cam	MCDR
Zinner	Lawrence Jos.		Nov. 22, 1928	Sep. 25, 1950	KY	KMIL
Zurschmiede	John		Sep. 20, 1889	Mar. ??, 1972	Jef	MCDR
Zuverink	John		Jan. 15, 1903	July 8, 1988	Jef	MCDR
Zwosta	Robert		Apr. 7, 1902	Dec. ??, 1965	Ken	MCDR

INDEX OF MAIDEN NAMES

Our Ancestors of Cuyahoga County, Ohio, Volume 1
(with Patricia P. Nelson)

Ralls County, Missouri Settlement Records, 1832-1853

Records of Randolph County, Missouri, 1833-1964

Ten Thousand Missouri Taxpayers

*The "Show-Me" Guide to Missouri: Sources for
Genealogical and Historical Research*

CD: Dickson County, Tennessee Marriage Records, 1817-1879

*CD: Index to the Arkansas General Land Office, 1820-1907
Volumes 1-10*

CD: Missouri, Volume 3

CD: Tennessee Genealogical Records

CD: Tennessee Genealogical Records, Volumes 1-3

7962509R0

Made in the USA
Lexington, KY
27 December 2010